THE PROVOCATION OF LEVINAS

WARWICK STUDIES IN PHILOSOPHY AND LITERATURE
General editor: DAVID WOOD

It used to be a commonplace to insist on the elimination of the 'literary' dimension from philosophy. This was particularly true for a philosophical tradition inspired by the possibilities of formalisation and by the success of the natural sciences. And yet even in the most rigorous instances of such philosophy we find demands for 'clarity', for 'tight' arguments, and distinctions between 'strong' and 'weak' proofs which call out for a rhetorical reading. Equally, modern literary theory, quite as much as literature itself, is increasingly looking to philosophy (and other theoretical disciplines such as linguistics) for its inspiration. After a wave of structuralist analysis, the growing influence of deconstructive and hermeneutic readings continues to bear witness to this. While philosophy and literature are not to be identified, even if philosophy is thought of as 'a kind of writing', much of the most exciting theoretical work being done today, in Britain, Europe and America, exploits their tensions and intertwinings. When one recalls that Plato, who wished to keep philosophy and poetry apart, actually unified the two in his own writing, it is clear that the current upsurge of interest in this field is only re-engaging with the questions alive in the broader tradition.

The University of Warwick pioneered the undergraduate study of the theoretical coition of Philosophy and Literature, and its recently established Centre for Research in Philosophy and Literature has won wide acclaim for its adventurous and dynamic programme of conferences and research. With this Series the work of the Centre is opened to a wider public. Each volume aims to bring the best scholarship to bear on topical themes in an atmosphere of intellectual excitement.

THE PROVOCATION OF LEVINAS

Rethinking the Other

Edited by

ROBERT BERNASCONI

and

DAVID WOOD

Routledge
Taylor & Francis Group

LONDON AND NEW YORK

First published in 1988 by
Routledge
2 Park Square, Milton Park, Abingdon, Oxfordshire OX14 4RN

Published in the USA by
Routledge
a division of Routledge, Taylor & Francis
711 Third Avenue, New York, NY 10017

First issued in paperback 2014

Routledge is an imprint of the Taylor and Francis Group, an informa business

British Library Cataloguing in Publication Data
The provocation of Levinas: rethinking the
other.
1. French philosophy. Levinas, Emmanuel –
Critical studies
I. Bernasconi, Robert II. Wood, David, 1946–
194

Library of Congress Cataloguing in Publication Data
The Provocation of Levinas: rethinking the Other/edited by Robert
Bernasconi and David Wood.
p. cm.—(Warwick studies in philosophy and literature)
"Published in the USA by Routledge in association with Routledge,
Chapman & Hall"—P.
Bibliography: p.
Includes index.
1. Levinas, Emmanuel. I. Bernasconi, Robert. II. Wood, David
(David C.) III. Series.
B2430.L484P76 1988
194—dc19   88-327

ISBN: 978-0-415-00826-6 (hbk)
ISBN: 978-0-415-75501-6 (pbk)

Contents

Contents

Acknowledgments

The editors would like to thank Tamra Wright for her invaluable editorial assistance in the course of preparing this book, and the Research and Innovations Fund of the University of Warwick, without which it might never have seen the light of day. The index was prepared by Tony O'Leary.

Notes on the Contributors

ALISON AINLEY is a graduate student in the Department of Philosophy at the University of Warwick where she is currently working on a thesis on feminism and ethics. She has written on 'Woman' in Nietzsche in *Exceedingly Nietzsche* and has written poems included in *The Eric Gregory Anthology* (Salamander, 1987).

ROBERT BERNASCONI holds the Moss chair of excellence in philosophy at Memphis State University, and is the author of *The Question of Language in Heidegger's History of Being* as well as a number of essays on various aspects of Continental philosophy. He has edited a collection of Gadamer's essays on art and aesthetics under the title *The Relevance of the Beautiful and Other Essays*, and is currently preparing a book to be called *Between Levinas and Derrida*. He is the editor of the *Bulletin of the Hegel Society of Great Britain*.

DAVID BOOTHROYD did his graduate work on Levinas at the University of Warwick and is currently teaching in East Berlin.

TINA CHANTER is Assistant Professor of Philosophy at Louisiana State University. She has written articles on Levinas, Derrida and Heidegger. Her Stony Brook Ph.D. dissertation focused on Time in the philosophy of Levinas and Heidegger.

STEVEN GANS teaches Philosophy in and is Resident Director of the University of Maryland, Study-in-London Programme. He is a member of the Philadelphia Association and practises psychotherapy. He has published articles on Heidegger, Merleau-Ponty and Levinas.

JOHN HEATON is a psychiatrist practising psychotherapy in London. He has published *The Eye: Phenomenology and Psychology of Function and Disorder* and many papers on phenomenology.

CHRISTINA HOWELLS is Fellow and Tutor in French at Wadham College, Oxford. She teaches modern French literature and some Continental Philosophy, and is author of a study of *Sartre's Theory of Literature*, and *Sartre: the Necessity of Freedom*, 1987.

JOHN LLEWELYN is Reader in Philosophy at the University of Edinburgh. He is the author of *Beyond Metaphysics? The Hermeneutic Circle in Contemporary Continental Philosophy* and of *Derrida on the Threshold of Sense*.

NOREEN O'CONNOR is Director of Friends World College European Centre, the Philadelphia Association (London), and is in the Psychotherapy Training Programme of the Philadelphia Association.

Key to Abbreviations of Levinas's Texts

AEAE   *Autrement qu'être ou au-delà de l'essence,* The Hague, Martinus Nijhoff, 1974.

APB   'À propos de Buber: quelques notes', in *Qu'est-ce que l'homme? Philosophie/psychanalyse. Hommage à Alphonse de Waelhens (1911–1981),* Bruxelles, Facultés universitaires Saint-Louis, 1982, pp. 127–33.

BMP   'Martin Buber, Gabriel Marcel and Philosophy', translated by Esther Kameron, in *Martin Buber: a Centenary Volume,* edited by Haim Gordon and Jochanan Bloch, New York, Ktav Publishing House for the Faculty of Humanities and Social Sciences, Ben Gurion University of the Negev, 1984, pp. 305–21.

BP   'Martin Buber, Gabriel Marcel et la Philosophie', *Revue Internationale de Philosophie,* vol. 32, No. 126, 1978, 492–511.

DEE   *De l'existence à l'existant,* Paris, Vrin, 1947.

DEHH   *En découvrant l'existence avec Husserl et Heidegger,* Paris, Vrin, 1974.

DL   *Difficile liberté: essais sur le Judaïsme,* Paris, Albin Michel, 1963.

DVI   *De Dieu qui vient à l'idée,* Paris, Vrin, 1982.

EE   *Existence and Existents,* translated by A. Lingis, The Hague, Martinus Nijhoff, 1978.

EeI   *Ethique et infini,* Paris, Fayard, 1982.

EI   *Ethics and Infinity,* translated by Richard A. Cohen, Pittsburgh, Pa., Duquesne University Press, 1985.

NP   *Noms propres,* Montpellier, Fata Morgana, 1976.

OBBE   *Otherwise than Being or Beyond Essence,* translated by A. Lingis, The Hague, Martinus Nijhoff, 1981.

TA	*Le Temps et l'autre*, Paris, Presses Universitaires de France, 1983.
TeI	*Totalité et infini*, The Hague, Martinus Nijhoff, 1961.
TI	*Totality and Infinity*, translated by A. Lingis, Pittsburgh, Pa., Duquesne University Press, 1969.
TIHP	*The Theory of Intuition in Husserl's Phenomenology*, translated by André Orianne, Evanston, Ill., Northwestern University Press, 1973.
TO	'On the Trail of the Other', translated by Daniel J. Hoy, *Philosophy Today*, vol. 10, No. 1, 1966, 34–46.

Additional abbreviations are indicated as used in separate articles.

Introduction

A few years ago many of us knew the name of Levinas only as the author of an important book on Husserl's theory of intuition. The 1980s, however, have witnessed an avalanche of translations and discussions of Levinas's work, and philosophers who once focused their attention on Nietzsche, Sartre and Heidegger are now being forced to consider Levinas as a figure of comparable status. The accelerating translation of his major works, beginning with *Totality and Infinity* in 1969, is both a symptom of this and a contributory factor. For many students of contemporary philosophy, however, it was Derrida's long and brilliant discussion of Levinas in 'Violence and Metaphysics' (in his book *Writing and Difference*) that served as their introduction. Derrida located Levinas firmly within the tradition of Kant, Hegel, Nietzsche and Heidegger, for each of whom the question of the nature and limits of metaphysical discourse is central. Derrida wrote Levinas into the history of deconstruction, but not without ambiguity and not without reservations.

Levinas, like Derrida, had begun his thinking with the most intimate and probing reading of Husserl, and had marked out his own position on the margins of the phenomenological map, neither quite within it nor completely apart. Levinas, like Derrida, had come to find in the 'principle of principles' – intentionality – an undiminished commitment to the founding privilege of the individual subject. Each moved to explode that sacred interiority. But while for Derrida that rupture was achieved by the development and deployment of strategies of deformative reading (in which all forms of semantic, epistemological and ontological closure were undermined, 'deconstructed'), Levinas chose a different *point d'appui*: the relation to the Other, the face-to-face relation.

Students of phenomenology have long recognized the critical nature of this question. A classic series presents itself: Hegel's account of the master/slave relation; the early Marx's account of human alienation; Kierkegaard's views on the ethical necessity of indirect communication; Nietzsche's treatment of friendship; Husserl's confrontation with the problem of intersubjectivity in his fifth Cartesian Meditation; Buber's account of the I/Thou relation; Sartre's discussion of the Look and his associated descriptions of the Self/Other relationship; Heidegger's treatment of 'das Man', and of the possibility of authentic solicitude. What is at stake in each case is the nature and possibility of human relatedness. And the question of possibility seems at once a transcendental one ('How is it possible?') and one that asks about levels, degrees and depths of possibility, about the 'possibilities'. Levinas's distinctive contribution could be said to be to have turned the question around, to have argued that the face-to-face relation, the ethical relation, is itself fundamental, and as such not only does not need metaphysical justification but is itself the 'original' enactment of metaphysics.

Levinas's work is an intriguing – and provocative – fusion of authority and fragility, neither term being simple. Its authority is that of a mystical vision, which is yet as concrete and empirical as one could wish, filled out with detailed 'phenomenological' descriptions and which carefully locates itself in relation to the philosophical tradition. Its authority lies equally, as Levinas says of God, in the absence of power, in the way it calls, commands, demands an ethical response. And yet it is an essentially fragile writing. No text can be protected from a reading which kills, and Levinas's writing more than most lives only at the mercy of its reader. To say what he wants to say as he wants to say it, Levinas has no choice but to enter and deploy the logocentric language of philosophy which constantly threatens his project. But what Derrida's reading of Levinas shows, in the course of exploring these difficulties, is that today – more than ever, perhaps – this predicament is unavoidable, and that even if Levinas's solution cannot be strictly speaking 'successful' it is a most serious response to the exigencies of philosophical discourse.

If Levinas provides us with an exemplary enactment of these *aporias*, what makes his work dramatic and compelling for so many readers is the central place it gives to ethics. Readers of Sartre, Heidegger and Derrida had become accustomed to having their hopes for ethical illumination disappointed. Ethics was either deferred, linked to a discredited humanism, or celebrated by its absence. The best we could hope for was some sort of affirmative Nietzschean amoralism. Levinas came to that scene as rain to the cracked earth of a parched landscape. Moreover, he accomplishes this miracle with the unpromising and uncompromising language of difference and alterity. With the subsequent publication of Sartre's *Cahiers*, and the taking up of ethical and political questions by Lyotard, Kristeva, Lacoue-Labarthe, Nancy and Derrida, the drought seems to be over. But the troubling, disturbing and provocative claims of Levinas continue to demand a response.

The contributors to this volume address all these issues and more. There are four papers relating Levinas to the work of other philosophers: David Boothroyd redraws the Heidegger/Derrida/ Levinas triangle, defending Levinas against Derrida's reading, and pointing out surprising convergences between Levinas and Heidegger; Christina Howells argues that Sartre and Levinas are closer than one would think and that Sartre's *Cahiers* can be seen as a response to Levinas's criticisms; Robert Bernasconi traces in detail the course of the 'dialogue between thinkers' between Levinas and Buber, showing how Levinas comes to acknowledge the 'saying' in what Buber has 'said'; while John Llewelyn locates Levinas within the broader tradition of 'ethical metaphysics', with special focus on Derrida's reading of Levinas. There are three papers addressing that most contentious area: Levinas's importance for contemporary feminism. Tina Chanter argues that on the whole feminists should treat Levinas as an ally and that Simone de Beauvoir's judgment of Levinas's philosophy (as a male philosophy) is too simplistic; Noreen O'Connor articulates a surprising complementarity between the views of Levinas and Foucault on power and sexuality; and Alison Ainley critically compares the attitude of equivocation towards the very concept of feminism evinced by Kristeva and Levinas. Finally, there are two papers which argue for the importance of Levinas's work for psychotherapy. Steven Gans, by bringing Levinas and Pontalis together, argues for the convergence of Levinas's phenomenological ethics and psychotherapeutic practice, while John Heaton enlists Levinas in the wider project of counteracting the synthetic ambitions of a reason which would obscure the otherness, the non-totalizability of the Other.

We are especially grateful to Emmanuel Levinas for allowing us to publish an important essay, 'Useless Suffering' (translated by Richard Cohen) and for answering some of our questions. Tamra Wright,

Alison Ainley and Peter Hughes interviewed him in 1986 and we publish the results here under the title 'The Paradox of Morality'. In 'Useless Suffering' Levinas begins with a phenomenological treatment of the radical passivity of suffering, and passes on the attempts of theodicy to make pain intelligible by drawing it into a metaphysical finality. The Holocaust seems to set a limit to such attempts, but Levinas, drawing on Fackenheim's account, allows that it may yet return us to our inter-human responsibility. The interview ranged over many issues: alternative phenomenologies of the face; the ethical status of non-human animals; the place of Judaism in Levinas's philosophy; the implications of his thinking for practical politics.

We hope the book is half as provocative as the thinking which inspired its appearance.

David Wood

· 1 ·

The Other and Psychotherapy

JOHN HEATON

The problem of the Other is crucial in psychotherapy, yet is covered over by most theoretical writing in the field which is occupied with various modes of treatment that endeavour to cure a pathology. Usually the texts of psychotherapy are part of a theoretical system and merely attempt to elaborate or add to it; its concept of cure and its methods of obtaining that cure are subsumed under the system. The cured individual and the psychotherapeutic system are simply correlated with each other. The system defines what cure is – integration and individuation, attainment of the depressive position, the ability to carry on one's own self-analysis, and so on – and the cure occurs because of the correct application of the method of cure generated by the system. As one influential book puts it, analysis depends on 'the state of mind of the analyst'; this is embodied in 'the psycho-analytic attitude' and 'the foundation of this attitude must be *dedication to the psycho-analytic method*'. 'The value of the analytic process derives from the degree to which it is determined by the structure of the mind.'[1]

But the Other cannot be subsumed in a system and cannot be reached by a method however dedicated one is to it. The desire for the Other is the fundamental desire; and therefore is most pertinent when a person consults an analytical psychotherapist. It is not a desire for satisfaction or for non-satisfaction, for success or failure; it has another intent. It desires beyond anything that can simply complete it. *Its desire is not for fulfilment by a method or to be determined by a structure but for deepening.*

The Other is not a simple presence of a self to a self; it is not contained in a relation which starts from a distance and ends in a bringing

5

together. The Other is radical only if the desire for it is not the possibility of anticipating it as the desirable or of thinking it out beforehand but if it comes aimlessly as an absolute alterity, like death. The Other cannot be described or subsumed in the theoretical language which is used in most psychotherapy. This language purports to describe various structures in the mind and processes which occur in the interaction of the subject and his 'others', some of which are pathological and drive him into a mental illness. So the psychotherapist who is well versed in his particular theory finds it wherever he looks. The Freudian finds Oedipal themes, the Kleinian the presence or absence of the depressive position, the Jungian various stages of individuation, and so on. Psychotherapy, wherever it looks, only finds itself: a form of violence to the Other.

It is notable that on the group of patients to whom the problem of the Other is most acute the effectiveness of psychotherapy is minimal. These patients are called narcissistic. Freud admitted that the fundamental problem yet to be resolved in psychoanalysis is that of narcissism.[2] There have been many attempts since then to solve this problem, all of which have failed except to show the narcissistic nature of the authors of the various theories and treatments. An obvious sense of frustration informs the literature, and all it has shown is how common narcissistic problems are in our society.

These attempts to 'cure' narcissism have all failed because their fundamental assumption has been that the problem is to 'get through' to the analysand. They assume that the state of mind of the analysand has to be got at in some way and altered. Narcissistic patients fail to respond to these seductions. They either are not seduced at all or are completely seduced but fail to respond in the sense that their deep unhappiness and frustration with living remains. Narcissistic patients fail to respond to attempts to 'get through' to them because this is simply an attempt to subsume them within the same, to bring them within the system of thought and language which the analyst uses, whereas their problem lies with the Other.

The Other is an infinity irreducible even to the representation of infinity, it exceeds representational thought. The Other is infinitely distant from my own reality yet without this distance destroying the relation or the relation destroying the distance as would happen in a relation within the same. It does not become a confusion with the Other or effect its identity.

No language can contain the Other, whom it is impossible to understand, explain or interpret. The absolute experience is not disclosure but revelation: a coinciding of the expressed with him who expresses, which is the manifestation of the Other of a face, over and beyond form. The manifestation of the face is already discourse, it speaks, it sees and is seen. So discourse is not primarily a yes or a no; it is not a modification of thought but an original relation with the Other.

The Patient

I will now quote some remarks made by a lady I saw for three years or so, who was wrestling in a particularly cogent and intelligent way with the problem of the Other. She was about thirty years old and had had much psychiatric treatment since she was fourteen, including an attempt at psychoanalysis.

Her Position

She could only be comfortable in the room with me when we were back to back, she in one corner of the room and I in the opposite corner; so we would each face the wall and speak facing the wall. When she left we might glance at each other as she went through the door, but even then she would always lower her eyes and say that I was staring at her. She could not bear to be stared at and felt that this was what people always did to her; she had broken off previous attempts at therapy because of this, although her difficulty had been 'interpreted' to her.

She was acutely conscious of the assymetry of inter-subjective space; for her the Other was the stranger who stares, the enemy, the powerful scientist who knows. But our separation, the apparent failure of communication, our disengagement from participation, evoked the Other for her which would otherwise be swamped. This absence of the Other is precisely his presence *qua* Other.

Vision

She made many remarks to me about vision – seeing and being seen:

'I don't want you to see me as if you saw my body it would not be me. It keeps it purer by not being seen.'

'People don't know how to look. I do. People only look at what they want.'

'As a child I used to cut the eyes out of people in magazines. The eyes are dead like dead people. I remember people staring at me when I was a baby in my pram.'

'Everyone and the furniture is part of the air. It is only the eyes which are nothing, it is as if they were another world.'

'I can't look at people's eyes as they are black and round. Round is a perfect shape while the rest of the body isn't, and black is no colour.'

'I have a festering boil in the middle of my eyes and I am staring at it.'

'My eyes are like two holes in the sky. They seem to point to a beyond. Does everything belong to me or do I belong to everybody?'

'Things are just shapes, objects look distant, they seem to quiver out of reach. They look as if teasing me.'

'I dream of darkness and then feel everyone has gone mad around me.'

'I dream that I am in my house and someone kept staring at me even if I draw the curtains.'

'When I was a child I felt we were all in a shoe box and the stars were the holes in the lid.'

'Things don't seem to be orientated from my body, they are not in reach. The whole world is too bright, like on a summer's day; everything is black and white. Therapy brings shadows, darkness to see better by and then I see some colours.'

'If I wear clothes I like I feel exposed. If I wear clothes "they" like then I don't feel exposed but then my husband is frightened of me.'

Dream: 'A man is throwing knives at me, he told me if I moved I would be hit. I moved my foot and the knife went through it. It bled, no-one could staunch it. I put a sock over it and it appeared OK but went on bleeding inside. Then I was a ghost, I could not materialize. But my foot was material. People were around and I could not make my foot disappear.'

Comment

The face sees and is seen, and a glance recognizes this. But a stare does not, and a person stared at may easily cease to be Other to the one who stares. The face resists possession. This resistance is not like the hardness of a rock that opposes my power by an equal resistance, but it defies my ability for power. It breaks through the form that would grasp it by inviting me to a relation incommensurable with an exercised power. The coinciding of the expressed with him who expresses is how the face manifests itself; the face speaks, and this is over and beyond form and is the Other.

The eyes break through the mask of the face which can lie, for the language of the eyes is impossible to dissemble. The eyes do not shine but speak, and it is their absolute frankness which gives the possibility of truth and lying. The grace of the face's radiance provokes the idea of infinity which is necessary for separation and the Other to break through.

Moreover, the exterior world being flooded with light is a violence which prevents the radiance of the face; this requires shadow and colour to provoke the Other.

The Relation with the Therapist

'Why do I come to therapy? I want to and I don't want to. I am being suffocated by the appearance. I am living a nightmare.'

'If you look at me I feel it is me looking at me.'

'I feel you are the most frustrating person I have ever met. I feel you are brainwashing me so I tell myself, "I must not let him brainwash me" but then I find I keep quoting you.'

'I feel you will catch me so I keep distant; I try and catch myself. I get in a big muddle on days when I don't see you.'

'I have a terrible fear, an energy, is it me? I feel I have to do what others expect me to do. Is that evil? It can't be, I don't believe in evil. I want to name it but can't.'

Dream: 'I can't find you.' *Association.* 'I have a feeling of pressure in my head and I point far away and feel I am rushing towards it but get no nearer.'

'I feel I am part of everything and yet feel apart from it all. Are you me? Am I everybody? To feel real I would have to trust you for no reason.'

Comment

Many of her remarks remind me of Wittgenstein in *On Certainty*[3] where he explores, much in the manner of the classical sceptics like Sextus Empiricus, the limits of our knowledge; for example, 'I know that I am a human being'. In order to see how unclear the sense of this proposition is, consider its negation. At most it might be taken to mean 'I know I have the organs of a human' (for instance, a brain which, after all, no one has ever yet seen). But what about such a proposition as 'I know I have a brain'? Can I doubt it? Grounds for *doubt* are lacking! Everything speaks in its favour, nothing against it. Nevertheless it is imaginable that my skull should turn out empty when it was operated on.[4] 'Strange coincidence, that every man whose skull has been opened had a brain!' (par. 207) 'My life shows that I know or am certain there is a chair over there, or a door, and so on – I tell a friend e.g. "Take that chair over there", "Shut the door", etc. etc.' (par. 7) Also remember the eerie feeling described by Kripke[5] when he contemplates the fact that there is nothing in his mind which instructs him to say 68 + 57 is 125 rather than 5. He feels sure that there is something in his mind – the meaning he attaches to the plus sign – that instructs him as to what to do in all future cases. When this 'feeling' is undermined by Wittgenstein's remarks he feels eerie. No wonder psychoanalysts who believe that meaning resides in the mind are so resistant to Wittgenstein's sceptical therapy. The Other is not in anybody's mind yet is the source of trust, of being sure.

Death

She was haunted by death.

'I am rotting away. I have got every disease and they are fighting for mastery. Am I a monster?'

'I see the whole of existence but there is a flaw in it and this flaw has me marked. I try and find the flaw but it is neither near nor far. Neither I nor you can do anything about it. I feel my death is marked. I can see my own death.'

Dream: 'There was lots of colour, a gay carnival but inside were beautifully made up corpses.'

Dream: 'I was in an old house with my parents. Suddenly undertakers came carrying a coffin. They had powdered faces, painted blue lips and eyes. One came to me and said "You look ill".'

Dream: 'I was dead and was lying in my wedding dress which was old and tattered. I asked my parents if I should put it on her. They said "There is no point now".' *Association.* 'I feel my corpse is an old friend. I am afraid of other corpses. I don't feel I am married.'

Dream: 'I am dead and doctors dressed as Elizabethans are killing me.'

Dream: 'There is a beautiful garden of an old house with magnolia bushes in bloom. My parents in a horse and carriage are driving round and round dead.'

Dream: 'I killed someone and then was annoyed that Dr Heaton did not stop me going to prison. Then I killed someone again.'

Dream: 'I was in a huge church. There was a brightly painted coffin on the altar with a head in it. We put the rest of the corpse in and went to leave but its eyes which were blue-gold chased me as if to grab me with its stare.'

Dream: 'I was at Canterbury. All the dead were to come alive. The day came, there was an eerie light and masses of people were busy. The dead began to materialize through the walls. They were transparent and in pale colours. It was horrible.'

'I am fighting death. Nothing else is real.'
Dream: 'An atomic bomb is going to drop. I was looking at the people and how they would react.'

Time

'My childhood never ended. Did it ever begin? Where was I before it began? Meaning is nothing to me, all is eternal. To ordinary people there are limits which is not nice.'
'Space and time are so big so why speak? Why don't you tell me what you think of me?'
'I feel everything is going into everything. Everything is turning itself inside out. Time and space are carrying on alone. Everything is me. Everything is nothing. I don't understand what I am saying.'
'I am becoming conscious of my agony, it is perpetual day and night. I am continually racing against time. I am being torn apart. A-PART: spelled backwards TRAP. I am not A-PART of the world.'

Comments

Is death the end of the Other? Can dying be passed through so that it is the point from which the separated being will continue by virtue of the heritage he has amassed? The death agony is precisely in this impossibility of ceasing, of being nothing but past. Dying is agony because in dying a being does not come to an end while coming to an end. He has no more time, he goes where he cannot go. The struggle with death is a struggle with the invisible. It is not to be confounded with the collision of two forces whose issue one can foresee and calculate.

To be conscious is to have time – that is, not to overflow the present by hastening to the future but to have distance with regard to the present. In suffering we are deprived of all freedom of movement, the pain of suffering lies in the impossibility of fleeing it, of being protected in oneself from oneself. This situation, where consciousness deprived of all freedom of movement maintains a minimal distance from the present, is patience: the passivity of undergoing and yet mastery itself. In patience we neither hover over our own history nor do we blindly engage in a struggle with some others. The being that does violence to me and has a hold on me is not yet upon me and continues to threaten in the future. But in this extreme consciousness extreme passivity can become extreme mastery and the will breaks through the crust of its egotism and, as it were, displaces its centre of gravity outside of itself. Death no longer touches the will so narcissism is overcome.

Insomnia

'I can't go to sleep, I try and keep in the middle in going to sleep, I fear dying, not death, the unbearable isolation.'

'I always fear people tampering with my consciousness, fear anaesthetics particularly. Only I can fall asleep and no one can do it for me.'

Comment

In insomnia we are no longer attending to objects, whether internal or external, but are vigilant. There is no longer any outside or inside, for vigilance is devoid of objects. Attention presupposes the freedom of the ego which directs it; the vigilance of insomnia has no subject. It is the reawakening of the 'there is' in the heart of negation. But an abstract being hovering in the air lacks an essential condition for falling asleep. To fall we must have a place to fall to. A place is not an indifferent somewhere but a base. In lying down and curling up we abandon ourselves to a place; *qua* base it becomes our refuge. Consciousness comes out of rest, out of this unique relationship with a place.

Thought and language

'I am a million echoes. My feelings are far more important than the words I apply to them. I use English like a foreign tongue. I have to think what word to apply to a feeling like sadness, what word would fit. How do you know what words fit, they have no meaning? You have been brainwashed by your training. All psychiatrists disappoint me. I can see the whole of you whereas you can only see part of me.'

'I look up in psychiatric books to tell me what I feel and to know what to tell you. But my blanket is too thick so I don't know where I am.'

'Knowing the light is on does not tell me the light is on.'

'My aim is total disintegration. You keep dodging me. Where do you stand?'

'I was taken to my GP and he told me there was nothing wrong with me. I felt angry. Doctors do not recognize despair unless I do something dramatic. One of my psychiatrists killed himself, it was the most terrible thing that ever happened to me. He kept wanting me not to "see" him and he told me my thoughts were silly and that I must not think them. Yet his letters which I saw after his suicide showed he had the same thoughts as I.'

'Everything is particular so there is nothing in particular. All is rubbish so I can't get rid of it.'

'What holds things together? I do. What is I? Everything is me. But what difference does it make? None.'

Later: 'What makes a thing complete? All are bits which are complete in themselves.'

'Am I what I think I am? My words say more than I think and this distresses me.'

'I can't see properly as my thoughts get in the way. As I speak I think thoughts and feel my speech betrays my thoughts.'

'When I was given psychological tests they were looking for what they wanted to find. They did not know what I meant. It was all a horrible game.'

'I used to be able to remember where my thoughts had got to, now I can't. I understand what I am saying but could not understand what I have said.'

Panic

'I can't tell how I am. I have no criteria to tell how I am. How do you know? What is your thought and what is mine?'

'I am a head wrapped in newspaper.'

'I keep thinking I must stop thinking what I am thinking.'

'I feel you are a gigantic game, how do I know you are not?'

'I am in limbo going round and round. What difference does it make my seeing you? What is the difference of difference? The impossible is happening. I am in the corner of the room, yet looking at myself.'

'I feel I am going mad. How do I stop it? Maybe the effort to stop it is the madness. Are you going to stop me? You have no right to meddle.'

'I read upside down and set myself obstacles to reading so as not to feel bored. If you fling sense it disappears, which is why I can't be content with space. I am everything, which is why I am so bored.'

Comment

The roots of language lie in the presentation of meaning. Meaning is the face of the Other. Exchanging ideas about the world, language as communication, presupposes the originality of the face, for the face signifies by itself, it offers itself in person. Discourse is not a modification of thought; it is not enacted within a consciousness but is an original relation with the Other. Meaning is not produced from the givens of the perceptual world, from representations in consciousness which is the thought of the same, but is said and taught by presence. And presence is an event irreducible to evidence for it dominates him who welcomes it and teaches its very novelty. To have meaning is to be situated relative to an absolute that comes from that alterity that is not absorbed in being perceived. It is to possess an inexhaustible surplus of attention.

Conclusion

Reason consists in the coherence of the one and the other in the unity of a theme, and this accord in the unity of a theme is called a system. The presence of a theme where the one and the other become significations is correlated with a subject which is a consciousness. So we have systems of therapy which significantly are called after the person who devised them – Freud, Jung, Klein and so on. Now scepticism shows that there is a rupture or split in reason, an incoherence which signifies that the thematic is not the ultimate framework of reason. The state and medicine try to surmount these ruptures by reason and knowledge. 'The said thematizes the interrupted dialogue or the dialogue delayed by silences, failure or delirium, but the intervals are not recuperated. Does not the discourse that suppresses the interruptions of discourse by relating them maintain the discontinuity under the knots with which the thread is tied again?'⁶

The invincible and evanescent force of scepticism does not permit us to confer any privilege on its said over against the presuppositions of its saying. This contradiction that opposes one to the other recalls the break-up of the unity of reason 'without which one could not *otherwise than be*'.⁷

Notes

1 D. Meltzer, *The Psycho-Analytical Process*, Scotland, Clunie Press, 1967, p. 79 (author's italics).
2 S. Freud, *On Narcissism: an Introduction* (1914), Standard edition, London, Hogarth Press, 1914, vol. 14, p. 67.
3 L. Wittgenstein, *On Certainty*, translated by D. Paul and G. E. M. Anscombe, Oxford, Basil Blackwell, 1969.
4 S. A. Kripke, *Wittgenstein on Rules and Private Language*, Oxford, Basil Blackwell, 1982, p. 21.
5 Ibid.
6 OBBE, p. 170; AEAE, p. 216.
7 OBBE, p. 171; AEAE, p. 218.

· 2 ·

Responding to Levinas

DAVID BOOTHROYD

It is often noted that Levinas's religious writings and his philosophical work exhibit a continuity and interrelatedness that deny the possibility of a strict distinction between the two. It is not surprising that a thinker who is deeply religious should attempt to work out the metaphysical foundations of his religious experience. However, we who are not religious, or those who are but consider their religious experience to be beyond the grasp of philosophical discourse, are quite likely to view Levinas's project as theological, and hence of no interest to philosophy, or as bad philosophy because it is based on theology. And yet, Levinas's work is clearly neither strictly theological nor strictly philosophical: theology as much as philosophy (*qua* ontology) is on trial in Levinas's work. As Derrida says, 'The complicity of theoretical objectivity and mystical communion will be Levinas's true target.'[1] Therefore, the undercurrent of messianism which runs throughout so much of his work, and which may or may not be merely an aspect of Jewish mysticism, should be understood only on the basis of an interpretation of its role in the texts. In other words, if Levinas's understanding of the *absolute* alterity of the Other, for instance, is esoteric or neo-religious, then its character as such can be exposed on the basis of our reading of his text. This should be possible firstly because of Levinas's (expressed) commitment to 'reason',[2] and secondly because of the explicitly non-intuitional nature of the experience which he places at the centre of his meditation – that of the Face.

Bearing this in mind, we are likely to greet Levinas's own reading of Heidegger with great consternation. His attack on Heidegger appears to be in response to what he takes to be the 'spirit' of 'Heideggerian ontology', a notion identified by Levinas on the basis of seemingly little attention to the letter of Heidegger's *Being and Time*.[3] I shall say more about this shortly. Levinas can similarly be charged with a selective reading of Husserl. As Derrida has noted in 'Violence and Metaphysics', Levinas, when discussing Husserl, constantly oscillates between what he refers to as the 'letter' and the 'spirit' of Husserlianism, adding that the former is most often contested in the name of the latter.[4] For example, in respect of Husserl's notion of intentionality, we may say that we commonly associate the 'letter' with the theoretical discussions of intentionality in terms of noesis/noema correlation and the 'spirit' with the descriptions of lived experience and the life-world – of our relation to alterity as intentional. In going against the 'letter' in this way, or at least in privileging the 'spirit' of Husserlianism, Levinas does not seek to challenge systematically or thematically the rigour of Husserl's analysis of intentionality. He seeks rather (indeed by means of a neo-Husserlian appeal to experience) to move away from the priority given to the objectifying reflection which, as it gathers itself into philosophical discourse in Husserl, assumes the neutrality of its own standpoint.[5] We do not wish to take issue here as to the precise meaning of Husserl's text or as to whether Levinas's emphasis fails to do justice to the 'letter' of the text at this point. We do wish to draw attention to the fact that it is no mere coincidence that these now perennial questions of the relation between the meaning and the text, the inside/outside of the text, and indeed the nature of the assumptions made by any text about such issues, are at the forefront of our response to Levinas. That is to say, it is not only because these issues characterize a certain theme of questioning but also because these issues themselves will not be left untouched by Levinas's work. Indeed, it is the challenge of Levinas's own texts that prompts Derrida himself, in speaking of *Totality and Infinity*, to wonder whether he is dealing with a 'treatise' at all and not a work of art.[6]

The difficulty encountered in responding to Levinas's work is partly due to the fact that the philosophical response we are apt to make is itself being put into question; it also arises because, beyond this, we are called upon to re-cognize (yet non-cognitively) a *silent* 'expression' (which is founded on speech). Redoubling the paradox, the inadequacy of the 'philosophical response', due to its 'ethical neutrality', can only be demonstrated on the basis of that which remains beyond it. Notwithstanding such an a-logical formulation, claims for the primacy of the ethical are presented as a critique of the tradition. Their force, however, would appear not to rest in the rigour of this critique –

an appeal to the intellect – but elsewhere; they achieve their effect by a means not so easily identified. Perhaps this should be described as an appeal to responsibility. However, the precise *understanding* of this term as we find it in Levinas is itself postponed in a significant way: we are led to think it in terms other than those of its intelligibility. For this reason the identification of the force which produces the movement in Levinas's discourse is problematic. It is neither dialectical nor hermeneutical nor analytical, nor yet does it call for poetic rapture. Perhaps Derrida is correct to point to Levinas's use of metaphor as the place which 'shelters within its pathos the most decisive movements of the discourse'.[7] If this is true – indeed, if this is possible – then it can be so because Levinas's language retains a foothold in the traditional *logos*: it exhibits a commitment to intelligibility; it is philosophical and yet seeks to express what in principle remains beyond the grasp of philosophy.

The commentary I offer here is intended to demonstrate the philosophicality of Levinas's discourse as it directs itself toward this so-called 'beyond' of philosophy. Firstly, I shall indicate certain points at which we can perhaps recognize, in a provisional way, the grounds for a genuine dialogue with Heidegger. In order to do this I shall identify and set aside what could be referred to as 'Levinas's Heidegger', which is a representation of Heidegger that functions internally within Levinas's own thesis. I set this aside in order to consider Levinas's own phenomenological analyses to see if the kind of claims they lead him to make are as radically opposed to Heidegger as he clearly thinks. In questioning the philosophical status of what Levinas is doing and saying, I ask whether there are any 'structural' movements in *Totality and Infinity* which could be compared to the 'spiraling descent' of the hermeneutic circle in *Being and Time*.

What I understand to be at stake in our approach to Levinas is the possibility of regarding his work as a profound contribution to a body of thought which concerns itself with the 'end of philosophy'; a kind of sub-tradition whose key figures are Hegel, Marx, Nietzsche and Heidegger. What is so radical in Levinas is the way in which the issues which circulate within this sub-tradition, such as the relationship between the nature of language and the possibilities of a new way of thinking, are all illuminated in terms of the question of the relation to the Other. My general claim is that what emerges from a move in this direction is that in responding to Levinas we become reflexively tied up with the issue he is pursuing. That is, the problem of our own response to Levinas – as to whether we can find satisfactory 'discursive support' for his claims, and using this term does not pre-empt the nature of any such evidence – takes us directly to the heart of his own attempt to articulate something that disrupts the very possibility of 'philosophical satisfaction' with regard to the question of the other person.

Let us turn now to Levinas's relation to Heidegger and to what I referred to earlier as 'Levinas's Heidegger'. Levinas sets up a Heideggerian straw man and refers to it as 'Heidegger's ontology'. The definitive characteristic of this ontology, according to Levinas, is the priority afforded to Being over beings. From this alleged priority ensues the entire sustained criticism that in Heidegger the relation to the Other is subordinated to the relation to Being and hence ethics to ontology. It is this priority that he sought to reverse in *Existence and Existents* in the analyses of effort and fatigue, where he describes the moment in which the existent exhibits its 'mastery' over existence as does a 'subject over its attribute'. Levinas thereby takes the first step toward establishing ethics as 'first philosophy'. To read Heidegger's account of the ontological difference in this way (which, in fact, is not to attempt to think the *difference* at all) is crucial to Levinas's development of two of his central notions: those of the *separation* and *ipseity* of the subject *qua* 'substantive'. The kind of radical heterogeneity that is described by these two notions is insupportable on the basis of the *concept* of Being which Levinas attributes to Heidegger. He attributes to Heidegger an ontology in which Being functions as the excellent existent and is therefore supreme within a hierarchical economy of power. The comprehension of Being which Levinas identifies with this ontology signifies that it is equally a philosophy of the *same*, and in this sense an egology, in which the *question* of Being appears as the reflexive interlocution of the being of the same. Hence it is closed to alterity; to the possibility of an original difference – to Infinity. Levinas's reading of Being in Heidegger 'traditionalizes' Heidegger; by a peculiar irony, he makes Heidegger pre-Heideggerian.

Levinas 'needs' to read Heidegger in this way because the reversal of terms constitutes the basic move through which he will offer a critique of the entire (Greek) tradition and not merely of Heidegger. A consistent misreading of Being in Heidegger, particularly in *Being and Time*, does indeed make it appear as the most explicit formulation of a traditional preoccupation with being and therefore a very good target for Levinas's own attack on the tradition.

I do not wish to suggest that as Levinas sets out from a misreading of Being in Heidegger all of his criticisms aimed at Heideggerian notions are simply irrelevant to those notions. It is possible that they remain highly pertinent. This is possible precisely because, over and above the questions surrounding the difference between 'Levinas's Heidegger' and any other Heidegger, there remains the fact that they are both attempting to deconstruct/surpass/delimit/go beyond (bracketing the differences for the moment) the logocentric tradition, which exhibits a remarkable propensity for 'recapturing' any discourse which sets out to do exactly this. In his criticisms of Heidegger Levinas appears to take Heidegger's thesis as a frame on which to hang a very general critique of the tradition. The 'priority' of Being over beings in 'Levinas's Heidegger' is the priority of the general over the particular. The Other, grasped by means of the concept, is equated with his intelligibility, which is 'measured' by me. In such a schema I fail to regard him as an intelligence. He is an object of my intellection, as is any other (thing). The traditional identification of reason and cognition, coupled with Heidegger's 'comprehension of Being', harbours the implicit connection between intelligibility and the thinking of the same: light/illumination in association with theorizing and thematic representation are intrinsic components to Heidegger's thought according to Levinas. The reason why Levinas finds a profound need to leave the 'climate' of Heidegger's philosophy and yet not for a philosophy which would be pre-Heideggerian, is not that he sees Heidegger as having contributed to a break with the tradition as such. Rather, he sees in Heidegger its most extreme possibility, expressed by the phrase 'the comprehension of Being'. Heidegger is thus Levinas's 'last metaphysician'.

If we wished to defend Heidegger against Levinas's reading in a straightforward manner, we might reflect on Levinas's suggestion that there is a priority of Being over beings in Heidegger. To this we would say, with Derrida, that 'Being, since *it is nothing* outside the existent . . . could in no way precede the existent whether in time or dignity etc.'.[8] Neither is Being fundamental in Heidegger, such that the thought of Being is 'first philosophy'. It is the *question* of Being which is central in Heidegger.

However, the reading whose direction I would like to indicate here gets under way by holding our initial reactions to Levinas's peculiar reading of Heidegger at bay: by following him on to a wrong bus we may learn something about its route which will lead us to reconsider its destination. There is a sense in which this gesture corresponds to the suspension or postponement of our critical response called for when we consider the quasi-phenomenological analyses in *Existence and Existents*. There we are invited to attend to 'certain moments in human experience'.[9] Notice that he says *in* experience. Such moments, which prove to be decisive for Levinas, are essentially constitutive of human experience but are also essentially prior to its constitution as such. Of course, without the account of time as a series of Instants, rather than a temporal flow or ecstasis, it would make no sense to say that these moments were *experienced* at all. We are told that what these moments signify (that is, exemplify) can only be thought from the perspective of their event. Levinas says, 'let us ignore all attitudes toward existence which arise from reflection, attitudes by which an already constituted existence turns back over itself'.[10] He suggests, for example, that by putting oneself in the moment of effort one 'directly perceives' the 'taking up of existence' as opposed to the reflective awareness or intellection of the experience. One is said to perceive the *event* itself and not merely its 'significance with respect to a system of references'.[11]

Levinas defers, however, any transcendental justification of this proposed 'method'. He says, 'our investigations will bring the necessary clarifications of this principle by the application they shall make of it'.[12] We could say that Levinas is blindfolding us here, which not only makes us more sensitive to what cannot be seen, to what, due to our preoccupation with the visible (namely, the already constituted) we might ignore, but it also compromises our demands for intelligibility and the comprehension of the whole. Levinas evokes the connection between the metaphor of the sun and Western thinking, the thinking which associates light and illumination and the possession of what is with intelligibility.

Such demands are apt to make us less responsive to what is 'immediate' in Levinas's sense of the term. He is saying more here than that his claims will be substantiated if we remain patient; more importantly, he is saying that what we might ordinarily regard as substantiation may prove to be inappropriate here. Precisely what will prove to be appropriate will of course depend on what we ultimately come to consider to be the nature of the claims in question. Now, to compromise one's expectations of intelligibility, one might suspect, is to sail dangerously close to the wind of mysticism. But would this not be an unavoidable danger and a necessary risk for any thinking which is attempting to transcend the distinction between the 'mystical' and the 'philosophical'? I shall now pursue this characterization of the problem and see if there are any interesting parallels to be made with what I understand to be the nature of Heidegger's 'task'.

In *Being and Time* the project of an existential hermeneutic gets under way on the basis of the 'hermeneutic circle' which is decisively joined by and thus founded upon the precomprehension of Being proper to Dasein. Being is both disclosed and dissimulated in and by the question of Being – in language. The 'necessity' of dissimulation opens the 'possibility' of disclosure. Being both circulates within language and hides within language *qua* ontic metaphor. However, this 'ontic metaphor' within which Being is dissimulated is not a displacement of the literal meaning of Being because Being is *nothing* outside of this ontic determination, in the same way in which it is nothing outside of the existent. Being is the trans-categorical ground of the 'metaphoricity' of metaphor, and this indicates to us the sense in which Being both transcends metaphysical (ontic) determination and appears within it. There is no 'ideal' disclosure or full presence of Being in language, in philosophy, but only a *trace* which marks the withdrawal of Being within ontic metaphor.

To say that ontic metaphor is not a displacement of the meaning of Being is to say that it does not have an 'origin' *as such* – which would be Being *itself*. We must rather think of Being as enduring in an originary way as the history of its discursive dissimulation, a history which can be traced in and through the development of this metaphor. Therefore, any discourse which seeks to speak against, to distance itself from or go beyond this metaphor, must in a sense go beyond history. To neutralize history by means of a *reduction* was criticized by Levinas, in *The Theory of Intuition in Husserl's Phenomenology*, for *assuming* its neutrality in the form of the 'liberty of theory'; at that time he turns toward Heidegger's analyses based upon the historicity of Dasein.

By the time of *Totality and Infinity*, however, Heidegger's own attempt to think the historicity of history by means of the meta-history of Being is understood to involve the 'dissolution' of the subject in his historical situation. Levinas says of *Totality and Infinity*, 'This book's insistence on the separation of enjoyment was guided by the necessity of liberating the "I" from the situation into which, little by little, philosophers have dissolved it.'[13] It is against this trend and armed with his misreading of Being in Heidegger that Levinas develops his metaphysics of separation and exteriority, which locates the 'origin' of meaning *outside* of history (which is the history of Being) in the face of the other which, he argues, is *beyond Being*: 'When man truly approaches the Other he is uprooted from history.'[14]

Levinas's commitment to a philosophical rather than a mystical understanding of the beyond history/Being is expressed in the following: 'This beyond the totality and objective experience is, however, not to be described in a purely negative fashion. It is reflected *within* the totality and history, *within* experience.'[15] It is therefore the 'proper object' of philosophy. In so far as infinity is reflected within the totality, the impossible has, so to speak, already occurred; the moment of totalization has already been deferred or postponed by the face of the Other. Now, if Levinas sought merely to draw attention to the face by means of a phenomenology of the face and to attempt to base *an* ethics on such a study, then he would indeed be engaged in the kind of ethical philosophy that Heidegger says, in his *Letter on Humanism*, will flourish only when 'original thinking has come to an end'.[16] This is clearly not the intention of Levinas's enterprise. Metaphysics is ethics *first*, says Levinas. The relation to the Other is the originary event in Levinas.

Against the perpetual movement of disclosure and appropriation of Being in (historical) time, Levinas is offering an account of a concrete relation to the infinite in the face-to-face relation. It is the 'irreducibility' of this event which secures its axiological centrality in Levinas's metaphysics. This difference, if indeed it is a genuine difference, could be represented by the different understanding of time in Heidegger and Levinas, or more explicitly, in Levinas's understanding of Heidegger's notion of time as 'historical'. The Instant, on the other hand, is not thought of in terms of *duration* at all. Consequently, Levinas is able to say that the relation to the face of the other does not endure as such but is perpetually *recommenced*.

There are, nevertheless, similarities here. For example, this relation is not thought in terms of the *presence* of the infinite within totality. Similarly in Heidegger: 'the "openness" [which] grants to the movement of speculative thinking the passage through what it thinks',[17] is characterized by a play of light and dark, of the visible and the invisible, of presence *and* absence.

In order to maintain a radical difference between Heidegger and Levinas on this point of the relation between the Infinite or Being and totality, one would have to read Heidegger's disclosure and appropriation of Being in terms of thematization, of grasping and possession, which is contrary to his most explicit intention. Derrida puts it well when he says,

the Being *which is in question* is not a concept by which the existent (e.g. someone) is to be submitted (subsumed). Being is not the concept of a rather indeterminate and abstract predicate seeking to cover the totality of existents in its extreme universality: firstly, because it is not a predicate, and it authorizes all predication; secondly, because it is 'older' than the concrete *presence* of the *ens* and thirdly, because belonging to Being does not cancel any predicative difference but, on the contrary, permits the emergence of every possible difference. Being is therefore transcategorical and Heidegger would say of it what Levinas says of the Other: it is 'refractory to the category'.[18]

Derrida goes on to absolve the Heideggerian thought of Being of the charge of violence toward the existent as such (that is, of any ethical violence), but it is not the details of that particular move that interest me here. What indicates at least some measure of proximity between Heidegger and Levinas here is that they both place that which is refractory to thematic representation at the 'origin' of meaning.

What we are seeking all along is the justification for Levinas's identification of the Other as this origin. Is there any ground upon which such a move may legitimately be made? Can Levinas only make this move on the basis of his misconception of the thought of Being in Heidegger? Derrida reminds us that it is implicit in this thought that Being permits the emergence of *all* difference (and hence that of the I/ Other). In conceptualizing Being, does not Levinas thereby deny himself every determination from the outset? asks Derrida. Furthermore, with regard to Levinas's failure to grasp the significance of the ontological difference, is not Derrida correct in saying that 'Levinas confirms Heidegger in his disclosure: for does not the latter see in metaphysics (in metaphysical ontology) the forgetting of Being and the dissimulation of the ontological difference?'[19] Levinas's reading of Heidegger certainly supplies us with the grounds for such a remark, but we are puzzled by the thought that there is also a sense in which this emphatic assertion of the ethical neutrality of the thought of Being could be said to confirm Levinas's discourse with regard to the 'impersonal' and the 'neuter'; not because Being functions as a 'neutral power' denoting the tyranny of the same, but because of its absolute indifference to the infinitude of the Other. It is true that the thought of Being is no more politics than it is agriculture or ethics,[20] but does this not imply, correctly or incorrectly, a degradation of the ethical in relation to the thought of Being?

In order to answer this question we would have to be sure that we could understand the meaning of the term 'ethical' in such a way as to wrest it from the thought of Being, and it is not at all clear that this can be done. For us to accept Levinas's account of the relation to the Other as originary and as not based on an ontic ethnocentrism, this thesis must adequately describe the antecedence of the ethical relation to any determination of the other (in general). Without this his thesis would apparently be akin to negative theology: a philosophy *pointing* to what is explicitly understood to lie beyond philosophical determination. When this objection is similarly put to Heidegger's thought of Being we say, with reference to *Being and Time*, that the ontological interpretation proceeds not merely by negation upon negation but (on the basis of a precomprehension of Being) 'in movements of increasing explicitness'.[21] Levinas denies himself such an explanation because, in appealing to the primordiality of the face-to-face, he implicitly appeals to its ahistoricity. Interpretation, on the other hand, as a movement of increasing explicitness, is a movement within history (or even the movement *of* history) which at the outset dissimulates what it discloses (rather than 'pointing' to it) in the interpretation itself. Once again, I think the key to understanding Levinas's claim lies in his notion of time as a series of Instants.

In such phenomenological studies as those of effort, fatigue, indolence and labour in *Existence and Existents*, and those of enjoyment and habitation in *Totality and Infinity*, we are given an account of the relation to being and to the 'element' which aims to account for the (pre-phenomenological) anteriority of such relations to the world *qua* 'constituted'. Terms such as 'living from' and 'enjoyment' are used to describe these. The 'level of life' which these analyses indicate is said to be anterior to the system of constituted relations within which the very appeal for this anteriority comes. The justification for this illogical claim is quasi-phenomenological in that it appeals to something which is implicitly prior to phenomenological representation. In these analyses objects are described as being primarily objects of enjoyment. In the analysis of labour we find evidence for time as a series of Instants. The combination of these two enables Levinas to say:'The incessant turning of ecstatic representation into enjoyment . . . in each instant *restores the antecedence* of what I constitute to this very constitution.'[22] What I constitute 'antecedently' here I constitute on the basis of my originary separation and ipseity, which were seemingly derived theoretically from the phenomenological studies rather than being what gave rise to them. I return to this part of Levinas's account, to the relation to Being, in order to show the way in which this model occurs at different levels in the text.

Firstly, in the description of our relation to the element in terms of enjoyment, Levinas gives us an account of the 'condition' for the separation of the existent. The existent is capable of sustaining its 'mastery'[23] over existence and thus maintaining its separation through the satisfaction of its needs. In this description of enjoyment we are referred to a 'level of life' and to a relation to the other (in general) which is antecedent to the world as *constituted*. Separation itself is 'restored' to this level and is seen not merely to be a product of conceptual representation. This model serves to help us understand the 'functioning' of the face-to-face. Levinas's understanding of speech is crucial here: speaking (conversation) is understood to do the work of restoring the antecedence of the ethical relation. Speaking is at once the interruption of a 'hitherto' uninterrupted relation and yet requires the antecedence of the relata prior to this speaking. Speaking interrupts the relation and restores the antecedence of the relata *qua* relata in each Instant. Paradoxically, the relation recommences *un*interrupted; it can do so precisely because time is conceived as a series of Instants. With each new Instant the antecedence of the ethical is restored – in the face-to-face.

It may be objected that this paradoxical anteriority can only be stated theoretically and therefore only has meaning in relation to the 'system' in which it is presented – in this case Levinas's *Totality and Infinity*. More poignantly, it may be objected that in so far as the face is articulated at all, it is subjected to the (non-ethical) violence of ontic metaphor. Derrida emphasizes and re-emphasizes this point because the intertwining of the finite and the infinite, which is supposed to have its epiphany in the face-to-face, would thus be an ideality. As such it could indeed be said to be outside of history, but could not (itself) be *said* at all, as to be outside of history is also to be outside of language. Furthermore, that which is beyond linguistic expression must be subject to a mystical understanding, almost by definition. What is being said here is that either the face-to-face is an ontic determination of what in principle cannot be accounted for, and hence cannot be what it is claimed to be, or it is outside of language and therefore radically unintelligible, namely mystical.

The relation between these two alternatives, which is central in Levinas, also characterizes the general problem of transcending the control which philosophical conceptualization exercises over thinking, without abandoning the demand for intelligibility. This problem constitutes the framework of his appeal for the primacy of the ethical and his attempts to describe the metaphysical foundations of experience (religious or otherwise). Levinas does not seek merely to give this relation between philosophy and any beyond-philosophy an ethical context, but also to describe this relation which occurs as a rupture of totality, as ethical (or ethics).

Understanding the interrelations and structure of Levinas's terminology, understanding the nature of his claims systematically or philosophically, necessarily falls short of the 'understanding' called for of that which is untotalizable in any system.[24] This restates the problem that I claim is central to the question of our own response to Levinas. Neither philosophical nor mystical, the metaphysics in which Levinas is engaged attempts to occupy the space between these two extremes. Does not Levinas's discourse get recaptured by the logocentric demand for intelligibility which gives priority to the philosophical, in that, against his best intentions, he constructs a classically metaphysical system whose circular movements can be described and approved, but one which is essentially 'closed' in so far as its terms do in fact only have meaning within its own system of reference?

One way of responding to this suggestion might be to ask whether there is anything in Levinas similar to the movements of 'increasing explicitness' which are characteristic of the 'interpretation of interpretation' in *Being and Time*, to this kind of reflexivity. Such movements are associated with a 'distancing' of oneself from any traditional mode of inquiry. I would like to speculate that something equally consistent can be seen to be going on in Levinas. I hinted at it above when I suggested that the model for understanding what happens in the face-to-face is already given in the account of the relation to Being. Firstly we are given an account of the relation to the element in terms of enjoyment, which, it is said, is beyond the grasp of phenomenological representation (in the sense of being at a level prior to it). At that point 'justifications' of this 'method' were postponed. Secondly, in the face-to-face we see how the separation of existents is both the prerequisite of speaking (conversation) and yet this relation is always already entered into. Thirdly, the structure of model governing these movements of 'restoration' serves analogously for the way in which Levinas understands the relation between philosophy and what is beyond philosophy: metaphysics is 'ethics' first.

Now, bearing the above in mind, we can think of this 'first' in terms other than those which would construe it as a metaphysical fundamentalism of the excellent existent (or *event* in Levinas's case). We can understand it in the sense that the relation to the other as *life* is prior to its conceptual representation. This is the plane on which responsibility and hospitality are to be found without having to account for themselves. Of course, when we say 'prior to conceptual representation', to philosophizing, we realize that we are always already philosophizing. This is reflected in the fact that the call to responsibility is not a call to silence, nor is it a call for 'more responsibility and less philosophizing'! On the contrary, what Levinas is saying is that the relation between philosophy and its other deserves to be placed at the centre of thinking. What he is attempting to show is that this is the event of the ethical, and is, in a sense, a metaphorical displacement of the empirical I–Other conjuncture: 'Metaphysics is *enacted* in ethical relations.'[25] Ethics, in Levinas, is the very 'substance' of metaphysics, a relation between 'substantives'.

How should we understand such a claim? Is this an empirical claim, or even a claim for empiricism? Derrida seems to think that despite Levinas's clear protestations to the contrary his 'empiricism' indicates a choice having been made, a choice Derrida himself 'hesitates' to make, between 'opening and totality'.[26] He sees Levinas as ultimately having opted for the 'incoherence' of empiricism raised to the level of philosophy. His adherence to such 'incoherence' is effectively mystical. Derrida finds in Levinas's empiricism the profound revelation of empiricism to itself as metaphysics: the pretension to non-philosophy exposes the necessity of the solicitation of the *logos*. Levinas's discourse thus militates against itself; it fails to respond to the fact that the emphasis placed on radical exteriority demonstrates more clearly than ever that the non-simple relation to the Greek *logos* dominates all thinking, including that which locates itself within the closure of philosophy.

Derrida charges Levinas with having chosen the incoherence of 'opening' and, therefore, with a mystical understanding of the infinite exteriority of the Other. At the same time he credits him with the recognition of the 'dangers' that such a choice involves. Despite the 'impossibility' of such a choice according to Derrida, Levinas's having made it, he acknowledges, demonstrates the nature of the question of the relation between the Greek *logos* and thought. That Levinas needs simultaneously to identify and differentiate thought and language but cannot do so; that to go the way he does he must respond to this problem (even if not by making of it a thematic as such); that his work implicitly deals with the issues which philosophy at its closure puts to itself 'as problems philosophy cannot resolve'[27] – for all these reasons, Levinas is indeed an important figure in the 'end of philosophy' tradition with which we commonly associate Hegel, Marx, Nietzsche and Heidegger. To see his work as an important contribution to a 'community' which concerns itself with the 'death', 'end' or 'closure' of philosophy is correct, but is there not a danger here that one may, in this highly philosophical response, fail to give weight to the fact that in Levinas the 'origin' of meaning does not ensue merely from the relation between philosophy and its other, but from the relation to the other *qua* Other.

In other words, to regard Levinas's emphasis on the absolute alterity of the Other as mystical or as a Judaic idiosyncrasy[28] would be to fail to take seriously what is most radical in Levinas. How we come to regard what Derrida identifies as Levinas's empiricism requires much qualification; perhaps I may briefly indicate the direction in which that qualification might go. Derrida describes empiricism as the 'inability to justify oneself [or] to come to one's own aid as speech'.[29] When we consider this description in relation to Levinas's account of the face-to-face we find that the face-to-face is presented as a relation not calling for 'justification' (justification always involving the 'third', or reason). The silence of this relation, as we saw above, is not a failure to come to one's own aid as speech because it is a silence which, as Levinas tries to show, is founded upon speech (conversation). Levinas's empiricism is more radical than the mere exposure of empiricism to itself as metaphysics, for it reflexively seeks to respond to the fact of this exposure's occurrence *within* the 'empirical' I–Other conjuncture and experienced *as* the face-to-face.

In locating the 'origin' of meaning in the relation to the Other, Levinas attempts to make thought inhabit the fullness of life. Such an attempt is not alien to Heidegger's own concerns. In his book *The Mystical Element in Heidegger's Thought*,[30] Caputo recalls some early remarks of Heidegger which appear in the Duns Scotus book and bear this out. For instance, 'Philosophy lives at the same time in a tension with a living personality and draws its content and claim to value out of its depths and fullness of life.'[31] The 'fullness' of life here transcends the distinction between the 'spiritual' and the 'worldly', between what is experienced mystically and what is experienced through conceptualization. Levinas similarly speaks of an 'intersection' of the human and the divine in interpersonal relationships. In the same place he says that this represents 'the entire spirit of the Jewish bible'.[32] Whether or not such an 'intersection' can be assimilated to Judaism remains a question for Jewish theology. However, that such an intersection described in terms of exteriority and separation can find 'resonance' in modern European thought makes it a matter for all of us.

The difficulty of knowing how to respond to such a thought is perhaps adumbrated in the word 'provocation' in the title of this volume. The 'philosophical approach' might at first sight appear to be in keeping with Levinas's commitment to reason, but this response carries along with it the sense of its own inadequacy to the stirrings of the heart *provoked* by the appeal for the sanctity of the Other – an appeal whose jurisdiction, it is said, resists any philosopheme. Of course I did not expect to be able to give an answer as such to the question of what is and what is not appropriate, but by articulating the problem it becomes clear that it is not simply a case of overcoming the peculiarity of Levinas's style and figure in order to uncover the truly philosophical core of what he says. As Derrida says, in Levinas's writing, 'stylistic gestures less than ever can be distinguished from intention'.[33]

It is perhaps the peculiar indeterminacy of the provocation we feel on reading Levinas and on contemplating his claims for the ethical that indicates the extent to which we need to defer the critical demands with which we are likely to greet his work. Perhaps un*reasonably* we have to undertake a Levinasian meditation in advance, as it were. What I think is involved in this notion of 'suspension' is very difficult to express because it is both akin to the Husserlian *epoché* and keen to mark out its difference from this. It is made more difficult by the fact that this suspension (itself) in a sense exemplifies the ethical for Levinas in so far as it is an 'element' of a reprieve from totalization. We might similarly say that the question of Being, in Heidegger, is its own interlocution: it holds the 'opening' open. The *provocation* of the ethical reflects the fact that *I* am already implicated in this discourse which focuses on the I–Other conjuncture. It is *I* who am being called to responsibility and not merely to engage myself in a philosophical discourse on ethics.

Notes

1 'Violence and Metaphysics: an Essay on the Thought of Emmanuel Levinas' (VM) in *Writing and Difference*, translated by Alan Bass, Chicago, University of Chicago Press, 1978, p. 87; 'Violence et métaphysique. Essai sur la pensée d'Emmanuel Levinas' (VeM) in *L'Ecriture et la différence*, Paris, Seuil, 1967, p. 130.

2 Cf. TI, p. 204; TeI, p. 179.

3 Martin Heidegger, *Being and Time* (BT), translated by J. Macquarrie and E. Robinson, Oxford, Blackwell, 1973.

4 Cf. VM, p. 86 (VeM, pp. 128–9). In the same place Derrida is also quick to point out that the struggle between the 'letter' and the 'spirit' of intentionality is to be found in Husserl's own writings, a fact not so much overlooked by Levinas as not given the correct emphasis. Indeed, it may seem strange that Levinas does not stress that for Husserl it is the experience of the other person which disrupts the totalizing propensity of phenomenological representation, particularly if this is, as Derrida says, 'the most manifest and incontestable meaning of the fifth Cartesian meditation' (VM, p. 123; VeM, p. 182).

5 Cf. TIHP, p. 157, 'Husserl gives himself the *freedom* of theory just as he gives himself theory.' (My emphasis).

6 VM, fn. 7, p. 312; VeM, fn. 1, p. 124.

7 Ibid.

8 VM, p. 136.; VeM, p. 200.

9 EE, p. 22; DEE, p. 27.

10 EE, p. 24; DEE, p. 30.

11 EE, p. 30; DEE, p. 41.

12 Ibid.

13 TI, p. 298; TeI, p. 275.

14 TI, p. 52; TeI, p. 23.

15 TI, p. 23; TeI, p. xi.

16 *Basic Writings*, edited by David Farrell Krell, London, Routledge & Kegan Paul, 1978, p. 195.

17 'The End of Philosophy and the Task of Thinking', in *Basic Writings*, p. 384.

18 VM, p. 140; VeM, pp. 205–6.

19 VM, p. 142; VeM, p. 209.

20 Cf. VM, p. 137; VeM, p. 201.

21 Cf. TI, p. 146; TeI, p. 120.

22 TI, p. 147 (my emphasis); TeI, p. 121.

23 Cf. EE, p. 18; DEE, p. 17.

24 Cf. TI, p. 175; 'The face has turned to me – and this is its very nudity. It *is* by itself and not by reference to a system' (TeI, p. 147).

25 TI, p. 79; TeI; p. 51.

26 Cf. VM, p. 84; VeM, p. 125.

27 VM, p. 79; VeM, p. 118.
28 Cf. VM, p. 152; VeM, p. 226.
29 VM, p. 152; VeM, p. 226.
30 Athens, Ohio, Ohio University Press, 1978.
31 *Fruhe Schriften*, Frankfurt-am-Main, Klostermann, 1972, pp. 137–8. Also cited by Caputo, *Mystical Element*, p. 146 (this is his translation).
32 *Difficile liberté: essais sur le judaïsme*, Paris, Albin Michel, 1963, p. 36.
33 VM, fn. 7, p. 312; VeM, fn. 1, p. 124.

· 3 ·

Feminism and the Other

TINA CHANTER

This chapter[1] has three main sections. The first section discusses feminism in general, and some problems associated with the way in which it is currently perceived. In the second section I deal more directly with Levinas; I attempt to present what Levinas says about the feminine. The third section tries to answer some of the questions which will have been raised about Levinas's notion of the feminine and its relation to feminism.

I

'Feminism' has become a confused and confusing term. The media are proving adept at pointing to the growing number of women who shrink from being labelled feminists. Indeed, the disclaimer 'I am not a feminist, but . . .' can be heard increasingly to preface any one of a number of injustices remarked by women. It is a remark characteristic both of those 'career women' who, despite any sexual discrimination, are doing very well for themselves, and of the traditional working-class housewife. The popularity of this all-purpose qualifying remark is indicative of the threat that feminism poses. The flourishing stereotypical images of feminism seem to have created a new problem, that of overcoming the alienation of women for which feminists themselves are deemed responsible. Identifying with other like-minded feminists undoubtedly builds confidence and facilitates solidarity, and the strengths of group-identification should not be underestimated. These strengths are not in dispute here; the concern is rather to consider a less propitious side-effect accruing from them. Whether the image is that of the 'brown bread and sandals brigade' that has made feminism unpopular, or that of the 'middle-class trendies', in a position to leave household chores behind and flaunt their new-found freedom; whether it is resentment over suggestions that women spend too much time caring about how they look, or resentment of the 'liberation' enjoyed by Ivy League/Oxbridge graduates comfortable in their privileged professional positions; whatever the reason, it must be admitted that across the social spectrum, women are anxious to distance themselves from feminism. In short, there appears to be division not only between men and women, but also between women who embrace the feminist movement and those who reject it. If the liberation that feminists see themselves as working towards for the benefit of all women is inhibited by the reluctance of a number of those very women to accept feminism, what is the future of feminism?

Part of the problem lies in the diverse and multiple strands of thought which help to make up that movement we identify as feminism. At the moment, one of the more heated debates among feminists concerns the acceptance or the rejection of the term 'post-feminism'. Is it 'a clever little linguistic trick cooked up by the mass-media' which represents an attempt to 'pack up and file away once and for all something that they've never been very comfortable with'?[2] Or could it be that post-feminism designates a more productive attitude, an attitude to which Julia Kristeva gives expression, where 'the very dichotomy man/woman as an opposition between two rival entities may be understood as belonging to *metaphysics*'?[3] This attitude would not discard feminism as outmoded; feminism would coexist with the attitude of post-feminism, parallel to it (WT 51). It would be concerned, 'along with the *singularity* of each person . . . with the *relativity of his/her symbolic as well as biological existence*, according to the variation in his/her specific symbolic capacities' (WT 53). Post-feminism is an attitude which necessarily 'involves risks' – not least if it should degenerate into an excuse for no longer seeing feminism as a social problem involving all women – but this 'should not hide the radicalness of the process' (WT 52).

Despite the fact that the conflict we have sketched, between what is wanted by many women for themselves and what feminism wants for women as a whole is a conflict between individual interests and the interests of the whole, it is not necessarily an unproductive conflict, just as the fact that feminism is not drawn from a single coherent body of thought, but is informed by psychology, philosophy, linguistics, semiotics and so on is not necessarily disadvantageous. Bearing in mind the pluralism that exists within the feminist movement, and the variety of responses that individual women experience in relation to feminism, I want to consider Levinas's thoughts about the feminine. The question I want to bring to Levinas's account of the feminine is this: do we find there an articulation of the relation between the social whole (totality, in Levinasian terms) and the individual (the Same, the one, egoism) that helps us to think through the problems that contemporary feminism is encountering? One of these problems, I am suggesting, is the fact that while feminism in fact embraces a number of more or less distinct approaches to women's sexuality, the rejection of feminism tends to assume the unity of feminism as a discourse.

Asked to identify the most distinctive feature of Levinas's philosophy, one might point to his elaboration of the Other in its relation to the I. Because this human relationship is so important for Levinas, it is tempting to regard him as a 'social philosopher'. But considerable care should be taken to distinguish what Levinas means by 'social' from a philosophy which treats the Other in terms of the collective whole.[4] According to Levinas even Durkheim, whom he regarded as having avoided reducing the relation with the Other to objective knowledge, nevertheless ultimately treats the relation of I and Other in terms of the collective whole. Levinas's challenge is to just such a reduction. He is critical of any theory that presupposes the sameness or similarity of individuals, and which does so by taking for granted the priority of the whole. If one works within the framework of the social whole, the relations between individual and society are played out in terms of freedom and equality which are interpreted as rights. Feminism, for example, can focus upon the rights of individual women to have opportunities that are equal to those of men. But for Levinas, to start from the ideal of social equality avoids the problem of how I am related to others – it already assumes too much. It leaves unquestioned the justification for assuming certain rights – the right to freedom, for example. It pre-empts any consideration of the relation between subjectivity and sociality. To follow Levinas's account of the otherness of the Other, an entirely different conception of society is called for – starting not with equality, but with the asymmetry of the face-to-face relation. In order to think about the relation of self to Other, within the face-to-face relation we are required to re-think traditional ideas of subject, freedom and consciousness.

In this chapter I attempt to show that the face-to-face relation, undeniably important for Levinas's philosophy, nevertheless draws heavily on another account of the Other: that of the feminine. In highlighting the role of the feminine, I am not trying to diminish the significance of the Other as understood in the face-to-face relation; the feminine is presupposed by the face-to-face relation. What I am trying to do, in terms of an interpretation of Levinas, is to tackle the problem of how to reconcile Levinas's description of the I in enjoyment with the account of the I as answerable to the Other. The familiarity of the welcome which appears in Levinas's description of dwelling, in the midst of enjoyment, seems to run contrary to the absolute otherness of the Other in the face-to-face. The difficulty is expressed in the following statement from the preface to *Totalité et infini*, where Levinas presents 'subjectivity as welcoming the Other, as hospitality' and immediately goes on to say, 'in it the idea of infinity is consummated' (Tel, p. 17; TI, p. 27). How can the I remain I in the face of the Other? This question is important not only in terms of understanding *Totalité et infini*. It also addresses the question of woman that inevitably poses itself to feminists reading Levinas.

The precedent that has been set for such readers by one eminent feminist is dismissive of Levinas. Simone de Beauvoir judges that he 'deliberately takes a man's point of view'.[5] The traditional attitude of male dominance is characterized, according to de Beauvoir, by the assumption that 'He is subject, he is the Absolute, she is the Other'. She adds, in a footnote, that Levinas 'expresses this idea most explicitly', and quotes as evidence a section from the essay *Le Temps et l'autre*. Levinas says there, 'Otherness accomplishes itself in the feminine, a term of the same rank of consciousness but of opposite meaning'.[6] By interpreting this as an affirmation of what Levinas distances himself from more clearly elsewhere – namely, 'the ancillary status of woman'[7] – Simone de Beauvoir shows herself unwilling to take up the challenge he is making to philosophies of consciousness.

One can see the force of de Beauvoir's objection: Levinas's portrayal of femininity seems to fall prey to very traditional assumptions about the role of woman. The domain in which the face of the feminine makes its appearance for Levinas is the realm to which woman has been consistently relegated; the relatively serene abode of the domicile, the dwelling as preserved by the 'feminine touch'. Not only does Levinas appear to sketch out the arena for the woman in the most traditional way (by identifying the woman with domesticity, keeping her at home), but he also deprives the feminine face of the facility of verbal speech. He accords that privilege to the face-to-face encounter with the Other. A catalogue of the attributes ascribed to the feminine by Levinas only serves to reinforce the impression that Levinas's attitude to women is reactionary. His account reveals the lack of authority, dominance and self-assertion of the feminine. The distinguishing characteristic of the feminine face is identified, by Levinas, as 'discretion'.

However, if Levinas's philosophy succeeds in its attempt radically to rethink the Other, then we cannot understand Levinas's account of the otherness which 'accomplishes itself in the feminine' as a restatement of the traditional domination of the Other by the same. In other words, by identifying the feminine with discretion, Levinas is not unthinkingly reasserting the invisibility of women; he is making of this historical invisibility a philosophical positivity – in a move that protests the virile world in which everything is 'clear as day'. Against the reign of supremacy enjoyed by logic, where conversation, taking its cue from reason, irons out ambiguity, against the talk that is 'man to man', Levinas posits the primacy of the ethical relation, as face to face. For Levinas, ethics is prior to logic, the Other comes before the I. Once it is understood that the main attempt of Levinas's thinking is to depart from the model of the Other as determined by the I, it is also necessary to recognize that to think the feminine as other takes on a new meaning in Levinas. The otherness with which the feminine has always been associated is rethought by Levinas. Levinas is upsetting, not accepting, the traditional values which identify the egoism of male dominance as superior to female sufferance.

To say that Levinas upsets these categories is not to indicate a simple reversal of the terms. It is not to suggest that Levinas merely envisages a subversion of male superiority by feminine alterity. That would be the principle informing the view that feminism's only hope is to fight men on their own terms, as it were – that is, in terms of professional and financial success. Nor does Levinas affirm that the feminine is the weaker sex. This would be the rationale of those feminists who, in their refusal of male values, concentrate upon the development of characteristics they claim to be specific to women.

Kristeva expresses this divergence with reference to linguistic phenomena. Speaking in an interview in 1980 she said,

Certain feminists, in France particularly, say that whatever is in language is of the order of strict designation, of understanding, of logic, is male. Ultimately, theory or science is phallic, is male. On the other hand that which is feminine in language is whatever has to do with the imprecise, with the whisper, with impulses, perhaps with primary processes, with rhetoric – in other words, speaking roughly, the domain of literary expression, the region of the tacit, the vague, to which one would escape from too-tight tailoring of the linguistic sign and of logic.[8]

Kristeva goes on to give her view that

One must try not to deny these two aspects of linguistic communication, the mastering aspect and the aspect which is more of the body and of the impulses, but try, in every situation and for every woman, to find a proper articulation of these two elements. What does 'proper' mean here?[9]

The answer for Kristeva is 'that which best fits the specific history of each woman, which best expresses her. . . . We have to talk in terms of individual women and of each one's place inside these two poles.'[10] I think Levinas's account of femininity develops that notion of individuality. This is not to say that Levinas shares Kristeva's reasons for stressing the importance of the individual. It is clear that Levinas does not see himself as primarily concerned with feminism, Kristeva's or anyone else's. We are given some idea of his position in *Le Temps et l'autre* where he says, 'I do not wish to ignore the legitimate claims of feminism. . . . What matters to me in this notion of the feminine is [its] mode of being which consists in slipping away from the light' (TA, p. 79; TO, pp. 89–90). What does it mean to say that the way of the feminine is a slipping away from the light? Levinas is reacting, in part, against Heidegger for whom, says Levinas, 'Ontology becomes ontology of nature, impersonal fecundity, faceless generous mother, matrix of particular beings, inexhaustible matter for things' (TeI, p. 17; TeI, p. 46). The neutrality of Heideggerian ontology is regarded by Levinas as characteristic of what he calls 'the Heideggerian thesis that every human attitude consists in "bringing to light" ' (TeI, p. 270; TeI, p. 294). It is not the aim of this paper to account for Levinas's interpretation of Heidegger's work, which is problematic in some of its aspects, to say the least. Suffice it to say that although phenomenology profoundly influences Levinas, on many occasions it is also that from which Levinas decisively and deliberately distances himself.

Another discourse of which Levinas proves himself keenly aware is that of Marxism. I do not intend to dwell on Marx any more than on Heidegger in this paper, but I would like to mention one of the most essential elements of Marxism that Levinas could be said to take further. That is the fusion of the social with the natural that Marx's analyses achieve and which, appropriately, radical feminists have taken up. Nancy Hartsock writes, for example:

The Marxian category of labour, including as it does both interaction with other humans and with the natural world can help to cut through the dichotomy of nature and culture, and for feminists, can help to avoid the false choice of characterizing the situation of women as either 'purely natural' or 'purely social'.[11]

There is of course a difficulty in suggesting that Levinas may have gone 'beyond' Marxism in some sense. It is the same difficulty, perhaps thrown into sharper relief, in talking of Levinas and feminism in one and the same breath. While feminism and Marxism are overtly political, Levinas is not primarily concerned with politics. Although ethics, in the sense that Levinas gives it, does not exclude the political, the inclusion of politics within the ethical undercuts the very primacy politics would claim for itself. Pursued for its own sake, the political would be guilty of the same offence as Heidegger's philosophy of Being, according to Levinas. Politics too expresses the 'domination of the panoramic' (TeI, p. 270; TeI, p. 294), as Levinas calls it. By questioning, as Levinas does, whether politics provides its own justification, Levinas questions what is fundamental to Marxism.

II

Two problem areas for feminism are, first, the possibility of affirming a specifically feminine experience and, second, the danger of this degenerating into a crude biologism. If language is male, the alternative to male language for feminists would be to construct a 'female' language. But such a language would still be governed by male language in so far as it attempts to be what male language is not. Any attempt to stand outside male domination would still be governed by the opposition male/female, and the female pole therefore judged inferior. Even if it were possible to find a way to embrace specifically female values on their own terms, the danger of defining women biologically in affirming their difference from men may lead women to collude with patriarchy. If it is not social convention alone that constitutes femininity, feminism risks endorsing the view that women's natural capacity as childbearers, for example, proves that their proper place is in the home.

Is it possible to take account of a specifically female experience without resorting to biological reductionism, *and* to leave space for the differences between individual women to be aired? Can feminine specificity be embraced by women without glossing over race, class, age, sexuality, disability? Can feminism foster the uniqueness of individuals without sacrificing the strength of the collective identity of women? Can solidarity be preserved without resorting to the totalization that comes of interpreting individuals solely in terms of the social whole? Perhaps post-feminism can answer some of these questions affirmatively, and perhaps Levinas's thought can help to raise the question of otherness anew.

In the remainder of this second section of the chapter I consider the feminine first as it occurs in Levinas's discussion of habitation, and then in his description of eros. The next few pages are taken up with an account of how self-consciousness is accomplished according to Levinas.

Levinas says of self-consciousness, 'Prior to every vision of the self it is accomplished by holding *oneself* up (*se* tenant); it is *implanted in itself* as a body and it keeps itself (se tient) in its interiority, in its home' (TeI, p. 276; TI, p. 299). In the section of *Totalité et infini* entitled 'La Demeure' (The Dwelling), Levinas characterizes interiority in terms of enjoyment. The life of enjoyment, says Levinas, is 'a vibrant state of exaltation in which dawns the self' (TeI, p. 91; TI, p. 118). The relation one has with the elements in this 'egoism' of enjoyment is prior to one of (complete) mastery; it is not yet labouring. Living from the elements is, says Levinas, 'mastery in dependence'. It is this activity and the dimension in which it occurs that he calls interiority.

The life of enjoyment brings to the I a certain independence, and yet in the fluidity of its elemental existence the I is also threatened by insecurity. However, through domestication this instability decreases. The permanence of domesticity eliminates, along with spontaneity, the risk that obtained previously, in the flux of the elemental life. The happy acceptance of enjoyment, so far gratuitous, gives way to a different pleasure. At home now, the I's freedom is no longer derived from 'the agreeableness of the elements' (TeI, p. 127; TI, p. 153). The spontaneity of living from the elements is exchanged for an 'intimate familiarity' which is produced not as the gratuitousness of a non-definitive I, but as 'a gentleness that spreads over the face of things . . . a gentleness coming from an affection (*amitié*) for that I' (TeI, p. 128; TI, p. 155). In recognition of human sociality a distance is created between the I and its enjoyment. This is, as we shall see, a distance across which gentleness flows.

A loss of spontaneous freedom is experienced, then, in the abolition of immediate enjoyment. In its place is produced the satisfaction of the worker in his or her work, the execution of which forestalls death (by keeping hunger at bay). That is, the immediacy of enjoyment is replaced by the rhythm of work. The movement of the 'economy of being', a movement from the I's enjoyment of the elements to the familiarity that embraces it in the home, is a bestowal of permanence on what was previously enjoyed 'freely' but by chance. At the same time, the movement serves to identify the I as an I to itself, gives it distance from itself. The establishing of a home not only makes goods durable by suspending the temporary enjoyment of elements. It is also where the I gains a welcome, and a familiarity, in the intimacy of a relation with someone. At the risk of oversimplifying Levinas's own complex analysis, I will try to sum up the passage from habitation to the face-to-face, the encounter with the Other. It seems to be guided by a question Levinas asks in the section on dwelling just reviewed. He asks there, immediately before the sub-section entitled 'Habitation and the Feminine', 'how does habitation . . . make labour and representation . . . possible?' (TeI, p. 127; TI, p. 154).

It might at first seem that it is the body which makes possible labour and representation in habitation. Before anything else, what makes a thing mine is the fact that something 'keeps a certain proportion relative to the human body' (TeI, p. 134; TI, p. 161). What separates a thing from the chaos of the elements is the relation it keeps to the body, its closeness or distance. Most specifically, it is the hand which subjects elemental qualities to its 'grasp'. A distance is thus effected between the elements and the I; out of the elements possessions are created. Levinas says, 'The hand . . . gathers the fruit but it holds it far from the lips, keeps it, puts it in reserve, possesses it in a home' (TeI, p. 135; TI, p. 161).

However, a difficulty emerges. Did we not see that it is the welcome of intimacy that creates a distance between the I and the elements from which it lives? Levinas does indeed say that this distance begins with an 'intimate familiarity' (TeI, p. 128; TI, p. 154). It becomes clear that the I discovers the feminine as Other only after its relation, as intimacy, has been accomplished in dwelling. Levinas says, 'I must have been in relation with something I do not live from. This event is the relation with the Other who welcomes me in the home, the discreet presence of the feminine' (TeI, p. 145; TI, p. 171).

What then are we to make of these two different answers Levinas provides to his own question, the question as to how habitation makes labour and representation possible? On the one hand the body is said to be the condition of labour and representation, while on the other hand the feminine is their condition. The importance of resolving this difficulty bears upon the central issue introduced at the beginning of this chapter; that is, the possibility of the I maintaining its identity while at the same time being responsible to the Other. The whole of *Totalité et infini* can be read as an elaboration of this situation, where the I both exists as a separated being and is called into question by the Other in the relation of the face-to-face. Here we find an expression of that situation; the I is caught up in the life of enjoyment and yet it is in relation to the Other, the feminine Other.

Levinas describes this contradiction by means of a recurrent metaphor, that of the ring of Gyges, the ring which is reputed to have made the wearer invisible. He says,

Gyges's ring symbolizes separation. Gyges plays a double game, a presence to the others and an absence, speaking to 'others' and evading speech; Gyges is the very condition of man, the possibility of injustice and radical egoism, the possibility of accepting the rules of the game, but cheating (Tel, p. 148; TI, p. 173).[12]

The ambivalence that Levinas presents in terms of his reference to Gyges, in which the I is both present and absent, both speaks and evades speech, is announced repeatedly throughout *Totalité et infini*. The following are just two instances of many. First, Levinas says that matter, in the grasp of labour, both 'announces its anonymity and renounces it' (Tel, p. 133; TI, p. 159). Under the work of the hand, matter remains at the same time 'indefinite' and becomes 'identifiable'. Second, there is what Levinas calls the 'simultaneity' of corporeity, where 'to be at home with oneself in something other than oneself' (Tel, p. 139; TI, p. 164) characterizes the existence of the I. What do these two exemplary descriptions have in common with the figure of Gyges? The phenomenon to which Levinas directs our attention through his descriptions of the I's dissimulating identity, the ambiguity of the body, and the simultaneous anonymity and identifiability of the matter that is worked in labour – is equivocation. The equivocal, for Levinas, is the domain of the feminine. 'Equivocation', he says, 'constitutes the epiphany of the feminine' (Tel, p. 241; TI, p. 164).

So equivocation is the way of the feminine. How does this contribute to our understanding of how habitation makes possible labour and representation? Levinas says that it is, 'separation' that makes labour and property possible (TeI, p. 130; TI, p. 156). Indeed, we could present more of his assertions about what it is that conditions labour and representation. 'Dwelling conditions labour,' says Levinas (TeI, p. 135; TI, p. 161), and again 'dwelling makes acquisition and labour possible' (TeI, p. 139; TI, p. 165).But our question is, *how* does habitation make labour and representation possible?

As far as the activity of labour is concerned, its achievement consists in making time for itself through the concrete production of goods. The significance of such a procedure is the entry into the market-place which it makes possible. As soon as things can be bought and sold, the status of anonymity can be conferred upon them by virtue of the reduction of their value to quantities of money. Hence Levinas's claim that the grasp which labour maintains over matter can signal its indeterminacy, as when the labourer relinquishes the fruits of labour which thereby become the possessions of another. However, when things become property, the change they undergo does not have its source in the labourer who produced them but in the other who acquires them. As property, things invoke a relation to the Other, or, in Levinas's own words 'the possession of things issues in a discourse' (TeI, p. 136; TI, p. 162).

It is not the feminine but the I of enjoyment whom Levinas characterizes as the one who gives. It is the I of enjoyment who gives to the Other when called upon in the face-to-face relation. But until the I has learnt to identify itself as an I and as distinct from that which it enjoys, there can be no bread to give to the Other. The feminine being is the one who encourages the I to break from its life of pure enjoyment and conserve its goods. It is in this sense that the feminine is presupposed by the face-to-face.

The equivocation of the body comes into play in more dramatic circumstances than those described so far. At its most extreme, the time – the time for living – that labour creates for the I puts off death, not just by keeping hunger at bay, but in defending itself when faced with a more immediate threat. In the violence of war the I relies upon its 'suppleness', a skill which is 'inscribed in the very existence of the body' (TeI, p. 200; TI, p. 225).

In the feminine, equivocation occurs as a kind of 'withdrawal' (TeI, p. 145; TI, p. 170) from being, as hiddenness (TeI, p. 242; TI, p. 264) which, according to Levinas, 'says less than nothing' (TeI, p. 238; TI, p. 260). To put this another way, the feminine has a language, but it is a silent language. That is the language of love. Associated with the relation of love is the movement of eros, a movement which takes place both as voluptuosity and as fecundity. It is in the difference between these two planes, voluptuosity on the one hand, and fecundity on the other, that the equivocation of the feminine is produced. Of this we shall have to say more, but first, and by way of introducing the following discussion about the feminine in voluptuosity and in fecundity, I want to look at another metaphor of *Totalité et infini*. The image is used several times by Levinas to address the way in which the I can at one and the same time be separated and answerable to the Other; interior, while open to infinity.

The elements in and from which I live are also that to which I am opposed. The feat of having limited a part of this world and having closed it off, having access to the elements I enjoy by way of the door and the window, realizes extraterritoriality and the sovereignty of thought, anterior to the world to which it is posterior (TeI,p. 144; TI, p. 170).

Again, Levinas says, 'In the separated being the door to the outside must hence be at the same time open and closed' (TeI, p. 122; TI, p. 148). The ambiguity of interiority indicated by means of this image of a door both open and closed is worked out in terms of the body. Just as the position described here by Levinas refuses logic, so his account of the feminine way of being is 'refractory' to 'universalization' and, by the same token, refractory to 'society' (TeI, p. 242; TI, pp. 264–5). That is, the relation to the other as feminine takes place as intimacy, behind closed doors. Nevertheless, despite its withdrawal from the light of day, the intimate relation has implications that are far-reaching for the world it excludes by its secrecy. 'The in appearance asocial relation of eros will have a reference – be it negative – to the social' (TeI, p. 240; TI, p. 262), says Levinas.

Developing this reference of asocial to social, let us turn now to a more thorough examination of equivocation as portrayed in the feminine. We have seen that Levinas associates the feminine with eros, in his description of the relation between lovers. How does voluptuosity on the one hand and fecundity on the other hand occur within the relation of love? The distinguishing feature of voluptuousness, for Levinas, is that it amounts to a return to self. As such it is not a relation to infinity, it is a relation with another; but it is not the face-to-face relation. Levinas says, 'it is voluptuosity of voluptuosity, love of the love of the other . . . . If to love is to love the love the Beloved bears me, to love is also to love oneself in love, and thus to return to oneself' (TeI, p. 245; TI, p. 266). So the voluptuousness of love does not go beyond the Other, but precisely reflects the I itself. However, in fecundity, the relation between lovers does become a movement toward the infinite. 'The feminine presents a face that goes beyond the face' (TeI, p. 238; TI, p. 260), Levinas says. And, a little later, eros 'goes beyond the face' (TeI, p. 242; TI, p. 264). The accomplishment of the relation with the beyond in fecundity speaks for itself; it is the engendering of a child (TeI, p. 244; TI, p. 266).

I have described these two aspects of the erotic relation one after the other, but in doing so I have not meant to imply that they exist in distinction from each other. Voluptuosity is nothing but the relation that exists between lovers; and fecundity is the other side of this relation. It is not that one exists without the other, in the relation of love. Rather, Levinas is pointing to a fundamental ambiguity; the relation between lovers is characterized by femininity. It goes toward infinity while at the same time it is marked by a return to self. Therefore it 'resembles' (TeI, p. 245; TI, p. 267) but is not the same as the relation of the face-to-face, precisely because it involves this return to self. Yet, as every reader of Plato knows, that which imitates is both like and unlike. So, as with fecundity, the relation of love is a relation of transcendence. Levinas says that 'in love transcendence goes both further and less far than language' (TeI, p. 232; TI, p. 254). That is to say, since language is founded by the face-to-face (TeI, p. 182; TI, p. 207), the feminine face goes both further than the face-to-face relation, and less far. The relation with the feminine is face-to-face and is not face-to-face. It is face-to-face in that it produces the I as 'infinitely recommencing' (TeI, p. 250; TI, p. 272), or it is fecund. It is not face-to-face because it does not 'contest' possession. 'For this', says Levinas, 'I must encounter the indiscreet face of the Other that calls me into question' (TeI, p. 145; TI, p. 171).

III

As we have seen, just as Levinas stresses two aspects of habitation – that is, bodily enjoyment and the familiarity of the welcome – so he presents the two sides of love. Voluptuosity represents a *return to self* – the lover loves not only the beloved but also itself, in love; and fecundity represents a *transcendence of self*, which goes beyond the transcendence of language. This feminine transcendence, fecundity, is not confined to the biological. (I will say more about this shortly.) What, then, are we to make of Levinas's account of woman? That is the question addressed in the third and final part of this chapter.

For Levinas, the presence of woman is at the same time an absence (TeI, p. 128; TI, p. 155), for the speech that the feminine face initiates, unlike that of the Other in the face-to-face relation, is not verbal speech. Levinas calls the language of the feminine a 'silent language' (TeI, p. 129; TI, p. 155). It is presence in withdrawal, 'discreet' presence. The art of self-effacement, it would seem, constitutes the essence of woman for Levinas. Her silent demeanour is one of gentleness , welcome and kindness.

Are we then forced to agree with Simone de Beauvoir and dismiss Levinas's point of view as typically male? What I have tried to show is that in characterizing the feminine as Other, Levinas is far from simply assuming the dominance of the male as ego or sameness. I have tried to show this by examining what Levinas says about the feminine in *Totalité et infini*, a text which was published after Simone de Beauvoir's remarks, and which elaborates a position Levinas had only sketched in *Le Temps et l'autre*. It becomes clear, from a reading of *Totalité et infini*, that to criticize Levinas for 'disregarding the reciprocity of subject and object', as Simone de Beauvoir does, rather misses the point. If there is anything that Levinas is at pains to stress it is the asymmetry of the relation between I and Other. The effort to repudiate the notion of individuality that is based upon reciprocity is at the heart of *Totalité et infini*. For Levinas, the reciprocal assumes the priority of the whole, whereas the singularity of the feminine, despite its return to self, is that in fecundity the I 'is not purely and simply dissolved into the collective' (TeI, p. 251; TI, p. 273).

But in characterizing transcendence in the erotic relation as fecundity, and in identifying this dimension as feminine, is Levinas not simply reinvoking traditional values? Does he not thereby confine women to the role of child-bearer, and, like Plato, relegate childbearing to a role subordinate to the begetting of laws and political states (which is the business of men)? Why does Levinas, for example, revert to the language of 'paternity', 'filiality' and 'fraternity' when it comes to discussing the significance of fecundity? Although there is not a simple answer to these questions, I want to gesture in the direction in which I think an answer could be framed. A full answer would have to address the issue of how justice, which is 'the presence of the third party, the whole of humanity' (TeI, p. 188; TI, p. 213) and which 'looks at me in the eyes of the Other' (ibid.) can also, as the 'reasonable Order' of things, cause cruelty by its very reasonableness.[13] But since such questions exceed the scope of this chapter, I will only indicate how I think an answer might be developed in terms of the present discussion – specifically, in terms of eros. Again I can do no more than intimate how Levinas might be read here by making the following suggestion. Perhaps the most obvious way of understanding what Levinas means by the 'Ambiguity' of love (TeI, p. 232; TI, p. 254) might be to take our cue from the description of dwelling. Here Levinas gives us to understand that one way in which the feminine is equivocal is that the feminine being is both *qua* feminine and *qua* human being. This reading is supported by the following statement by Levinas about the feminine: 'the discretion of this presence includes all the possibilities of the transcendent relationship with the Other' (TeI, p. 129; TI, p. 155). But does this not oversimplify things when it comes to understanding not only the way in which the feminine is 'a delightful lapse in being' or that it signifies 'less than nothing', but even more so when we try to understand Levinas's account of the erotic caress, which 'consists in seizing upon nothing, in soliciting what ceaselessly escapes its form toward a future never future enough, in soliciting what slips away as though it *were not yet*' (TeI, p. 235; TI, pp. 257–8)? Levinas indicates with the phrase 'future never future enough' the possibility of a time which is being towards the future not through fecundity, not through being other in my child; but precisely in the inevitable failure to grasp the other, a failure which nevertheless contains within it a constantly renewed attempt to do so. Perhaps, here, Levinas has caught sight of an alterity which is still more radical than the otherness of the Other in the face-to-face? And yet it is less radical, for there is nothing more cruel than the dissipation of love as desire into love which reduces itself to need (TeI, p. 232; TI, p. 254).[14]

I think Levinas's account of feminity can apply to gays, just as I think it can apply to heterosexuals of either sex. In the first place transcendence, I have just suggested, seems to characterize eros not just in fecundity but as the erotic itself; but that is not all. Levinas states quite clearly, at the end of the section in *Totalité et infini* called 'The Home and Possession' that his description of the discreet welcome of the feminine which the separated being receives in habitation does not imply the 'empirical' presence of the 'human being of "feminine sex" ' (TeI, p. 131; TI, p. 158). If that is the case, then there is no reason to suppose, I suggest, that paternity implies the empirical presence of a human being of the masculine sex. Indeed, Levinas says in an interview that

allusions to th·· ontological differences between the masculine and the feminine would appear less archaic if, instead of dividing humanity into two species (or two genders), they would signify that the participation in the masculine and in the feminine were the attribute of every human being.[15]

However, the fact that femininity or masculinity cannot be reduced to the physical distinguishing characteristics of the sexes does not divest gender of all equivalence with the body. Rather, it means that it makes no sense to imagine gender as solely determined by physical characteristics. The significance of these characteristics necessarily comes from our relation with others; it is unavoidably social from the start. There is a sense in which the woman-body is essential to femininity in general, but this is not to say that there can be no femininity without the feminine body. Thus Levinas speaks of feminine tenderness as a 'way', a 'regime' (TeI, p. 233; TI, p. 256). (Just as 'effemination' (TeI, p. 248; TI, p. 270) can implicate the virile subject, despite what he would wish, so the way of the feminine cannot be seen as exclusive to the feminine sex.)

Nevertheless, the fact that Levinas employs a distinction between sex and gender does not by itself make everything fall into place. We still have to reckon with the difficulty of identifying what it is, if not biological sex, that determines femininity as opposed to masculinity. To say that gender is not exclusively determined by biological sex does not entail that it bears no relation whatsoever to biology. It is only to say that gender is not limited (TeI, p. 256; TI, p. 279) by sexual identity as determined biologically. Thus paternity, Levinas says, can be 'borne by the biological life, but lived beyond that life' (TeI, p. 225; TI, p. 247). This is an important observation, and Levinas returns to it in one of the concluding paragraphs of *Totalité et infini* (TeI, p. 283; TI, p. 306). It reveals not so much an attempt to confine the role of the feminine to the home while affirming that the mastery of the elements is a masculine task. Rather, biological reproductive capacities that are seen as a function of fecundity, so that specific sex differences come to be seen in terms of, not as based upon, fecundity. In terms of elaborating how fecundity founds biological difference rather than vice versa, the achievement of Levinas's discourse is its recognition that on the one hand any absolute distinction between nature and culture is invalid from the first, and that on the other hand this does not imply the elimination of either spiritual or material existence. Whereas Marx posits a fusion of social and natural forces in the activity of reproduction, and then has difficulty in maintaining the socialist ideal for a universal class of individuals working according to their 'nature', Levinas refuses to admit the social as a founding concept in the first place. It is in the productive capacity of labour, both in the sense of procreation and in the sense of reproducing the self in goods which sustain life, that the significance of the Marxian category of labour lies. For it is here, in the various manifestations of the labour process, that alienation – from self, others, work, and goods – occurs.

Like Marx, Levinas recognizes the power with which money is invested to make anonymous, or render invalid, the particularity with which goods are fashioned (TeI, p. 136; TI, p. 162). Unlike Marx, Levinas envisages a situation where the relinquishing of goods to the other does not take the form of exploitation. The ethical dimension in which this occurs would be, for Marx, just another form of alienation: 'The more man puts into God, the less he retains within himself.'[16] Not so for Levinas. To say that Levinas does not admit the social whole as a basic category is not to deny Levinas's recognition of the role of language in shaping thought and thereby precluding any life outside of the social existence of thinking and speaking beings. It is rather that, at the level of enjoyment, for example, or in the erotic relation, the language that exists is a clandestine, and inverted language, which already refers to the spoken word, but does not submit to that universal authority. Instead there is a reversion to the hidden. In an essay written in 1982, Levinas describes the way in which being at home with oneself (*chez soi*) in the interiority of the dwelling brings us back to the feminine face through an 'inflexion of the I'.[17] The way in which the feminine subtends the masculine is elaborated in an earlier essay 'Judaism and the Feminine Element', which first appeared in 1969. Levinas says there,

To overcome an alienation which, fundamentally, results from the very masculinity of the universal and conquering *logos* that stalks the very shadows that could have sheltered it – such should be the ontological function of the feminine, the vocation of 'the one who does not conquer' . . . woman is the origin of all kindness on earth (DL, p. 55–6; JF, p. 33).

It is the 'secret presence' of the feminine in the Old Testament, the 'silent footsteps' of Sarah, Rebecca, Rachael (to name but a few) who, 'in the depth and opaqueness of reality . . . make the world habitable'

(DL, p. 53; JF, p. 32). These descriptions of woman, which recall the words which describe habitation and the feminine in the chapter on dwelling in *Totalité et infini*, occur in the first of the three sections of Levinas's essay. Here, woman 'answers to a solitude which subsists despite the presence of God – to a solitude in the universal' (DL, p. 33; JF, p. 35). Here there is a duality 'inscribed' in the very essence of the person. And although the conjugal friend 'can become the most terrible enemy' and happiness is 'not without risk' still, says Levinas, rehearsing the Oral Tradition, 'without woman man knows neither good, nor succour, nor joy, nor blessing, nor pardon'. Levinas adds: 'Nothing of what would be required for a soul!' (DL, p. 56; JF, p. 34).

In the second section of his essay Levinas goes on to discuss the appearance of Eve in terms of the social evil she brings. It is, says Levinas, an evil 'for which men carry responsibility'. He continues: 'If woman completes man, she does not complete him as a part completes another into a whole but rather, if one may put it thus, as two totalities complete one another' (DL, p. 58; JF, p. 35). Levinas has in mind the sense in which Eve comes from Adam's rib as a 'side' of Adam, interpreting this well-known biblical story as derivative of the image of those severed beings Aristophanes evokes in Plato's *Symposium*. Levinas recalls that in the Aristophanes myth the gods set about splitting up the originally spherical human beings into two, by way of punishment; in contrast, says Levinas, for the Jews 'separated existence will be worth more than the initial union' (DL, p. 58; JF, p. 35). But this leaves out of account two further characteristics of Plato's dialogue, the *Symposium*. First, on continuing his myth, Aristophanes has Zeus move the sexual organs of these unfortunate separated beings to their front, because they were perishing in this plight.[18] Second, and subsequent to the ability of this new bodily arrangement, humans were able to beget upon one another, thus propagating their species, and laying up immortality for themselves. In fact, Levinas's account of eros and desire draws so heavily upon Plato's *Symposium* that it almost reads as an extended footnote to that dialogue.[19] The 'ambiguity' (TeI, p. 232; TI, p. 254) that is at the heart of love for Levinas echoes the *metaxy* that Diotima ascribes to love, as halfway between divinity and mortal. But perhaps what is most interesting here is that while on the one hand eros, as child of *penia* (need, poverty), lies on bare ground and goes hungry, thirsty and without shelter, the poor one, on the other hand, eros as child of *poros* (plenty), is always in pursuit of truth, always weaving strategies (*Symposium* 203). Love both puts one in need and gives one the resources to provide for another. Not only do we find in Diotima's description of eros as *penia* a humorous reference to Socrates' habit of standing by the wayside in contemplation, as he did near the beginning of the dialogue; although the more obvious source is the biblical one, we also seem to find in Levinas's Other as widow, orphan, stranger Platonic echoes of the resourceless mother of love that Diotima depicts. Whether this discovery has any broader significance for understanding the relation between the feminine as other and the Other in the face-to-face relation, is a question whose answer will have to be delayed for another time. But perhaps we have gained a little headway in elaborating the feminine as it occurs in Levinas.

Conclusion

Because of the positive signification that Levinas attributes to the feminine, he is loathe to surrender its specificity up to the 'spirit in its masculine existence' (JF, p. 55; JF, p. 33); by the same token, he regrets the struggle for equality that characterizes the woman's movement – not because it has no integrity, but because it doesn't have enough; in opposing the differentiation of the sexes, it would group together men and women under the rubric of 'humanity'. And in doing so it would attest precisely to 'a certain priority of the masculine' (JF, p. 58; JF, p. 35); it would deliver to the inhumanity of reason that very tenderness that defines and supports life: perhaps, if we read carefully Levinas's description of the truly human as 'virile gentleness' we begin to understand the opening words of *Totalité et infini*: 'The true life is absent. But we are in the world' (TeI, p. 3; TI, p. 33).[20]

The value of Levinas's account of femininity lies in the originality of his description of identity, and his radical reworking of the concept of Otherness. For Levinas, the fact that woman is different from – other than – man does not imply her inferiority. Difference does not have to mean deference. As Derrida puts it, 'Secondariness . . . would not be that of woman or femininity, but the *division* between masculine and feminine'.[21]

In exploring the withdrawal of the feminine, Levinas claims to improve upon Heidegger's phenomenology of beings. This remains unsubstantiated as far as this paper is concerned, but significant in terms of the ontological status Levinas claims for the role of the feminine. In escaping the harsh light of reality, the feminine is said to have effected a withdrawal from being. This ability is provided for by way of the feminine, which has been the central notion of this paper – that is, by equivocation. It is the notion that Levinas takes up and examines in his treatment of the saying in the said, in *Autrement qu'être ou au-delà de l'essence*. Levinas says, toward the end of *Totalité et infini*, under the heading 'Phenomenology of Eros', that 'the "saying", and not only the said, is equivocal' (TeI, p. 237; TI, p. 260), and thus announces the theme of his next major work, *Autrement qu'être.*[22]

At the beginning of this paper I asked where the future of feminism lies, given the fact that significant numbers of women reject it. I went on to indicate that there is not only a variety of different reasons for the rejection of feminism but there is also a diversity of strategies within feminism itself. But this diversity, I suggested, does not necessarily constitute weakness. Plurality is essential to Levinas's notion of the feminine. From his description of the feminine in habitation, and his phenomenology of eros, woman emerges as fragmented and dissonant. But it is precisely this fragmentation and dissonance that Levinas affirms as feminine, in characterizing femininity as equivocation. Providing a welcome in the home, the feminine is both a discreet presence and a self-effacing absence. In the self-satisfaction of voluptuosity, the femininity of lovers returns to the self and it transcends every return to self, transcendent not only in fecundity but also in the inadequacy of the lover's caress, which would reach for, without ever being able to hold on to, the otherness of the Other. Fundamentally ambiguous, the feminine contradicts itself. It is both extremes at once, the ultimate return to self and the ultimate transcendence of self.

Levinas does not draw this conflict of extremes into a convenient whole, as if they were pieces of a jigsaw. Instead he identifies the feminine as the equivocal, recognizes that it is what it is not. In practical terms, to be other than what we are is an accurate description of women who find themselves objecting to what has been traditionally expected of us. It is, says Sigrid Weigel, 'necessary for woman to look in two diverging directions simultaneously'. Weigel continues:

She must learn to voice the contradictions, to see them, to comprehend them, to live in and with them, and also learn to gain strength from the rebellion against yesterday and from the anticipation of tomorrow.[23]

It is in learning to live the contradiction of looking two ways that woman is equivocal. The conflict of always having been understood as inferior to men, but beginning to understand herself not just as distinct from that definition but on her own terms, is expressed by Weigel as a transition from what de Beauvoir called the 'second' sex, to 'authenticity' (*Eigentlichkeit*) in the Heideggerian sense:

The utopia of woman as in 'authentic' [*eigentliches*] sex does not mean – to reverse patriarchal relations – claiming to be the only or the superior sex, rather it demands that woman is no longer defined in relation to man. Instead, she sees and experiences herself and with others as her own and not as deviant. With the transition from 'second' [*anderen*] to 'authentic' [*eigentlichen*] sex she will no longer have to identify herself as lack – although here too she is not imitating man but acting independently.[24]

There is no space here to describe how Levinas's account of otherness can be said to go beyond Heidegger's account of authentic existence; I have only been able to suggest that Levinas's account of the Other provides feminism with a voice that many feminists have already begun to seek: the voice of the radically Other. Lest it be thought that I am invoking a man to speak for us, as if we could not speak ourselves, it should be said that what Levinas says about the feminine remains fundamentally ambiguous, and in this sense the voice that Levinas provides is a silent voice. It is not, perhaps, for Levinas to break this silence. Rather, it is his silence which opens a space for others, those who have always been Other, and who are beginning to be radically other – women – to speak, to write their otherness. If women throughout history have been 'other' than men, that is, we have been judged as not counting, as different from, not the same as men; and if, for the most part, we have accepted that judgment, then what is it to be ourselves? It is to be other than what we have been, and still are to a great extent. Far from calling upon Levinas to speak on our behalf, I am simply pointing to a certain insistence in his work upon otherness, an insistence which appeals to what have traditionally been conceived as non-male values: gentleness, tenderness, welcome. Levinas's insistence upon otherness coincides with feminism's quest for women to be other than what they are. No one can do that for us.

Perhaps it will be said that one cannot *be* other: but that is what feminism asks of us, and if we cannot answer, at least we have heard the question. It is a question which provokes us to ask about the possibilities of post-feminism. It is thought-provoking because it asks whether, as feminists, we do not simply think of ourselves as other – that is, think of ourselves in male terms. Perhaps Levinas helps to make visible the limitations of male language for thinking the feminine precisely by thinking it as far as he can within that language. It is not that we can step outside male language, any more than we can step outside metaphysics. But we can try to think our otherness not *simply* as different from the sameness of male language. And that is why Levinas, by taking to the extreme the otherness of the feminine, can be said at the same time to have recognized a space for some kind of thinking of the other outside its opposition to the same.[25] One could indeed ignore the subtlety of Levinas's account and insist with Simone de Beauvoir that his is a typically male point of view. But once we understand Levinas's conception of the feminine in terms of the general attempt of *Totalité et infini*, as I have tried to do, Simone de Beauvoir's criticism is less convincing. Once we understand Levinas's statement that alterity accomplishes itself as the feminine in the context of the priority Levinas gives to alterity, otherness and exteriority over the same, the one, totality, we cannot say Levinas is simply keeping the woman at home, in her traditional place. Rather, he has taken femininity seriously and not merely defused the feminine either by putting it down as 'weak' or by dressing it up to make it acceptable but only on male terms. It is the world of male values, the universal rule of reason, the law of totality that Levinas is reacting against when he says 'the virile judgement of history . . . of "pure reason" is cruel' (TeI, p. 221; TeI, p. 243).

Abbreviations

JF Levinas, 'Judaism and the feminine element', translated by E. Wyschogrod, in *Judaism*, vol. 18, no. 2, 1969, pp. 30–8.
WT Julia Kristeva, 'Women's Time', translated by Alice Jardine and Harry Blake, in *Feminist Theory: a Critique of Ideology*, edited by Nannerl O. Keohane, Michelle Z. Rosaldo and Barbara C. Gelpi, Brighton, Harvester Press, 1982.

Notes

1 I am grateful to the Department of Philosophy at the University of Essex for providing me with the opportunity of reading a version of this chapter as an invited lecturer. I would also like to thank Margaret Whitford for her helpful comments on a draft of the chapter.

2 Jean Meyer, *Spare Rib*, No. 161, Jan. 1986, 8.
3 Julia Kristeva, 'Women's Time', translated by Alice Jardine and Harry Blake in *Feminist Theory: a Critique of Ideology*, edited by Nannerl O. Keohane, Michelle Z. Rosaldo and Barbara C. Gelpi, Brighton, Harvester Press, 1982, p. 51. This translation was first published in *Signs*, vol. 7, No. 1, 1981. The article was originally published as 'Le Temps des femmes' in vols 34–44, No. 5, Winter 1979, *Cahiers de Recherche de Sciences des Textes et Documents*, pp. 5–19.
4 Emmanuel Levinas, *Totalité et infini: essai sur l'extériorité*, 4th edition, The Hague, Nijhoff (1961), 1980; *Totality and Infinity: an Essay on Exteriority*, translated by Alphonso Lingis, Pittsburgh, Pa., Duquesne University Press, 1969.
5 Simone de Beauvoir, *Le Deuxième Sexe*, vol. 1, Paris, Gallimard, 1949, p. 15; *The Second Sex*, translated by H. M. Parshley, New York, Vintage Books: Random House (1952), 1974, p. xix.
6 Ibid. The reference is to Levinas, *Le Temps et l'autre*, Paris, Quadrige/Presses Universitaires de France (1947), 1983, p. 81.
7 Levinas, 'Le Judaïsme et le féminin' in *Difficile liberté: essais sur le Judaïsme*, Paris, Albin Michel, 1963, pp. 51–62 (the essay was originally published in *L'Age nouveau*, nos. 107–8, 1960); 'Judaism and the feminine element', translated by Edith Wyschogrod in *Judaism*, vol. 18, No. 1, 1969, pp. 30–8.
8 Kristeva, Interview with Elaine Hoffman Baruch, *Partisan Review*, vol. LI, No. 1, 1984, 122.
9 Kristeva, Interview, *op. cit.*, 123.
10 Ibid.
11 Nancy C. M. Hartsock, 'The Feminist Standpoint: Developing the Ground for a Specifically Feminist Historical Materialism', in *Discovering Reality*, edited by Sandra Harding and Merrill B. Hintikka, Dordrecht, D. Reidel, 1983, p. 283.
12 See Plato's *Republic*, stephanus nos. 359D–360D, translated by Paul Shorey, vol. 5, Loeb Classical Library, London, William Heinemann (1930), 1978, pp. 116–20.
13 Levinas, 'Transcendance et hauteur', *Bulletin de la Société française de Philosophie*, t. LIV, 1962, 102.
14 For some thoughts concentrating more on the erotic in Levinas than this chapter has done, see Luce Irigaray's essay 'Fécondité de la caresse' in her *Éthique de la différence sexuelle*, Paris, Minuit, 1984. Also see Catherine Chalier, *Figures du féminin: lecture d'Emmanuel Levinas*, Paris, La Nuit Surveillée, 1982.
15 Levinas, *Éthique et infini: dialogues avec Philippe Nemo*, Paris, Fayard, 1982, p. 71; *Ethics and Infinity*, translated by Richard A. Cohen, Pittsburgh, Duquesne University Press, 1985, p. 68. I am grateful to Peter Atterton for bringing this reference to my attention.
16 Karl Marx, 'Economic and Philosophic Manuscripts', *Early Writings*, translated by Rodney Livingstone and Gregor Benton, Harmondsworth, Penguin, 1974, p. 324.

17 Levinas, 'A propos de Buber: quelques notes' in *Qu'est-ce que l'homme? Philosophie/psychanalyse, Hommage à Alphonse de Waelhens (1911–81)*, Bruxelles, Facultés Universitaires, Saint-Louis, 1982, p. 132.

18 Plato, *Symposium*, stephanus no. 191, translated by W. R. M. Lamb, vol. 3 Loeb Classical Library, London, William Heinemann (1925), 1975, p. 139.

19 See esp. TeI 34–5/63, 87/114—15, 232/254. Although Levinas does not specify that it is Plato he has in mind in TI, he does acknowledge his debt to Plato in conceiving of eros as 'a child of need' in *De l'existence à l'existant*, Paris, Vrin (1947), 1984, p. 145; translated by Alphonso Lingis, *Existence and Existents*, The Hague, Nijhoff, 1978, p. 85. On the same page Levinas says that the Platonic interpretation 'completely fails to recognize the role of the feminine'.

20 Levinas, 'Aimer la Thora plus que Dieu', DL, p. 219; translated by Helen A. Stephenson and Richard I. Sugarman, 'To Love the Torah more than God', *Judaism*, vol. 28, No. 2, 1979, 205.

21 Jacques Derrida, 'Choreographies' (an interview with Christie V. Wood), *Diacritics*, vol. 12, 1982, 73. Also see the exchange between Verena Andermatt Conley and Derrida in *Boundary 2*, vol. 12, No. 2, 1984, 68–93, and Derrida's essay 'En ce moment même dans cet ouvrage me voici' in *Textes pour Emmanuel Levinas*, edited by François Laruelle, Paris, Editions Jean-Michel, 1980.

22 Levinas, *Autrement qu'être ou au-delà de l'essence*, The Hague, Martinus Nijhoff, 1974; translated by Alphonso Lingis, *Otherwise than Being or Beyond Essence*, The Hague, Martinus Nijhoff, 1981.

23 Sigrid Weigel, 'Der schielende Blick: Thesen zur Geschichte weiblicher Schreibpraxis', in *Der verborgene Frau*, edited by Inge Stephan and Sigrid Weigel, Berlin, Argument Verlag, 1983, p. 105; 'Double Focus: on the History of Women's Writing', translated by Harriet Anderson in *Feminist Aesthetics* edited by Gisela Ecker, London, The Women's Press, 1985, p. 73 (a partial translation). Weigel is refreshing in that, unlike many English-speaking feminists, she takes French feminists seriously. (See, e.g., Ann Rosalind Jones who has greeted Cixous, Irigaray and Kristeva with considerable suspicion in her articles: 'Writing the Body: Toward an Understanding of L'Ecriture Feminine', *Feminist Studies*, vol. 7, No. 2, Summer 1981, 247–63; and 'Julia Kristeva on Femininity: The Limits of a Semiotic Politics', *Feminist Review*, No. 18, Nov. 1984, 56–73.) Although Weigel too is ultimately critical of Cixous and Irigaray – for not making clearer the difference between what she calls the 'secondary' and the 'authentic' – she gives them a sympathetic hearing. When Weigel says that what she finds most problematic in their 'programmatic remarks' is their 'restriction of feminine praxis to writing', one suspects that it is her refusal of a post-Derridean understanding of writing that prevents her from going any further along the road they take.

24 Weigel, ibid., 112/79.

25 I am thinking here of the 'outside' to which Luce Irigaray has referred in discussing the mimicry of woman, where 'she keeps something in reserve'

even while 'she mimes so well what is asked of her' (Irigaray, *Ce sexe qui n'en est pas un*, Paris, Editions de Minuit, 1977, p. 148; *This Sex which Is Not One*, translated by Catherine Porter, Ithaca, New York, Cornell University Press, 1985, p. 152.) Irigaray continues, 'Because she doubtless needs to reenact it in order to remember what that staging has probably metabolized so thoroughly that *she* has forgotten it: her own sex' (ibid.). In an earlier essay, that which provides the title for the book, Irigaray says, '(Re-)discovering herself, for a woman, thus could only signify the possibility of sacrificing no one of her pleasures to another, of identifying herself with none of them in particular, *of never being simply one*' (30/30–1).

· 4 ·

The Personal Is Political: Discursive Practice of the Face-to-Face

NOREEN O'CONNOR

Introduction

The slogan 'the personal is political' constitutes a challenge to traditional notions of the human as political. Human rights theories, utilitarianism, contract theories, emotivist ethico-political theories retain the notion of interpretation as fundamental, thereby continuing the Aristotelian view of the relationship of man to the world – that is, the rational animal who has a capacity for political activity. What is stressed here is the notion of the individual who is fundamentally reasonable and through the exercise of his reason can direct his actions and be responsible for them. Justice is based on a notion of equality of persons and is to be achieved by the liberation of the person to be himself. The basic, operative assumption is that of a fixed, given, human essence or nature which can, in principle, be known.

The model of the human construed as fundamentally rational self-consciousness is subject to numerous reversals, refutations and critiques by contemporary European philosophers; particularly by Marxists and post-structuralists. In this chapter I shall focus on two philosophers whom I consider to offer radical contestations to foundationalist, logocentric notions of the 'human' and 'society'. Both Foucault and Levinas argue against the notions of the universality of reason, the unity of truth, the teleology of reason, time as gathered into 'presence', the human as self-conscious subject; positively, they stress disjunctions, differences, gaps, dispersions in time and knowledge which are refractory to unification or totalization. Philosophy, since Kant, has identified itself with transcendental reflection; that is, with the theme of origin and recuperation by which, as Foucault maintains, we avoid the differences of our present. Philosophy has avoided differences by focusing all questions on man's being and in doing this neglected the analysis of practice.[1]

For the ontological model of essential humanity Levinas and Foucault substitute an analysis of relationships – which are non-synchronizable in a unitary mind or consciousness. They consider relationships in terms of language, which is construed as discourse by Foucault and as *le dit* (the said, sedimentation) and *le dire* (saying, proximity) by Levinas. Both philosophers focus on the 'body' as the locus of linguistic/social conjunctions and disjunctions. Foucault argues that control of sexuality is central to modern power practice and that the political technology of the body can be read as the common history of power relations and object relations. For Levinas 'the body' is construed in terms of enjoyment and vulnerability. Enjoyment is, he argues, the pre-intentional satisfaction, a separation; it is the tasting of bread, the caressing of skin, and it is irreducible to quantification and to noetic–noematic correlation. Levinas construes the body as vulnerable in terms which are irreducible to knowledge or conscious self-possession; rather, as vulnerable, the body is caught in an anarchic time, a time which cannot be brought to presence and which disrupts the logical order of discourse. He elucidates this disruption by the use of metaphors such as the reflexive form of verbs, the time between heartbeats, growing old, and the relentless rivitation of suffering.

My strategy for this paper is the following: (1) I shall outline the principal features involved in Foucault's archaeology of knowledge since this is inextricably implicated with power relations; (2) I shall produce Levinas's argument in favour of the face-to-face relationship of proximity as that which is other than Being, other than essential; as such, the face-to-face relationship is outside of, yet cuts through, relations of power as possession which, in his view, are expressed in the language of Being; (3) I shall examine some gaps in Foucault's analysis of 'sexuality' with special reference to his account of transgression and I shall suggest a supplement, to use a Derridean term, to Levinas's account of the voluptuosity of the erotic relationship.

I

In this section I shall focus primarily on Foucault's analysis of the statement and the formation of discourse. Foucault defines archaeology as the systematic description of a discourse-object.[2] Archaeology analyses discourse as a practice which has its own forms of sequence and succession. Its aim is to analyse differences rather than overcoming them by thematization. Archaeology distinguishes four levels of events within a discourse: 'the level of the statements themselves in their unique emergence – the level of the appearance of objects, types of communication, concepts, strategic choices (or transformations that affect those that already exist); the level of the derivation of new rules of formation on the basis of rules that are already in operation – but always in the element of a single positivity; lastly, a . . . level at which the substitution of one discursive formation for another takes place'.[3]

Foucault begins with the unities that are already formed by history and then breaks them up to see what other types of groups could be formed; he does this, for example, with psychopathology in *The Birth of the Clinic* and *Madness and Civilization*.[4] In doing this he claims to open up the space and time within which they are specified, to break the infinite continuity of discourse. His point is that all manifest discourse is the repression of what is not said which, in turn, undermines all that is said.[5] Foucault distinguishes this pure description of discursive events from an analysis of language which he conceives as a system for possible statements – this is, a finite set of rules that direct an infinite number of performances. Discourse, on the other hand, is finite and specific. Discourse is not a matter of relating concepts or words with one another, nor does it establish a deductive or rhetorical structure between propositions or sentences.[6]

Discursive relations, although composed of signs, do more than simply use signs to designate things. Foucault analyses the 'statement' as that which allows for the surplus in discourse. His analysis of the statement is the key to all of his work, his practice, because it provides a model of discourse, relationships, which are irreducible to any foundational *a priori* principle, basic structures, dialectical principle or transcendental heuristic. The analysis of statements operates without reference to a *cogito*; it is not a matter of positing a free, speaking subject who reveals and conceals and yet is subject to the constraints of his own speech.

A statement is not a unit but rather a function that cuts across structures, unities, and which reveals them in time and space.[7] The relationship of the statement to what it states is not a group of rules of use and it is anterior to the relation of the proposition to the referent. A statement is not composed of 'facts' or 'realities' but of rules of existence for the objects that are designated within it and for the relations that are affirmed or denied in it.[8] A statement has substance, support and a place and date – it is part of a network of statements – there are no neutral statements. The description of a statement involves defining the conditions in which the function that gave a specific series of signs a specific existence can operate. The existence of the series of signs reveals it as a relation to a domain of objects and a set of possible positions for a subject.[9] The statement, ' . . . has the quasi-invisibility of the "there is", which is effaced in the very thing of which one can say: "there is this or that thing".'[10] Statements which are different, dispersed, form a group if they refer to the same object – emergent in individual and social experience.

For Foucault objects and subjective positions are specified in the analysis of a discursive formation. There are three rules operative in the formation of objects: (1) surfaces of emergence such as a family, social group, work situation, religious community; (2) authorities of delimitation such as law, medicine, education, religious authority; and (3) grids of specification which are systems which divide, relate, classify. There are historical conditions necessary for the appearance of an object of discourse since every object is involved in a matrix of relations of resemblance, proximity, distance, difference. Foucault emphasizes that one cannot speak anything at any time; for example, there could not have been a discourse about the object, rape crisis centre, in the thirteenth century. The relations that allow an object to appear are established between institutions, economic and social processes, behavioural patterns, systems of norms, techniques, types of classification. These relations are not present in the object, they are not its constituents, but rather place it in a field of exteriority. Discursive relations are at the limit of discourse, they characterize discourse itself as practice. Foucault argues that there are no 'things' anterior to discourse; there is the regular formation of objects that emerge only in discourse.

The formation of subjective positions is analysed in terms of the formation of enunciative modalities. Enunciation occurs whenever a group of signs is emitted – each of its articulations is individualized in space and time: 'if one must . . . question language, not in the direction to which it refers, but in the dimension that gives it: ignore the power to name, to designate, to show, to reveal, to be the place of meaning and truth, and instead turn one's attention to the moment which is at once solidified, caught up in the play of the "signifier" and "the signified" – that determines its unique and limited existence'.[11]

For Foucault discourse is not a matter of expression, a verbal translation of a previously established unity; rather, what he proposes are fields of regularity for various positions of subjectivity. Enunciations do not originate in or revert to the unifying function of a subject, whether conceived as transcendental or psychological ego. In the formation of enunciative modalities what matters is: who is speaking and with what status or by what right the person speaks; from what institutional site the speaking emerges. Foucault does not deny that a causal relation exists between an author and a system of signs; but he argues that the 'author' is not identical with the subject of the statement. There is a difference or gap between the author and the subject. He describes the subject of a statement as a particular function, but it is an empty function in that it can be filled by any individual when he formulates the statement and, furthermore, any one individual may occupy different positions and assume the role of different subjects in the same series of statements.[12]

The notion of originating subjectivity is reversed in Foucault's insistence on practice which is 'a body of anonymous, historical rules, always determined in the time and space that have defined a given period, and for a given social, economic, geographical or linguistic area, the conditions of operation of the enunciative function'.[13] Similarly, in his analysis of power Foucault argues that power is not a 'thing' that is possessed, it does not derive from assignable wills or interests. Power is constructed and functions in specific situations, events, but must not be analysed independently of processes and relations of production.[14]

II

The traditional task of reason is, Levinas claims, to ensure the coexistence of terms – that is, the coherence of both despite their difference – in the unity of a theme. Reason, in ensuring the accord of difference, without breaking the present in which the theme is held, permits both terms to be present as one signifying the other. Furthermore, the presence of the theme where both terms of relationship become meaning is the correlative of a conscious subject for whom subjectivity itself consists in making present.[15]

For Levinas the defection of identity, the subversion of essence, is the one-for-the-other. Meeting with the other is neither representation nor limitation nor a conceptual relation. Meeting, which he describes in terms of the face-to-face, is not encompassable by the question of essence, the question 'what is it?'. The face-to-face involves the enigma of responsibility for each other of two terms of an asymmetrical relationship where this responsibility between unequal terms contests the prerogatives of meaning-giving consciousness.

To focus on the enigmatic realm of responsibility and contestation is, Levinas argues, to move the notion of encounter outside the representationalism of intuition and concept to the dimension of separation. The face-to-face relationship both maintains distance and interrupts all totalities. Hence, the face is not a presence announcing an unsaid which, in principle, could be said.

Levinas's fundamental problem is one regarding the model of essence as adequate to the specification of social relations. How can one speak of the openness to the other than Being without this opening as such signifying immediately a gathering into conjunction, into the unity of essence, where could be read immediately the very subject to whom the gathering would be unconcealed? The schema of intentional subject is a constant danger, therefore, based as it is on a structure of interest and interiority to Being – immanence and transcendence.

If it is accepted that philosophy is a search for source, origin or foundation, then no horizon other than the comprehension of Being is possible. But to begin as if the meaning of difference were already established is to have no further problem because of the assumption that it is derived, controlled and ordered from the starting point of a being-present.[16]

Levinas, however, offers more than opposition to a tradition by posing a question about its foundational presuppositions. His treatment of the enigmatic irruption of the beyond Being, the face-to-face, offers a dimension outside of egological interest, initiative, recuperation, immanence and transcendence. Exposition to others in responsibility for them does not come from a decision of mine. It is a formless passivity of exposition. Even respiration, for example, is not a Sartrean all-inclusive *en-soi*, but exile, without repose. Neither is it reducible to biological description in the sense that in responding to a fundamental need of energy it carries to the tissues the oxygen necessary for the functioning of the organism and eliminates carbon dioxide. On the contrary, respiration, opening of 'self' to the other is not a conditioning or a foundation of self in some principle. It 'reveals' its meaning only in relation with the other, in the proximity of the neighbour which is responsibility for her and substitution for her.[17] Respiration, the movement from the self to the point of leaving, is a matter of being substituted for the other, to be responsible for her. In her otherness the other is not just a particular case, a species of alterity, but original exception. This is not to say that the other is a new, unsaid *quiddity*. Rather, novelty comes from the other: through the other, novelty signifies in being the other-than-Being.[18]

Without the proximity of the other in the face everything would be absorbed in Being. Progress would be fundamentally linear, for it would come in the same way, through the establishment of forms, or structures – totalities absorbing the very subject to which it is unconcealed.

Levinas's task is not one of distinguishing between the lived, as spontaneously operative, and efforts to account for it critically as operative totality. Even within the confines of traditional phenomenological investigation the notion of lived experience is not treated merely as repetition of that which has gone before. The work of Gadamer and Merleau-Ponty, for example, stresses that questions can be asked which challenge and which seek to overcome the insights held in our cultural store.

Levinas's claim is that responsibility of the one-for-the-other does not occur within the tension of a naïve, lived unreflection which would be available to thematization in some manner. For the interval, or difference, which separates one from the other, as well as the non-indifference of the one-for-the-other cannot be simply gathered into a theme, or else established as a state of the soul. Thus Levinas substitutes the relationship of proximity, the face-to-face, for that of intelligibility as *logos*.[19] Interpretation as *logos* is a thematizing, a synchronizing, a systematization, a being placed in Being. But the beyond Being escapes such categorization; here the time of philosophy is diachronic.[20] This has consequences for time such that instants are refused to the memory which recovers and represents. This traversion of rationality, or the logic of knowledge, is, in turn, a refusal to synchronize the affirmations already uttered. There is a contestation of the notion of linear time with its anticipation that between the already said and the present saying there is repeated synchronically the relation which links condition and conditioned. There is introduced between the said and the present saying not a mere interval as if both were correlatives, but a rupture, failure or impossibility of discourse.[21] Philosophy, in Levinas's view, is a breakthrough of categorization and recalls the rupture of synchronizable time – that is, the responsibility for the other.

Here, expression is not revelation. On the contrary, there is expressed the non-revealable that is beyond thematization, constitutive analysis, ontology.[22] In a culture dominated by the notion of *logos* there is no fundamental interruption, for all contestation and interruption of discourse is automatically translated in terms of the discourse itself.

Levinas's account of the face-to-face involves the notion of the 'self' as disjunction of identity rather than the constitution of a unity. The relationship of proximity is not a matter of subjectivity presented as the mysterious play of the essence of Being; rather, he says, the human is accused by the hyperbole, by the *dés-intér-essement* of essence. Thus, philosophical discourse does not pass from one term to the other in uniquely subjective horizons of that which is to be seen, but which somehow must embrace the conjunction of elements which break through the concepts upheld as presence, or subject.

III

What use are the analyses of Levinas and Foucault for the Women's Movement – a movement of discursive practices of sex/gender distinctions?

Does their substitution of matrices of relations for the notion of a unified subjectivity preclude the plausibility of a movement where primary status is accorded 'woman' since it might be argued that this is a reintroduction of an essentialist identity-structure?

Feminist analyses of power focus on the issue of men's power over women; in some cases this is expressed as men *having* power over women. Foucault argues against this notion of power as a 'thing' that can be possessed; rather, he says that we must free ourselves from an image of power as law if we are actually to examine *how* it works.[23] Power relations are matrices of transformation and immanent in every type of relationship. His point here is that it is a mistake to specify power as having a unitary locus which can be theorized. Again it is the analysis of discursive practice, the process, that he stresses. Sexuality became accessible to knowledge when power relations established it as a possible object in terms, for example, of control of reproduction, individual life and species life. The analysis of discourse practised by feminists in the area of reproduction and production do fulfil Foucault's requirement of specificity in time and space – for example, analysis of the contraception industry in terms of: surplus value, the effects and effectiveness of various methods of contraception, advertising, the media, the failure of technologists to develop a 'safe' contraceptive for men, the practice of heterosexuality. Along with Foucault's acknowledgment that all analyses of power relations must take account of the relations of production, feminists argue that all analyses of power relations must take account of sex/gender differences. This is not a matter of claiming that we know the answer in advance – that is, that we know how an individual man and men as a group relate to a woman and to women as a group – but now, in the latter half of the twentieth century, there is an established discursive object, namely, 'women's oppression', and as such it is open to analysis.

Power, for Foucault, is primarily exercised at the level of life, the species and the population; it is not, as I have already mentioned, simply a matter of a right of seizure but a matter of organizing forces, generating forces, ordering them.[24] Power over life evolved in two basic forms; firstly, in terms of the body as machine, disciplined and ordered according to what Foucault terms '*an anatomo-politics of the human body*'; secondly, the body considered as species life subject to regulatory controls which he calls 'a biopolitics of the population'. The techniques of power are present at every level of social relations and used by diverse institutions.[25] Foucault argues that in order to understand sex as a political issue it should be considered as the pivot of the above two forms of technologizing life: on the one hand tied to the disciplining of the body and, on the other, to the regulation of populations. He argues that for the past two centuries the politics of sex has advanced in four directions, each one combining disciplinary techniques and regulative methods: the sexualization of children was accomplished as a campaign for the health of the race, and the hysterization of women was a campaign for medicalizing our bodies and sex to serve the cause of the health of our children, safeguarding of the family and thus the stability of society. These two campaigns he specifies as disciplinary. The control of births and the psychiatrization of perversions he specifies as regulatory.[26]

Foucault cites Sade and Bataille as two of the most influential writers on sex as erotic. He argues that they conceive of the sexual in terms of death, the law, blood and sovereignty. Instead of this unitary analysis of sexuality Foucault proposes its analysis through the techniques of power which are contemporary with it.

In his essay, *Preface to Transgression*, Foucault defines eroticism as 'an experience of sexuality that links, for its own ends, an overcoming of limits to the death of God . . . at the root of sexuality, of the movement that nothing can ever limit . . . a singular experience is shaped: that of transgression'.[27] Transgression does not involve negativity but it does affirm finite being; it is neither violence nor victory over limits. Foucault claims that Bataille's extremity of language will serve as the basis 'for finally liberating our language'.[28] This language is not in control of itself; it breaks down and exposes a subject who is overcome, subjected by the language that he had tried to distance. Foucault specifies 'the philosophy of eroticism' as a description of the experience of the finitude of being. He praises Bataille's work for its exemplary attack on the notion of the predominance of the philosophical subject. By his exploration, transgression, Bataille's work proceeds to the limit which is the void, and this is the opening of communication. In *The Story of the Eye* Bataille uses the metaphor of the eye rotating in its socket and in Simone's vagina to describe the relation of language and death – where language discovers its being in the crossing of its limits.[29]

Foucault's exaltation of the movement of transgression in Bataille's work raises the question for feminists of how this eroticization of the body (in Bataille's text this is principally the female body) operates in terms of power relations between women and men. Some feminists who analyse male violence against women identify eroticism with pornography and argue that the juxtaposition of force and death is a romanticization of violence and a hatred of women's bodies.[30] Here the body is regarded as evidence, focus rests on representations of women's bodies *vis-à-vis* men; for example, Simone in *The Story of the Eye* is seen to exist in male sexual networks as a sadistic whore whose sexuality is murderous and insatiable but at the same time she is seen as a victim. Such a representationalist critique of pornography poses again the problem of essentialism. By only analysing representations there is the danger that the analysis of power practices will be ignored.

In other words, there will be neither an analysis of the conditions of the production and consumption of pornography (the pornography industry), nor of the fact that it is sanctioned by legal, medical and media institutions. This representationalist critique has been co-opted by right-wing fundmentalists because it is in line with their own essentialism. Oppositional practice can occur by shifting the debate to the fundamentalist opposition to mothers and wives in the work place, and to abortion. Furthermore, the representationalist construal of power as negativity must be supplemented by a positive politics of women's pleasure, and of women's different sexualities.[31]

Conclusion

In *Totality and Infinity* Levinas analyses the erotic relationship, and he does so within the context of a sex/gender distinction.[32] In specifying the voluptuosity of caressing the other as feminine he speaks of 'experience' which is not knowledge or the effect of an action. It is not the essential body of the woman that is caressed nor is it a matter of an object fulfilling an intentional, representational phantasy; rather, he says that it is an expression of love that cannot tell it. The otherness of the feminine cuts through the self's egoistic self-inherence: 'Equivocation constitutes the epiphany of the feminine – at the same time interlocutor, collaborator and master supremely intelligent, so often dominating men in the masculine civilization it has entered, a woman having to be treated as a woman, in accordance with rules imprescriptible by civil society. The face . . . in its feminine epiphany dissimulates allusions, innuendos . . . signalling the less than nothing.'[33]

Levinas argues that the relationship of lovers in voluptuosity is a matter of dual solitude which excludes the social relation, the third person. This account of voluptuosity is what must be supplemented by the feminine *dire*. Levinas identifies the dominant metaphor of vision with that of totalizing philosophy and he shifts to the metaphor of touch – where there is no 'object' available to possession, nor a centralized, unitary libido, but diffusion, disproportion and a breakthrough of activity/passivity dichotomies: it is by focusing on touching which is not possessive, nor teleological, that we can begin 'to think' the possibility of voluptuosity which does not exclude the social, the practice of differences.

Notes

1 Michel Foucault, *L'Archéologie du savoir*, Paris, Gallimard, 1969 (hereafter AS), p. 266; Michel Foucault, *The Archaeology of Knowledge*, translated by A. M. Sheridan, London, Tavistock, 1972 (hereafter AK), p. 204.
2 AK, p. 140; AS, p. 183.
3 AK, p. 171; AS, p. 223.
4 Michel Foucault, *La Naissance de la clinique*, Paris, Presses Universitaires de France, 1963; *The Birth of the Clinic*, translated by A. M. Sheridan, London, Tavistock, 1973. Foucault, *Histoire de la folie a l'âge classique*, Paris, Librairie Plon, 1961; *Madness and Civilization: a History of Insanity in the Age of Reason*, translated by Richard Howard, London, Tavistock, 1967.
5 AK, p. 25; AS, p. 35.
6 AK, p. 46; AS, p. 35.
7 AK, p. 87; AS, pp. 62–3.
8 AK, p. 91; AS, p. 120.
9 AK, p. 108; AS, p. 142.
10 AK, p. 111; AS, p. 145.
11 Ibid.
12 AK, p. 93; AS, p. 123.
13 AK, p. 118; AS, p. 152.
14 Cf. Jeffrey Weeks, 'Foucault for Historians', in *History Workshop* 14, Autumn 1982, 115.
15 AEAE, p. 170; OBBE, p. 133.
16 Jacques Derrida, 'La "Différence" ', *Bulletin de la Société française de Philosophie*, juillet–septembre, 1968, 88.
17 Noreen O'Connor, 'Human Encounter: Beyond the Philosophy of Male and Female', *The Crane Bag*, vol. 4, No. 1, 1980, 24.
18 AEAE, p. 229; OBBE, p. 182.
19 AEAE, p. 212; OBBE, p. 166.
20 It is important to note that Levinas uses the term 'diachronic' to describe speech which occurs in different, irreducible and irreversible, times; the term 'diachronic' does not refer to the unity of an object or speech through different times.
21 AEAE, p. 214; OBBE, p. 168.
22 Levinas argues that the phenomenological constitution of the other which Husserl carries out in the fifth *Cartesian Meditation* as well as the categorization by Sartre and Merleau-Ponty of the experience of the other in terms of encounter remains logocentric. The other is not constituted as a possession of the monadic subject, nor present as a behavioural style similar to mine. Rather, the ethical relation of the face-to-face is the emergence of an absolute alterity, of an exteriority which overflows the monadic Husserlian ego and the historically appropriating social subjects of Sartre and Merleau-Ponty.

23 Alan Sheridan, *Foucault: the Will to Truth*, London, Tavistock, 1980, p. 184.
24 Foucault, *Histoire de la Sexualité*, vol. 1, *La Volonté de savoir*, Paris, Gallimard, 1976, p. 179; *The History of Sexuality*, vol. 1, *An Introduction*, translated by Robert Hurley, Harmondsworth, Penguin, 1978, p. 136.
25 Ibid, pp. 183–4; translation, pp. 139–40.
26 Ibid., p. 195; translation pp. 146–7.
27 Foucault, 'Preface to Transgression', in *Language, Counter-memory, Practice*, edited by D. F. Bouchard, Ithaca, N.Y., Cornell University Press, 1977, p. 33.
28 Ibid, p. 39.
29 Georges Bataille, *Story of the Eye*, New York, Urizen Books, 1977.
30 Andrea Dworkin, *Pornography: Men Possessing Women*, New York, The Women's Press, 1981, p. 175.
31 Lesley Stern, 'The Body as Evidence' *Screen*, vol. 23, 1982, 38–63.
32 TI, pp. 256–66; TeI, pp. 233–43.
33 TI, p. 264; TeI, pp. 241–2.

· 5 ·

Amorous Discourses: 'The Phenomenology of Eros' and Love Stories

ALISON AINLEY

I would like to take up the possibilities of future understandings of feminism, ethics and subjectivity as they are raised in the work of Emmanuel Levinas and Julia Kristeva. Specifically I will consider the section entitled 'The Phenomenology of Eros' in Levinas's book *Totality and Infinity* and the essay 'Stabat Mater' in Kristeva's *Histoires d'amour*.[1]

Both Kristeva and Levinas put into question any assumed unity of subjectivity. This is an important area for feminism because of the way that patriarchal structures work to give priority to singularity, identity, 'full' presence and, co-extensively, the authorial authority of the writer. If feminism questions the unity of subjectivity then it may also question the power structures aligned with such unity. However, the unity of subjectivity cannot simply be replaced with multiplicity, because this may be reincorporated into existing structures. Consequently, Kristeva and Levinas attempt to theorize a mode of being which does not fall back into the old patterns but equally does not try to break away from them. In order to do this, they return to the site of the body and, particularly, the erotic realm and maternity.

Now it would be a dubious task to attempt to synthesize the work of Kristeva and Levinas, because Levinas is mainly concerned with ethical and phenomenological horizons whereas Kristeva is working at the interfaces between psychoanalysis, politics and linguistic theory. Nevertheless, both share a distrust of the way the 'I' apparently determines the other, especially when such a structure is conflated with 'male' determining 'female'. Kristeva's particular reading of psychoanalysis leads her to be critical of any identity which seems to be in danger of solidification. Moreover, she sees a transformation of such notions as essential if there is to be any sociopolitical change.[2] Hence it is as necessary to be critical of the notion of 'woman' as it is to be critical of that of 'man'. But Kristeva also refuses to endorse such notions as 'feminist' or 'feminism' because of the danger of slipping back into a pre-given distinction between man and woman which reinstates all the old prejudices.[3] However, this does not entail a complete deferral of action on the part of Kristeven feminists. It is necessary, in her view, to remain counter to patriarchal structures while at the same time questioning assumptions about 'woman as such'. Thus is seems that Kristeva is suggesting an attitude of equivocation, something which Levinas also seems to suggest.[4]

Levinas attempts to put into question all ethics which make reference to an abstract principle. He does this by returning oral considerations to the social dimension of the 'face-to-face' relation. Although Levinas is sympathetic to the aims of feminism, like Kristeva he reserves doubt about the threat of totalization and fixity which such a name may imply. An attempt to establish any kind of equality is suspect if it has failed to take into account the presuppositions upon which it is to be based. Despite this reservation, Levinas may prove to be significant to theoretical feminism. This is because, like Derrida and Adorno, he may be conscripted in the struggle for a critique of 'identity thinking' and essentialism in its various manifestations.

There is a two-fold problem within feminism in constructing such a critique. On the one hand, there is a danger of seeing identity simply as an ideological construction produced by the historical solidification of gender roles. On the other hand, rejecting the whole notion of sexual identity and trying to find an alternative is utopic and may fail to take into account differences which do exist not only biologically but socially.

However, social structures are clearly not static structures but processes in continual change. Both Levinas and Kristeva activate the creative and generative potentials they perceive in language, while at the same time taking into account the historical aspect of sexual identity. In this way they incorporate equivocation into their own work, moving between existing structures of sexual difference and possible new ones.

Kristeva's history of sexual difference considers the polarization of modes of thought between Hebraic and Hellenic and the attempt to synthesize them in Christianity. This gives a perspective on the mythical and cultural formulation of sexual difference as a continual attempt to regulate unruly equivocation, to make differences decidable.

Kristeva traces the way in which monotheistic communities held to a notion of communality which preceded, but eventually merged with, state unity and political law. Monotheism becomes fused with paternal, moralizing concerns, and this leads to a suppression of that which is counter to the specific interests of the collective. For women what this means is the repression of (paganistic) duplicity or multiplicity, or what Kristeva calls 'the polymorphic body, laughing and desiring'.[5] What is seen as diversifying, fragmentary and splitting is identified with the figure of woman in certain manifestations and, to ensure the continuity of communal interest, characterized as disruptive and undesirable. Without this move, the establishment of 'the principle of One Law – One Purifying Transcendent Guarantor of the ideal interest'[6] could not come about.

Hence it seems the bond of words – or the Word – ensures continuity. But this arises through the differentiation of the sexes and, more particularly, the differentiation of relation to the word. Men and women have a differential relation to God, and passivity is required, or demanded, of women to prevent the eruption of the outlawed elements which could then threaten the whole system.

But it is not simply identification and attempted outlawing which takes place. Kristeva indicates the extent to which these disruptive forces can also be incorporated and hence contained within the symbolic order, without a dangerous independent status. She suggests this occurs through the alignment of impurity and interiority of the body. This is then seen as signifying both femininity and maternity. In this way maternity can be co-opted for the continuance of the Law of the Father, reproducing it through reproduction.

Biblical impurity is permeated with the tradition of defilement . . . it *points to* but does not *signify* a force that can be threatening for divine agency. . . . Such a force is rooted historically (in the structure of religions) and subjectively (in the structuration of the subject's identity) in the cathexis of the maternal function – mother, woman, reproduction. But the Biblical text – and therein lies its extraordinary specificity – performs the tremendous forcing that consists in subordinating maternal power (whether historical or phantasmic, natural or reproductive) to symbolic order as pure logical order regulating social performance, as divine law attended to in the temple.[7]

In the Bible, the primary relation of man to God seems to indicate the secondariness of woman, created after him. However, Levinas suggests that it is not difference, but the relation to sexual difference, that is secondary:[8]

not that the feminine originates in the masculine but rather the division into masculine and feminine – the dichotomy starts with what is human. .... It is not woman who is secondary, it is the relation to woman as woman, and that does not belong to the primordial level of the human element.[9]

Here, in order to keep the possibility of an ethical relationship to the other, Levinas must also keep the notion of a prior 'human element'. Without this, ethics would seemingly fall to the partiality of one sex and lose its universal status. But at the same time, Levinas remains very much aware of the insidious nature of masquerading neutrality. One of the aspects of 'creating' dichotomous sexual difference is that it sets up a movement of 'war between the sexes' which permits the continuance of a notion of truth.[10] By occluding this process within the notion of a neutral truth, the actual masculine bias is either occluded or presented as the primary origin of sexual difference.

In order to expose the deceptive nature of the supposed neutrality of the other, Levinas openly comments on the primacy of the masculine access to spirit. As we are already contained in such a division, to occlude or deny it would be not only futile but dangerous. The alignment of language and cultural structures with patriarchal power structures reconstructs history as a journey from (primitive) nature to (sophisticated) culture. This characterization of nature as regressive and the alignment of women with the 'natural' means that the whole notion of difference is infected with positive and negative values which cannot simply be erased. The interrelated themes become entrenched to constitute a 'reality'. In this context, therefore, it is important to recognize that Levinas's writing is neither prescriptive, advocating the continuance of this 'reality', nor simply descriptive of the present situation.

Levinas follows his strategy of making femininity constitutive of the other for two reasons. Firstly, he must acknowledge the masculine bias of so-called neutral metaphysical desire and hence the masculine bias of language. Thus he is in a framework in which femininity is made to be other to these concerns and, in insisting on the importance

ALISON AINLEY

of keeping sexual difference an open issue in his work, he must necessarily fall into this pattern. However, his conscious appropriation of his place in such a pattern makes his position more complex than a simple reactionary attitude to women, an apparent reinstatement of women's traditional social roles and associated qualities such as passivity or kindness. If it is sexual difference which is secondary, not women, the requirement of an ethics which is a return to 'dwelling' (in the sense of both the home and presence), presently aligned with the feminine principle, is not necessarily reducible to 'putting women back in the home'. It expresses a desire for a community of reconciliation.

However, Levinas is not writing in this community but in a sexually differentiated one. Consequently, the paradox of writing which faces him is how to write as a constituted and authoritative subject, while simultaneously disavowing such a subject. This brings in the second reason. Because Levinas is present in a dichotomous structure of sexual difference, not apart from it, he writes as a man for whom the feminine is necessarily, but radically, other. Is this what Derrida means when he says *Totality and Infinity* could not have been written by a woman? Is it Levinas's attempt to be scrupulously honest in the face of ethical possibility, not pretending to write a neutral text?[11]

Derrida raises questions about the relationship between 'essential' sexual difference and the possibility of different strategies within language. But he also raises questions about what notions of such 'essential' truths about the two realms, and their division, might constitute. He advocates caution in reading Levinas straightforwardly, because of the number of different voices in his writing. But he adds another warning: 'The distance of this commentary is not neuter. What he comments upon is consonant with a whole network of assertions, or those by him, "him".' Levinas's attempt to deal with two features at once – a reasoned, critical, assertive space and a more ambiguous or uncertain one – means that this 'double strategy' is always open to the accusation that it is capable of being reincorporated into existing structures.

In a similar way, Kristeva adopts a split register of discourses in 'Stabat Mater'. Here there is a typographical differentiation between the theoretical/historical tracing of the model symbolism of motherhood and Kristeva's personal/poetic account of her own pregnancy. This split draws attention to a point which Kristeva makes regarding the 'double' aspect of maternity, corresponding in effect to the public

74

and private spheres. I will return to the questions raised by such writing strategies shortly. But first I want to consider the mythical aspects of the erotic and motherhood.

In Kristeva's analysis, what appears to constitute a rupture of the symbolic order is the very thing which is necessarily repressed: the figure of the active mother who is orgasmic as well as reproductive. It is by *removing* the aspect of *jouissance* – in the name of virginity – or *channelling* it into reproduction, that the security of unity may be maintained. What can be incorporated about motherhood is its symbolic significance for the community; what can be removed is the site of desire which permeates the community, yet threatens it. This desire can be displaced into a desire for the child, for the word.[12]

The myth of the Virgin Mary becomes a symbolic axis around which such a repression takes place. The conjunction of virginity and maternity may apparently represent a potential ambivalence with which to shake up the suppositions of Jewish monotheism and certain aspects of Greek thought, but in the Christian synthesis of the two into a totality virginity is co-opted for pure asceticism and maternity for the continuity of the community through the child. The conjunction of the two aspects is set up as an ideal model, a model which then fuses with the existing ideal of virginity in courtly love and the ideal of exclusive, devoted maternal love. What this means is that not only is the impossible totality of the virgin mother appropriated for a particular structure, but it is permeated into a social realm as the prototype for Western love relations.

Mary is made into an eternal virgin once her own immaculate conception is established in apocryphal sources. Through this ideal figure, the eternal Mary, the possibility of death is written out by making sexuality signify transience, sin and temporality, punished by death; while chastity signifies eternity and continual life. In this pure state Mary can become the mother not only of Christ but man and God as well. The totality, fused in one name, provides an apparent escape from mortality. The figure can pass in eternal flux from one metamorphosis to another.

However, Kristeva points out the underlying forces at work in this apparent extension of authority. When Mary is not only proclaimed Queen of Heaven but also charged with the care of the Church and given supreme earthly power, she becomes analogous to the noble lady of the medieval court. Such a figure demanded ardent and yet exclusive desire for a woman free of moral or physical sin, retaining authority over her suitors. But this disguises the severity of the law it is contained within. The agglomeration of desirable qualities in the virgin mother, an inaccessible totality, separates and opposes the woman to her own desires. With the introduction of the devout, tender mother-love, this high spirituality seems to be mediated by the signs of the human maternal body, signs such as the fluids of milk and tears. But Kristeva considers the milk and tears to be themselves contained within the horizon of an attempted escape from death. One way of displacing the unthinkable mortality is to hold to a purified maternal love which is eternal and unchanging.

The sorrow of Mary is never a tragic overflowing; joy and a certain triumph follow the tear, as if the conviction that death does not exist were an irrational but unshakable certitude upon which to base the principle of resurrection.[13]

Levinas suggests that this romanticized version of love is not present in the same sense in Judaism. However, this does not necessarily imply that erotic or sentimental love is suppressed, but rather that they are maintained in flux for 'the permanent opening of the messianic perspective'. The love which loves only for its own sake, idealized as a flight from death, would represent a closure of this possibility.[14] But Levinas reinstates something which lies *beyond* the immediacy of the erotic relation, something which can be conscripted for the interest of patriarchal structures.

Maternity is, in the Rabbinic interpretation of love, subordinate to a human destiny which exceeds the bounds of 'the joys of the family'; it is necessary to fulfill Israel, to 'multiply the image of God' inscribed on the faces of men.[15]

However, Levinas does not re-endorse this view in a straightforward manner. Instead, like Kristeva, he tries to move away from romanticized and deified notions of the erotic and towards an image of women which does not *exclude* the aspect of potential maternity, but equally does not make it into a determining factor. Is such a reclamation possible, given the networks of myth and history called up in its wake? To consider this question we may examine what Levinas and Kristeva offer towards possibilities of the future.

In attempting to establish ethical possibilities of the future, it would seem that allowing sexual difference in would threaten the whole project, because it seems to differentiate 'ethical actors' according to gender. But Levinas's rebellion against neutrality takes up sexual difference as the *very possibility* of ethical relations. It is in the realm of 'exteriority' of being that ethical relations seem to take place, the 'public' realm. But Levinas suggests that the equivocal (feminine) realm puts this exteriority into disarray; it establishes an uncertainty and a continual shifting which disrupts any clear fixity of identity. Exteriority would be a closure without the undecidable 'interior' space, a space which for Levinas is aligned with the erotic. The relation of the face-to-face shows the other *as* other via distance through which expressive signification can take place. It is not I who determine the other, but the other who calls upon me to name myself. However, in the erotic realm, this process is one of equivocal tenderness, so that clarity is put into question in the boundaries between shadow and light.[16] Levinas joins this realm with 'the feminine'. It is a dimension of uncertainty and postponement. 'The essentially hidden throws itself towards the light, without becoming signification. Not nothingness – but what is not yet.'[17] The simultaneity of that which is clandestine and exposed results in a loss of distance. The search for presence is given up, the will to dominate the otherness of the other (as in Sartrean erotic relations) is surrendered.[18]

But interiority is not mere introspection. The renewed encounter with the other prevents this. Interiority does not seek to make alterity into identity, but remains a process of longing for what is remote, a state of being fascinated by otherness.

Now it may seem that Levinas is aligning 'the feminine' with a realm of silence, in that signification belongs to the exterior realm, not the erotic. But Levinas wants to suggest that the erotic realm equivocates on the borders *between* 'speech and the renouncement of speech'.[19] Hence he holds that equivocation is not merely within language, in allusions, innuendoes and puns, but also in the scintillation of silence and language.

Two facets of the erotic relation which Levinas describes are voluptuosity and fecundity. Voluptuosity corresponds to a return to self. It is the pure enjoyment of love, 'complacent, pleasure and dual egoism'.[20] The dimension of fecundity, however, is the possibility of moving from one identity to another, or to something which lies beyond the face. This is not merely a replica of the self, but a new self, the child. The shift to the child which, Levinas suggests, offers a glimpse of 'an endless recommencement of a different order of time', cuts across voluptuosity. But Levinas wishes to ensure that his notion of fecundity is not reducible to a biological *telos* realized through erotic desire, since it does not belong to a sphere of projects or desires to be projected *on to* the world. The notion of fecundity Levinas proposes is not entirely subordinated to a deathless ideal, because it is expressed within the dimension of interiority, but nor is it enclosed within itself.

This participation of the present in the future takes place specifically in the feeling of love . . . [which] leads it beyond the instant and even beyond the loved person. This end does not appear to a vision exterior to the love, which would then integrate it in the plan of creation; it is in the love itself.[21]

Here we see a problem with Levinas's proposal. If we are to understand the balance of voluptuosity, which is the self's immersion with itself, as fecundity, or that which expresses a 'beyond', it seems that inherent within Levinas's schema is a specifically heterosexual formulation of love relations, containing the possibility of parenthood. Levinas wants to maintain that the possibility of a 'beyond' is not exterior to the love relation, but within the relation itself. But the title of the section in which 'the Phenomenology of Eros' appears, 'Beyond the Face', indicates an intention towards that which exceeds. Because of this Levinas must face the charge that the continuity of identity via fecundity expresses not only the continuity of the Law of the Father, but also a presupposition of a heterosexual relation, albeit symbolically rather than biologically expressed. Levinas wants to keep accounts of maternity and paternity which are linked to a biological projection but not governed and determined by it, but the qualifying point which Derrida raises is still valid. Perhaps metaphysical desire is essentially virile.

Kristeva's notion of positionality situates subjectivity other than within a reductive biological determinism, and yet without recourse to something which lies beyond material relations. In terms of the heteronomy of drives that Freud establishes, Kristeva maintains that

Drives are material, but they are not solely biological since they both connect and differentiate the biological and symbolic within the dialectic of the signifying body invested in a practice.[22]

Drives are 'simultaneously assimilating and destructive', making the 'semiotised body a place of permanent scission'.[23] Such a reinscription of desire makes it a process of continual transgression and renewal.

Nevertheless, Kristeva's notion of the semiotic chora seems to be aligned with the pre-Oedipal mother's body. But Kristeva is not returning to a simple correlation of 'the feminine' with the originary place of the subject, and entry into the symbolic as masculine.

The chora is, according to Kristeva, a fluid and undifferentiated realm, containing aspects of both femininity and masculinity. But because it is positioned prior to the 'thetic rupture' of subjectivity into the Law of the Father, the entry into language, it is capable of being aligned to the figure of the mother. Kristeva writes, 'The mother's body is therefore what mediates the symbolic law organizing social relations, and what becomes the ordering principle of the semiotic chora.'[24]

Levinas refers to 'an unrecuperated, pre-ontological past of maternity'.[25] As in Kristeva's analysis, this nostalgia for a matriarchal order is not reducible to an ontological first cause, nor to a reinstatement of motherhood under the principles of bourgeois values. Rather, it functions as a myth turned in on itself and inside out; a utopian gesture to counteract the cynicism and reductionism of patriarchal social relations.

Both Levinas and Kristeva activate conceptions of maternity from within, in order to displace certain preconceptions about the solidification of its symbolism. For Kristeva, the exposition of what has generally been excluded constitutes a rethinking of maternity for feminism, not reducible to its biological materiality. She writes,

There might doubtless be a way to approach the obscure place that maternity constitutes for a woman . . . one might equally try to see more clearly into the incredible construction of the maternal which the West elaborates through the Virgin . . . concerning every woman's body, this heterogeneity that cannot be subsumed by the signifier nevertheless explodes violently with pregnancy (threshold of nature and culture) and the arrival of the child (which extracts a woman from her unity and gives her a chance – not a certainty – of access to the other, of ethics).[26]

The possibility of a future in which feminine impulses could be allowed requires, within Kristeva's schema, the necessity of a reconstituted (and so repressed) subject, to bring about a transition. Writing alone cannot effect it, although it is within disruptions of the symbolic order that the elemental semiotic drives may be glimpsed. But the addition of writing and subjectivity equals a new manifestation of oppression, if the very notion of the subject is seen as a phallocentric phenomenon. Consequently Kristeva does not want to adopt a metatheoretical position which would suggest a disguised patriarchal authority. For her, maternity is constant disruption, the entry of the genotext into the phenotext, the negativity and persistence of space and silence and the repeated disintegration and reconstitution of the subject.

One problem which the heterogeneity of the subject raises is the possibility of its reincorporation into the oppressive structures which it is trying to disrupt. In this form it is simply an anarchy which is the negation of totalitarianism, and would lead to the exploitation and suppression of maternity rather than an openness towards it. Levinas escapes this charge, but perhaps at the expense of introducing a justification of patriarchy in the form of continuous vistas of infinite time.

But both Levinas and Kristeva seem to remain optimistic about the strategic appropriation of a 'double life' in present social relations; both appear to claim that women have a privileged access to a realm of experience linked explicitly to biology which nevertheless has wider implications. It is the relation of a woman's desire to herself and others in a private sphere, which involves a recollection and remembrance of her own abandonment, and a potential, as Kristeva says, of access to the other, of ethics.

Notes

1 Kristeva, 'Stabat Mater' in *Histoires d'amour*, Paris, Denoel, 1983. Translated by Leon S. Roudiez in *The Kristeva Reader*, edited by Toril Moi, Oxford, Basil Blackwell, 1986.

2 'In the twentieth century . . . we should have learned that there can be no sociopolitical transformation without a transformation of subjects.' (Kristeva, 'Woman Can Never Be Defined', in *New French Feminisms*, edited by Elaine Marks and Isabel de Courtivron, Brighton, Harvester Press, 1981, p. 141.)

3 'The very dichotomy man/woman as an opposition between two rival entities may be understood as belonging to metaphysics. What can identity, even sexual identity mean in a new theoretical and scientific space where the very notion of identity is challenged?' (Kristeva, 'Women's Time', translated by Alice Jardine and Harry Blake, *Signs*, vol. 7, No. 1, Autumn 1981. Reprinted in *The Kristeva Reader*, edited by Toril Moi, Oxford, Basil Blackwell, 1986, p. 209.)

4 'This simultaneity of need and desire, of concupiscence and transcendence, tangency of the avowable and the unavowable, constitutes the originality of the erotic, which in this sense is *the equivocal* par excellence.' (Levinas, TI, p. 255; TeI, p. 233.)

'A constant alternation between time and its "truth", identity and its loss, history and the timeless, signless extra-phenomenal things which produce it. An impossible dialectic, a permanent alteration; never one without the other.' (Kristeva, *About Chinese Women*, translated by Anita Barrows, London, Marion Boyars, 1977, p. 38. Originally published as *Des Chinoises*, Paris, Éditions des Femmes, 1974.)

5 Ibid., p. 19.

6 Ibid.

7 Kristeva, *Powers of Horror, an Essay on Abjection*, translated by Leon S. Roudiez, New York, Columbia University Press, 1982, p. 91.

8 This is also suggested by alternative translations of the Bible, in which 'Adam' is taken as referring to a sexually undifferentiated human. Within Jewish tradition, the *Midrash* (Genesis Rabbah 8:1) interprets the verse 'Male and female created He them' (Gen. 1:27) as meaning that Adam was originally a hermaphrodite, a position which is taken up and discussed in the Talmud (Er. 18a).

9 Levinas, 'Et Dieu crée la femme', in *Du sacré au saint*, Paris, Éditions de Minuit, 1977.

10 'Did not God give the name Adam to man and woman joined together, as if the two were one, as if the unity of the person were able to triumph over the dangers that lie in wait for it only by a duality inscribed in his very essence? Dramatic duality – for conflict can well up into catastrophe and the friend can become the most terrible enemy.' (Levinas, 'Judaism and the Feminine Element', translated by Edith Wyschogrod, *Judaism*, vol. 18, No. 1, 1969, 30–8.)

11 Derrida writes

Let us note in passing that *Totality and Infinity* pushes the respect for disymmetry so far that it seems impossible, essentially impossible, that it could have been written by a woman. Its philosophical subject is man (vir). . . . Is not this principled impossibility for a book to have been written by a woman unique in the history of metaphysics? Levinas acknowledges elsewhere that femininity is an 'ontological category'. Should this remark be placed in relation to the essential virility of metaphysical language? But perhaps metaphysical desire is essentially virile, even in what is called woman.'

'Violence and Metaphysics: an Essay on the Thought of Emmanuel Levinas', in *Writing and Difference*, translated by Alan Bass, London, Routledge & Kegan Paul, 1981, p. 320, fn. 92 ('Violence et métaphysique: Essai sur la pensée d'Emmanuel Levinas', in *L'Écriture et la différence*, Paris, Éditions du Seuil, 1967, p. 228, fn. 1).

12 Kristeva writes

Patrilinear descent with transmission of the father's name centralizes eroticism in the single goal of procreation, in the grip of an abstract symbolic authority which refuses to acknowledge the fact that the child grows and is carried in the mother's body, which a matrilinear system of descent kept alive in the mind by leaving certain possibilities of polymorphism – if not incest – still available. (*About Chinese Women*, p. 20.)

13 'Stabat Mater', p. 239, my translation.
14 Levinas writes
    The dimension of the romantic, where love becomes its own end; where it remains without any 'intentionality' which spreads beyond it, a world of pleasure, or a world of charm and grace, which can co-exist with a religious civilization (and even be spiritualized, as in the cult of the Virgin Mary in medieval Christianity), is foreign to Judaism. . . . The feminine will never take on the aspect of the divine, neither the Virgin nor even Beatrice. The dimension of intimacy is opened by women, not the dimension of loftiness. ('Judaism and the Feminine Element', p. 27.)
15 Ibid.
16 'the feminine face joins this clarity and this shadow. The feminine is the face in which trouble surrounds and already invades clarity.' (TI, p. 262; TeI, p. 240.)
17 TI, p. 256; TeI, p. 235.
18 'It grasps nothing, issues no concept, does not *issue*, has neither the subject–object structure nor the I–Thou structure.' (TeI, p. 238; TI, p. 261.)
19 The equivocation of the erotic relation is 'between speech and the renouncement of speech, between the signifyingness of language and the non-signifyingness of the lustful, which silence yet dissimulates'. (TI, p. 260; TeI, p. 238.)
20 'If to love is to love the love the Beloved bears me, to love is also to love oneself in love and thus to return to oneself.' (TI, p. 266; TeI p. 244.)
21 Fecundity is 'self-identification', but also a distinction within identification. It 'does not "discover", beyond the face, another, more profound I which this face would express; it discovers the child.' (TI, p. 267; TeI, p. 244.)
22 *Revolution in Poetic Language*, translated by Margaret Waller, Columbia University Press, 1984, p. 167.
23 Ibid., p. 26.
24 Ibid., p. 27.
25 AEAE, p. 95; OBBE, p. 76.
26 'Stabat Mater', p. 245, my translation.

· 6 ·

Levinas and Pontalis:
Meeting the Other as in a Dream[1]

STEVEN GANS

Simply stated, the aim of Levinas's phenomenological ethics is no different from the aim of psychotherapeutic practice: both show the way toward the transformation of egoic *need* into interpersonal *desire*; both seek to subvert and transform cultivated violence into living celebration. In this chapter I show that both approaches belong together. But, must we not say of Levinas and Freud what Pontalis, quoting André-Green ('a practised expert on Freud and an attentive reader of Merleau-Ponty') says of Merleau-Ponty and Freud, that they missed the rendezvous?[2] Yet is not this deferred meeting between phenomenology and psychoanalysis eagerly awaited to this day, inasmuch as these separate but convergent discourses both hold the promise of releasing us from the oculo-centric predicament that has characterized the Western metaphysical and messianic traditions from their utopian origins to the present time of technocratic impoverishment? The 'dream' has ended, but we can but dream on. And so I propose to dream up a meeting on the question of meeting between Levinas and Pontalis, who epitomize and bespeak in their deference and subtlety the highest qualities of phenomenological and psychoanalytic praxis.

In the essay, 'Between the Signs,' Pontalis retrieves Merleau-Ponty's gesture toward psychoanalysis in his last writings in the *Visible and Invisible*, saying, 'it was as if, in the end, the paradigm of perception were dreaming and the original perception an oneiric one'.[3] He then concludes that, 'Following this line of thought, one can claim that all dreams are images of the mother, or that the mother is a

. dream'.[4] Resonating to Freud's thesis that dreams are wishes, Pontalis argues that 'Dreaming is above all the attempt to maintain an impossible union with the mother to preserve an undivided whole, *to move in a spacing is above all the attempt to maintain an impossible union with the mother to preserve an undivided whole, to move in a space prior to time.*'[5]

This space is thought within the psychoanalytic tradition as the nucleus of infantile omnipotence and remains the primal core of all subsequent stages of subjectivity. The paradox of the dream, hence of all productions of consciousness, is that it is created as given. Winnicott, for instance, argues that 'The breast is created by the infant over and over again out of the infant's need'.[6] 'Need', 'drive', 'instinct', 'wish' are the words used within psychoanalytic discourse to describe the dynamics of the coming into being of egoic consciousness. This tradition remains within the realm of the imaginary, where wishes form images to appear in dreams and the self always finds itself already in the world. The question of how the given is created as given is the paradigmatic transcendental problematic that also informs European thinking to the present day. It is at this intersection of Freud's Oedipal quest to penetrate the secret of the already thereness of the world that is given as mine, that the phenomenologies of Husserl, Heidegger and Merleau-Ponty converge, and it is this position of thought that Levinas characterizes as totalizing and indicts as the epitomization of violence.

From within this perspective of egology, others seem to have no other status than that of stimulus to my own pleasure, a state of mind illustrated for Pontalis by the solitary dreamer, Rousseau of *The Confessions*. And even Merleau-Ponty, who attempts to articulate a more embodied phenomenology, can say, 'Our relationship with the day before, with things, and especially others, are by principle of a dreamlike nature, the others are present like dreams.'[7] The ego's self-identification and reduction of difference (the not me) to the same (the for me) is the totalization process *par excellence* which Levinas undertakes to critique in *Totality and Infinity*.

Levinas launches his critique by describing the position of egoic interiority as the Gyges syndrome. From within the closed circuit of interiority, Western man *looks* out for his enjoyment. From the invisible centre of his hidden presence, he represents and constitutes a world which he in turn penetrates, manipulates and controls, so that he can accumulate power and might in order to deploy resources to satisfy his needs and defend against loss.

Levinas dares propose a break with the Eleatic Onto-theological tradition by reintroducing the Socratic Good which is beyond Being. His ethical discourse exhorts us to leave archaeological egologies, nostalgia, memory, history, retrieve and deconstruction, so that we may enter the face-to-face encounter with the Other. Only in this way will we achieve the aim of the therapeutic, which is to break with the narcissism of the imaginary in order to live in the promised land of the real and the good.

It is a worthwhile exercise to recapitulate the main stages of Levinas's eschatological itinerary in a way that will reveal his ethics as an indispensable foundation for therapeutic practice, a practice which seeks to overcome neurosis by moving the client from self-involvement to relatedness with the Other.

The negative stage of Levinas's paradigmatic movement toward meeting is the overcoming of deficient desire, which he calls need. Need is a void in the heart of interiority. It is that which initiates the objectification process as defence against loss, limitation and death.

To flesh out the stages of need, the insatiable demand for un-obtainable satisfaction, which is the wellspring of the totalization pro-cess, I turn to Pontalis and his discussion of the fetish, which he takes as the model of perversion. Fetishism is an obscenity because it is literally a turning away from the scene, from situatedness, from living persons. It is instead a turning to the abstract, detached, isolated and fixed cult object. The fetishist seeks to gain power over the source of his own pleasure; he seeks to be the sole activator of his pleasure. As Pontalis states, 'The fetishist is trying to found and maintain at all costs a belief which would authenticate in his eyes the power of the fetish object ensuring his pleasure.'[8] For Freud, the fetish equals the woman's phallus, symbol of absence, lack and loss, the so-called per-ceived absence.

It is his very own need, lack and deficiency that the fetishist attempts to deny by means of objectification, sexualization and embodiment of insatiable interiority. The culmination of fetishism is wealth, the accumulation of might and power, which grants the ever-present availability of immediate and unlimited satisfaction. This is the deficient eschatological vision or, rather, the scatological dream of the contemporary world. At this point of man's ultimate *hubris*, Levinas, following Plato's rejection of Aristophanes' myth of the androgynous, suggests that Socrates' account of the parents of eros reveals the poverty of wealth. Again calling on Pontalis, we see need or deficient desire denying its own essential nature in the myth of bisexuality.

The hermaphrodite regards as intolerable any desire, since any foreign body is seen as a threat, and violation of its own faultless self-contained gratification system. By rejecting sexual differentiation, the hermaphroditic consciousness does not admit of the deprivation, real or imaginary, of what the other sex has. In this way, the hermaphrodite or original circle man/woman of the Aristophanian myth becomes invulnerable, immortal and, phoenixlike, remains the same through all its possible transformations, never wanting anything to be complete in itself. Hermaphroditic plenitude is the culmination of need. The hermaphrodite of old was regarded as a neutered, loveless monster, who had no place in human relatedness.

Genuine desire, as opposed to need, originates from the Other: 'Desire is desire for the absolutely other.'[9] Here Levinas develops Heidegger's notion of the call of Being, but not in terms of an anonymous Being process, rather in terms of the Other, who is beyond any subordination. The Other calls forth desire which exceeds any idea or image we may have of the Other. This is the point at which Levinas parts company with the classical phenomenological methodology and tradition, which he argues is based on the ocular and logo-centric denial of the Other. The desire for the Other is beyond need, and above enjoyment or happiness, although desire presupposes both attaining and a non-attachment to my own enjoyment. To meet the Other face to face means I must leave my egocentricity behind and enter a play space of welcome, discourse and intercourse.

To allow the Other to be means to let someone speak independently, apart from any other aim we have in regard to that person. We cannot place the Other in our own light, and incorporate the Other into our own story, without destroying the possibility of meeting in the genuine sense. Hence, recognizing the Other, as Levinas says, is to give.

It can be said, following Pontalis, that the work of psychoanalysis is to move the client from the position of need (from suffering), to desire (to becoming an agent), able to meet, give to, speak to and love an Other.

Is the Freudian psychoanalytic model adequate to its aim? I argue that Levinas in fact provides a more adequate framework for psychoanalytic praxis. Freud emerges as Oedipal in the way he penetrates (analyses) dreams, which are the displaced maternal body. He attempts to conquer and possess their secrets, in order to become master of the dream machine. His analysis murders the dream by reconstructing it and subjecting it to the law and order of paternal interpretation. Pontalis, in search of a gentler, more feminine (in Levinas's sense) way to approach dreams and analytic practice follows Winnicott to the place of dreams, to transitional space where dreams have the potential to open a space between analyst and client. The way the client relates dreams to the therapist, how the client relates to or sees the Other – for example, as a distant witness, close accomplice, reliable container, persecutor, rubbish dump, ideal . . . all the ways that prevent open meeting with the Other, perpetuating a cover story of false self-esteem.

For the client to awaken out of this dream, or waking dream, he/she must recognize the Other and be recognized. In other words, the client must enter the ethical relationship. Levinas shows the way toward the ethical in his discourse on dwelling, language and love.

Dwelling is a stage beyond the solipsism of enjoyment, of 'living from' the things within the world, of property, possession and totalization. Dwelling is prior to the degeneration of desire into need, since it provides the window which gives the occasion for the objectifying look which seeks to grasp, dominate, possess and transform the world into a storehouse of products for use.

I find myself, at first, at home in the intimacy of the familiar, opened through the welcome of the Other. The welcoming one *par excellence*, Levinas states, is the feminine being. The woman inhabits the dwelling and offers hospitality with characteristic gentleness, warmth and intimacy. Feminine presence is the *sine qua non* of dwelling and being with someone. She keeps silent and stills the need for self-assertion. As a refuge without expectations, the feminine accepts, welcomes and enables meeting between persons. This meeting can never occur in an anonymous nowhere between neutered anybodies, such as the interchangeable beings of commercial interchange. A place must open in the world that is close to our heart, that gives a *raison d'être* and structure to our relation with the world. It is, of course, essential not to equate feminine presence with empirical females who may or may not embody the feminine welcome, any more than we ought to exclude males from instituting dwelling. Habitation is a radical break with fetishism, hermaphroditism and narcissism. It is the condition of meeting, speaking and loving. Either we are at home with someone in the between of human relatedness, or we are nowhere, passing messages as anonymous and disembodied observers, tourists or scorekeepers.

I argue that dwelling is the healing resource in the analytic-therapeutic relationship. If the analyst dwells, a bridge is provided for an Other to realize his or her potential for relatedness with the Other. Dwelling is the necessary and sufficient context for analytic-therapeutic or ethical relatedness. Dwelling is the occasion for desire to come to expression, as each addresses the other in what Levinas calls the primordial face-to-face of language.

I am called by the face of the Other to awaken as if from a dream. I must drop my cover story, my defences, my masks; I must cease living 'as if' by going through the motions, turned away from my fellow man in despair, and instead respond to the address of the face which touches my heart and asks me to tell the truth, or at least not to do violence by diminishing the Other to a mere cipher, an interchangeable instance of a neutered anybody. What you mean to me in terms of who you are enables me to say who I am, to move from the explicit and predetermined orders of social conventions to the implicit order of discourse where I can respond to the questioning gaze of the Other. I find myself speaking with you of what is between us, of the world of which and in which I speak.

Every attempt to reduce the Other to a symmetrical *alter ego* initiates violence and war and kills desire and relatedness. I lose respect for the Other by absolving myself of responsibility to be open to their Otherness in the ultimate sense – a sense beyond intelligibility, a sense that is infinite and inexhaustible, a sense that cannot be reduced to commerce, exchange, *quid pro quo* manipulation or control. The Good, as Socrates says in the *Phaedo*, is the only thing worthy of our consideration and each and every Other is the embodiment of the potential good to be realized between us through love and freedom.

Love is the culmination of Levinas's discourse with the Other, as well as the culmination of the psychoanalytic process. Levinas treats us to a masterful 'phenomenological' account of erotic unfolding, the denouement of his ethics for which the analytic encounter is a propaedeutic.

Words like 'frailty', 'tenderness', 'fragility' and 'vulnerability' permeate the text which leads us on the way toward the subterranean depth that resonates to the theme of feminity. Levinas advances feminity as counterpoint to male egoic conceptual languages. We are led beyond the male-oriented scientific and metaphysical *look* through touch. For Levinas, 'The caress transcends the sensible.'[10] The caress does not originate from need; it is not like scratching an itch to relieve an intolerably sensitive and charged hunger for relief or satisfaction. The caress searches, anticipates and opens the gates of embrace and passion. The caress reaches beyond the face, through the between of being-with toward a future in the present, toward a mystery beyond limit, toward an infinite richness as if entering another reality, an evanescent vertiginous depth without light. The caress generates and amplifies waves of tenderness which culminate in voluptuous abandonment of the I and the Other, breaking with concentricity and eccentricity – that is, with positionality in general. The caress engenders desire as such as the infinite renewal in each moment of the expression of love.

In loving, there is no attainment, no possession of the hidden secret at the depth or height of expression and disclosure, rather the reverse; the enfolded flesh resonates and celebrates the multi-dimensional subtleties of its inscrutability, unfathomability and infinite variegation. The voluptuous breaks with the orders of discourse; yet in its silent saying beyond the meaningful gives access to the source of meaning itself, namely, to the lightning birth of ecstasy that is both the precondition of and the fruit of entry into the world.

The relationship between lovers cannot be socialized or amalgamated into a generalized social space. Lovers inhabit a dual intimacy and solitude which is refractory to onlookers. It is through the bond of coupling, which resists any attempt at generalization, unification or subsumption, that regeneration and renewal occur. A child is born beyond any intelligibility, purpose or use – the child is a dream come true, born of the profundity, depth and delight of mutuality.

Levinas in the final analysis proposes to confront the violence of the masculine machine with the gentleness of feminine tenderness in order to bring about a reversal at a micro- and macro-social level of war – that is, the depersonalization of relatedness, and to move toward an ethics of love, toward the celebration of our interrelatedness. To generate this movement he engages in a discourse that is at once phenomenological and therapeutic, yet beyond both – he points toward a discourse beyond discourse – toward a meeting of discourses, an intercourse which is pregnant with what must forever remain unsaid, even as it expresses the infinite richness of what we each can and do mean to one another.

Notes

1   This chapter is based primarily on a reading of two texts: Emmanuel
    Levinas, *Totality and Infinity*; and J. B. Pontalis, *Entre le rêve et la
    douleur*, Paris, Editions Gallimard, 1977; *Frontiers in Psychoanalysis:
    Between the Dream and Psychic Pain*, translated by Catherine and Philip
    Cullen, London, The Hogarth Press, 1981.
2   *Frontiers in Psychoanalysis*, p. 67.
3   *Frontiers in Psychoanalysis*, p. 65.
4   *Frontiers in Psychoanalysis*, p. 66.
5   *Frontiers in Psychoanalysis*, p. 29.
6   *Frontiers in Psychoanalysis*, p. 142.
7   *Themes from the Lectures at the Collège de France*, translated by J. O'Neill,
    Evanston, Ill., Northwestern University Press, p. 15.
8   *Frontiers in Psychoanalysis*, p. 74.
9   TI, p. 34; TeI, p. 4.
10 TI, p. 257; TeI, p. 235.

· 7 ·

Sartre and Levinas

CHRISTINA HOWELLS

What I hope to show in this chapter is that the conceptions of the Other held by Sartre and Levinas are less antagonistic than they might at first appear, and more particularly that Sartre's own view of the role and importance of the Other has an affirmative 'Levinasian' side almost ignored in *L'Être et le néant*, and for which new evidence is only now appearing. My argument will have three main thrusts: firstly, an attempt to show that Levinas's description of relations with the Other is Sartrean in its non-evaluative aspect – in other words, that Levinas has formulated his description of the role of the Other in, for the most part implicit but none the less specific, response to Sartre's analysis, and that it is a response which necessarily takes over much of that analysis. Secondly – and in consequence – that it is in their *evaluations* rather than their *descriptions* of relations with the Other that Sartre and Levinas come into conflict, and that this is in fact a conflict which is based on a curious paradox. And thirdly, that Sartre's 600-page notes for an ethics, written in the late 1940s and published in April 1983 as *Cahiers pour une morale*, show a more creative, affirmative aspect to his view of the role of the Other, and moreover reply explicitly – and positively – to a couple of specific criticisms made of him by Levinas. Finally, I hope to suggest reasons why, despite the *rapprochement*, Sartre can never entirely embrace the optimism of Levinasian ethics.

In the first place, what are the grounds for agreement between Sartre and Levinas over my relations with the Other? Let us start, perhaps, with *me* rather than the Other: both Sartre and Levinas agree that there is no possibility of self-coincidence, of self-identity. 'I am what I am not and am not what I am' (EN, p. 100);[1] 'The self . . . is an other'

(TeI, p. 6). Self-identity would be the death of the subject, *ennui* (TeI, p. 284; AEAE, pp. 9–10): being human is precisely not being a *being* (EI, p. 107). This much at least is as true of the Other as it is of me (EN, p. 102).

And the impossibility of self-identity is certainly one of the reasons why both Sartre and Levinas refuse to envisage relations with the Other in terms of knowledge (TA, p. 8, p. 13). It is not so much that the Other is unknowable, as if he had some content which was incommunicable (TA, p. 21); it is rather that the terminology of knowledge is inappropriate to describe relations between two transcendent, nonidentical free consciousnesses. I cannot ever know the Other 'as he is' for he precisely *is* not (EN, p. 290). Similarly, both Sartre and Levinas criticize Heidegger's conception of *Mitsein*: it is true, of course, that for Sartre *Mitsein* is singularly inappropriate in its optimistic overtones, but his objection is not simply to the positive connotations of the term. In Sartre's view, *Mitsein* suggests a kind of 'ontological solidarity' (EN, p. 302), which he sees as philosophically impossible in so far as it implies that the Other has some kind of 'ontic reality' which would make of him an object and thereby impede precisely that very reciprocity which was being asserted. As a *pour-soi* the Other is fundamentally unknowable; Heidegger may be attempting to escape the conception of objective knowledge, but, Levinas and Sartre both argue, his portrait of *Mitsein* still ultimately involves a notion of ontological comprehension (TeI, p. 39), and moreover envisages intersubjectivity in terms of an unacceptable notion of coexistence (TeI, p. 39).

Relations with the Other cannot then be defined in terms of knowledge or of *Mitsein* for either Sartre or Levinas. Moreover, the Other for both Sartre and Levinas puts my freedom and my possession of the world into question (EN, p. 608; TI, pp. 13, 48). I am born into a world already structured, patterned and possessed by others; my interpretation of it must necessarily take into account the interpretation of others: my freedom to make the world is limited, its application cannot be self-sufficient and arbitrary. In Sartre's terms, 'the Other steals the world from me' (EN, p. 313); he implies the total metamorphosis of the world (EN, p. 328); like me, he transcends the world, but with a transcendence which is precisely not mine (EN, p. 329). 'He has already given the world significance' (*Cahiers*, p. 630). As Levinas puts it, the Other represents 'une notion de sens antérieur à ma Sinngebung' (TeI, p. 22), a notion of meaning anterior to the meaning

I bestow on things. Through the Other my anarchy is limited: 'the world becomes objective' (TeI, p. 72). It must be clear that such a conception has necessarily both a negative and a positive aspect: the Other limits my freedom but at the same time allows me to live in a world which is not purely subjective. Both Sartre and Levinas recognize the positive aspect which such a limitation necessarily implies. Both writers, thereby, recognize the ambiguity of my relations to the liberty of the Other. In love, Levinas explains, I desire the freedom of the Other, not controlled, objectified and reified but rather *indomptée* (TeI, p. 243) – in its very freedom. Indeed, for Levinas, it is not so much the *pour-soi* as the *Other* who is the very source of freedom. And this is less opposed to Sartre's view than popular simplifications might suggest: for Sartre, since it is the freedom of the Other that invests me with objectivity, that founds my being, I want to take hold of that freedom without removing its essential characteristic of freedom (EN, p. 430). The freedom of the Other may alienate me, but it is none the less his freedom which constitutes my being (EN, p. 433):

I cannot experience my alienation without at the same time recognizing the Other as transcendence. And this recognition would have no meaning were it not *free* recognition of the freedom of the Other. . . . Thus I cannot recognize the Other as freedom except in the free project of so doing, and the free project of recognition of the Other is indistinguishable from the free assuming of my being-for-others. (EN, p. 609)

It is this same ambiguity, of course, which means that my work and products only become objective in so far as they are apprehended by the Other and are at once alienated and removed from me and given independent status.

In undertaking what I intended I have brought about so many things that I did not intend . . . my works grow out of the discarded remnants of my work. . . . So the product of my work is not my inalienable possession and may be usurped by the Other. My works have a destiny which is independent of me.' (TeI, pp. 150–1)

This is Levinas: it could as well be Sartre at any time from *Qu'est-ce que la littérature?* to *L'Idiot de la famille*.

These then are some aspects of what Levinas and the early Sartre have in common. Where they differ fundamentally is, of course, in their evaluations of what they describe. The non-coincidence of self with self in time is seen by both as inadequation, paradox, distance, 'unquenchable aspiration' (TA, p. 10), 'useless passion' (EN, p. 708), and this non-coincidence is described by Levinas as 'good', 'precious' and 'better' than self-coincidence. Now logically Sartre is bound to agree, since self-coincidence would entail the death of consciousness, but he often prefers to focus on the eternally unsatisfied yearning of desire rather than on the freedom it represents. It is for similar reasons that Levinas criticizes the existentialists for stressing human solitude as despair rather than dignity (TA, p. 35); and he is right as far as Sartre's early philosophy is concerned, though we know that elsewhere Sartre has maintained, with precisely that Byronic romantic psychology Levinas is regretting, that 'human life begins on the other side of despair' (*Les Mouches*).

Levinas's main quarrel with Sartre is of course over the question of human conflict: he contests in the first place the negative overtones of the proposition that man is *condemned* to be free (TI, p. 57), and goes on to argue that the Other does not impede my freedom but rather ratifies it (TeI, p. 60). On its own the self is, Levinas agrees with Pascal, hateful (TeI, p. 61) – egoistic, arbitrary, unjustified – it is only in relations with the Other that it has the opportunity of becoming moral. The Other is not then primarily a threat or a rival: such a pessimistic picture depends on an overvaluing of arbitrary, anarchic liberty and a misunderstanding of the creative potential of responsibility (TeI, p. 171). Levinas reinvests with value precisely those elements of the existential world-view which seem to Sartre most negative. Even the inability to communicate fully with others is transformed into an affirmation of the precious specificity and inalienable subjectivity of each individual (TA, p. 89). As Levinas recognizes, the 'good' is presented in his ethics as dependent on and emerging from what initially appears most negative, 'une apparente diminution' (TeI, p. 76). We might notice here that Levinas none the less denies that he is engaged in a form of negative theology (TA, p. 91). It would seem that few 'negative theologians' are prepared to recognize themselves as such. I have argued elsewhere that despite their strenuous denials both Sartre and Derrida engage in precisely this transformative activity which consists in revaluing failure as success, absence as presence, loss as gain.[2] What is important in this context is that Sartre's own powerful pattern of *qui perd gagne*, loser wins, which perpetually transforms the negative into the positive (the nothingness of consciousness into the key to freedom; the poet's inability to communicate conceptually into a higher form of communication, and so on), does not seem to be operative, at least in *L'Être et le néant*, with respect to relations to the Other. There is no attempt in this sphere to turn failure into success.

Nonetheless, Sartre cannot entirely escape the implications of his own thinking elsewhere; and Levinas is clearly engaged in a process of re-evaluation which Sartre might be expected to approve. In particular, Levinas's stress on the way in which subjectivity escapes totalization and system is a theme dear to Sartre's own heart. Human transcendence shatters totality (TeI, p. xiii). Levinas will claim against Kierkegaard that it is the Other and not I who is inassimilable to the System (TeI, p. 10), but his conception is none the less fundamentally Kierkegaardian in so far as it is subjectivity which escapes the totality of history (TeI, p. 23), interiority which cannot be reduced to a concept, consciousness which introduces discontinuity into the whole (TeI, p. 28). And all this is worked over explicitly by Sartre in his essay on Kierkegaard and Hegel[1] where he permits the paradox of 'loser wins' to have its full corrosive and creative force. We might then say that despite (or in this case perhaps even because of) its opposition to Hegel and to totalization, *L'Être et le néant* is still excessively Hegelian in terms of its conception of relations with the Other primarily as conflict; and that it is when Sartre allows the full implications of his own specifically paradoxical and detotalizing thinking to take effect that he both comes closest to Levinas at the same time as being most true to his own fundamental intuitions.

It is in the *Cahiers pour une morale*, written around 1947–8, and published in 1983, that we can see the clearest evidence for Sartre's affirmative quasi-'Levinasian' stance. In the first place we might note that Sartre refers explicitly to Levinas on two occasions in the *Cahiers*. On the first he quotes a passage on *nourritures* from *Le Temps et l'autre* and supports Levinas in his opposition to Heidegger's view of the primacy of the world as utility or as a structure of tools (*Cahiers*, p. 397). On the second occasion he cites Levinas's criticism of his own (Sartre's) description of the future, and concedes that there is in fact a plurality of structures in the future, including those of alienation and the unknown that Levinas wishes to stress (*Cahiers* p. 431).

But what is more interesting is the large-scale reappraisal of the nature of human relations since *L'Être et le néant*. Sartre writes at length about love, joy, generosity and sacrifice in terms that bear little resemblance to his earlier analyses. What seems to have happened is that the notion of *conversion* which was briefly referred to in *L'Être et le néant* has come to take a much larger place in Sartre's conception of human reality. In *L'Être et le néant* he alludes to this conversion on only two occasions, and significantly enough both times in footnotes. The first is in connection with *mauvaise foi* when he concedes that we are not doomed to remain forever in bad faith and can achieve authenticity, by 'une reprise de l'être pourri par lui-même' (EN, p. 111), a recovery of the corrupted being by itself. The second comes at the end of his analysis of the failure inherent in all types of relations with the Other, from hatred to love: 'These considerations do not exclude the possibility of an ethics of deliverance and salvation. But this must be reached after a radical conversion which we cannot speak of here' (EN, p. 484).

Sartre is certainly referring to the project for an ethics which the *Cahiers* represent. In the *Cahiers*, conversion has become a constant theme and reference point. It seems to have become a genuine human possibility rather than a mere afterthought. This means, of course, that Sartre is bound to take an explicit distance from many of the analyses of *L'Être et le néant*. Human conflict is seen in the *Cahiers* not as an ontological necessity but rather as an adjunct of alienation. Of man's sado-masochistic relations with others, seen earlier as the essence of human relations, he now writes:

Sadism and Masochism are the revelation of the Other. They have sense – like the conflict of consciousness – only *before* conversion. Once we assume the fact that we are both free and an object for others (for example the authentic Jew) there is no longer any ontological reason to remain in the domain of conflict. (*Cahiers*, p. 26)

Overall, Sartre's analyses of relations with the Other are immeasurably more positive in the *Cahiers*. The Other is described as he who *recognizes* me (*Cahiers*, p. 76). He is an unpredictable freedom (*Cahiers*, p. 128) through whom I make myself: 'I create myself by giving myself to the Other', 'So I must lose myself to find myself' (*Cahiers*, p. 136). True freedom is a gift, not a demand; it is a recognition of the freedom of the Other (*Cahiers*, p. 146). It is evident that *qui perd gagne* has penetrated and transformed Sartre's analysis of human relations. An extreme example of this is given in one of his notes for a plan: 'The for-itself and the Other: self-giving [le Don]. In sacrifice I am, and I prefer the Other. I prefer what I do not prefer. But I *am* my gift to the Other – Joy' (*Cahiers*, p. 156). Sartre acknowledges that *L'Être et le néant* was criticized for neglecting the affirmative aspect of life, and argues that it was not so much denied as envisaged as dependent on the negating power of consciousness (*Cahiers*, pp. 155–6). The *Cahiers* will redress the balance. It is probably in his analysis of love that Sartre's evolution is clearest. Without denying the sado-masochistic element described in *L'Être et le néant*, Sartre recognizes the incompleteness of his original analysis: 'There is no love without deep recognition and reciprocal understanding of freedom: this is the dimension lacking in *Being and Nothingness*' (*Cahiers*, p. 430). He will even describe the classless society in terms of mutual love:

The Ego must lose itself: that is the nature of self-giving. Reconciliation with Destiny is generosity. In a classless society it may also be love – that is to say the trusting project that other freedoms – valorized and willed as such – will take up and transform my works and thereby my Ego which loses itself in the absolute dimension of freedom. (*Cahiers*, p. 434)

The text is a little obscure; what is clear is that the loss of self entailed in the love and trust of others is valorized, and indeed seen as the key to a potentially more authentic existence. Sartre constructs a schematic hierarchy of values with liberty and generosity at the top. He imagines a post-conversion society in which alienation would be rejected and there would be mutual and reciprocal recognition of freedom (*Cahiers*, pp. 486–7). It is in this society that what he calls *authentic* love would be possible: a love which would involve recognizing the aims of the Other, celebrating his world-view without attempting to appropriate it, and protecting him with my freedom.

It is perhaps easy to understand why Sartre never allowed the *Cahiers* to be published in his lifetime. They put forward an optimistic picture of the possibility of ethics which is potentially vulnerable to accusations of utopianism. However, this would be to misunderstand the nature of and conditions for conversion as Sartre describes them in the *Cahiers*. On the one hand, conversion is still identified with a kind of purifying reflection – 'la réflexion non complice' – and therefore still presupposes the analyses of inauthenticity given in *L'Être et le néant*; indeed, it is yet another example of the *qui perd gagne* pattern for it is born out of failure: the failure of *réflexion complice* (*Cahiers*, p. 489), and the failure of self-coincidence (*Cahiers*, p. 488): 'Theme of conversion: the impossibility of self-recuperation' (Cahiers p. 486). 'Conversion may be born from the perpetual failure of all attempts by the For-itself to achieve *being*' (*Cahiers*, p. 488). On the other hand, conversion is frequently envisaged as a social rather than a purely individual phenomenon: it involves not merely purifying reflection but also a rejection of alienation: 'The meaning of conversion: a rejection of alienation' (*Cahiers*, p. 486). It is virtually possible for all oppressed peoples' (*Cahiers*, p. 488). This means that ethics which are necessarily dependent on conversion can no longer be envisaged as an individual enterprise: 'The suppression of alienation must be universal. Impossibility of being moral alone' (*Cahiers*, p. 487). 'One cannot carry out conversion *alone*. In other words, morality is possible only if everyone is moral' (Cahiers p. 16). Morality is defined as preparing the (Kantian) kingdom of ends through finite, creative, revolutionary politics (*Cahiers*, p. 487). Revolution necessarily transgresses the rules of (established) morality, but it is in this that its moral function lies: 'It is not possible for the revolutionary not to violate the rules of morality' (*Cahiers*, p. 110). Morality is a theory of action, it is always concrete and situated. It is fundamentally historical. And conjointly, conflict too has been replaced firmly in the historical domain: it is *not* part of human ontology.

The *Cahiers*, then, mark two kinds of break with *L'Être et le néant*: they imply an ontology which comes far closer to Levinas than the Hegelian emphasis on conflict prevalent in *L'Être et le néant*; but they also promote a politics of revolution which Levinas does not espouse. Levinas, one might say, describes as already implicit what for Sartre is only possible in a post-conversion society. Indeed, Levinas himself recognizes that he is writing an ethics of and for peace: 'The state of war suspends morality' (TeI, Preface, p. ix). It is perhaps in their assessments of the *present* possibility of such peace or conversion that Sartre and Levinas ultimately part company.

Abbreviations

Cahiers Jean-Paul Sartre, *Cahiers pour une morale*, Paris, Gallimard, 1983.
ED Jacques Derrida, *L'Ecriture et la différence*, Paris, Seuil, 1967.
EN Jean-Paul Sartre, *L'Être et le néant*, Paris, Gallimard, 1943.

Notes

1 All translations are my own; page references are to the French editions.

2 See 'Sartre and Negative Theology', *Modern Language Review*, July 1981; and 'Sartre and Derrida: *qui perd gagne*', *Journal of the British Society for Phenomenology*, 1982.

3 'L'Universel singulier', *Situations*, ix, 1972, 52–90.

· 8 ·

'Failure of Communication' as a Surplus: Dialogue and Lack of Dialogue between Buber and Levinas

ROBERT BERNASCONI

'Strife among thinkers is the "lover's quarrel" concerning the matter itself'[1]

Introduction

The proximity between Martin Buber and Emmanuel Levinas which is so striking to the external observer was not always so apparent to Buber and Levinas themselves. The present essay surveys Levinas's numerous studies of Buber, and in particular compares an essay predating *Totality and Infinity* with another post-dating *Otherwise than Being or Beyond Essence* in order to explore both the continuity and change not simply in Levinas's understanding of what Buber wrote, but also in the way in which Levinas approached Buber. The relation between Buber and Levinas has already given rise to a few studies,[2] but these commentaries predate Levinas's most recent discussions of Buber and so are unable to take account of essays which, as I shall try to show, introduce a new stage in Levinas's relation with Buber. Levinas was initially preoccupied with differentiating or separating his own position from that of Buber. But having established the points of difference, he found himself then able to re-read Buber in another way. Although Levinas continued to focus on many of the same issues in his treatment of Buber, his approach – his way of relating – appeared to undergo a transformation. It is my contention that

Levinas's recent essays on Buber are important not only for an understanding of the relation of these two thinkers, but also because they serve as a valuable introduction to the question of what might provisionally be called 'a Levinasian hermeneutics'.

The Question of Relation in Buber

Heidegger wrote that 'we are not in a position – or if we are, then only rarely and just barely – to experience purely in its own terms a relation that obtains between two things, two beings. We immediately conceive the relation in terms of the things which in the given instance are related'.[3] It could be said that Buber in *I and Thou* takes up the task of thinking the relation *qua* relation. One of the characteristics of the I–Thou relation is that it cannot be reduced to the terms related, the relata. Indeed, whenever the terms related are pre-eminent, the I–It already dominates.[4]

The crucial sentence for this interpretation of Buber runs, 'In the beginning is the relation' (DP, p. 22; IT, p. 69). The sentence can be understood to express both the priority of the I–Thou over the I–It and the priority within the I–Thou of the relation over the relata. Buber offered two models or parallels for thinking the I–thou as a 'genuine original unity' in this sense (DP, p. 22; IT, p. 70). The first is that of primitive peoples amongst whom, Buber suggested, the basic word I–Thou is spoken in a natural unformed or preformed (*vorgestaltlich*) manner prior to any self-recognition of an I (DP, p. 26; IT, p. 73). By contrast, the I–It presupposes a self-recognition such as takes place in the detachment (*Ablösung*) of the I. Buber conceded that the primitive man affords only brief glimpses into the temporal sequence of the basic words I–Thou and I–It and is anyway only a metaphor for what he calls 'primal man'. He suggested that 'more complete information' is given in the child (DP, p. 28; IT, p. 76). Indeed, Buber went back beyond the child to the pure natural association of prenatal life, where he found evidence of the originality not so much of the relation as such as of the 'longing for relation'. But it would seem that prenatal life is also appealed to only as a metaphor for 'the womb of the great mother – the undifferentiated preformed primal world' (DP, pp. 28–9; IT, p. 76). In any case, 'In the beginning is the relation' does not refer to the I–Thou – which is how the sentence has often been understood – but to this longing for relation. 'In the beginning is the relation – as the category of being, as readiness, as a form that reaches out to be filled, as a model of the soul; the *a priori* of relation; *the innate Thou*' (DP, p. 31; IT, p. 78).

The question of the genetic order of the I–Thou and I–It is a complex one, as Buber himself indicated when he wrote that 'the genesis of the thing is a late product that develops out of the split of the primal encounters, out of the separation of the associated partners – as does the genesis of the I' (DP, p. 31; IT, p. 78). The 'primal encounters' (*Urelebnisse*) are not to be understood as the I–Thou and the I–It, but rather as 'the vital primal words I–acting–Thou and Thou–acting–I' (DP, p. 25; IT, p. 73). The I–Thou is a return to what is primal, rather than the primal itself. In the beginning is not so much the *relation* itself as the *a priori* of relation. There follows from this beginning the splitting of the 'primal encounters', giving rise both to the thing and to the I. But the I *is* only in the I–It and the I–Thou and is not the same I in both. The issue could only be pursued in a lengthy commentary on Buber's text, but these details are surely sufficient to disturb the standard picture of Buber. Furthermore, if the 'innate Thou' appears to serve as a principle which lends priority to the I–Thou, it should be recalled that Buber also acknowledged a rival principle which accounts for 'a progressive increase of the It-world' (DP, p. 39; IT, p. 87). He expressed it in the sentence, 'every Thou must become an It' (DP, p. 20; IT, p. 68). The formulation is carefully phrased to suggest that the I–Thou retains a residue of priority and that the I–It is only supplementary in its effect. But the I–Thou and the I–It both arise from the 'relation' which is in the beginning and which is itself not the I–Thou.

I have focused on the interpretation of Buber's phrase 'in the beginning is the relation' because it assumed so much importance in Levinas's reading of Buber. It is possible to find in Levinas what might at first appear to be a parallel formulation. He wrote in *Totality and Infinity* that 'the priority of the orientation over the terms that are placed in it (and which cannot arise without this orientation) summarises the present work' (TeI, p. 190; TI, p. 215). Similarly, Levinas's frequent references to the 'relation without relation' might seem to be doing the same work of freeing the relation from being thought in terms of the relata. But the crucial word here is 'orientation'. My relation with the Other is a relation of transcendence such that the dimension of height is always in favour of the Other by virtue of my responsibility for him or her. Levinas would be cautious about assigning priority to the relation as such, because it might suggest something like a dissolution of the terms in the relation. On his account the Other is absolute within the relation, which is to say absolved from it. Similarly, my responsibility for the Other *separates* me from the relation. Indeed, it was with reference to this notion of separation that Levinas introduced the phrase 'relation without relation' (TeI, p. 52; TI, p. 60 and TeI, p. 271; TI, p. 295). It will be found that these notions of *separation* and *orientation* govern Levinas's relation to Buber.

Levinas's Initial Response to Buber

Writing in 1964, Derrida in the essay 'Violence and Metaphysics' touched on the question of Levinas's relation to Buber. In the course of a discussion of alterity he observed how having opposed the magisterial height of the *Vous* to the intimate reciprocity of the I–Thou, Levinas appeared to move in the 1963 essay 'The Trace of the Other' to a philosophy of the *ille* or of the third person. Then, in a footnote, having summarized in three points Levinas's repsonse to Buber's account of the I–thou relation, Derrida proceeded to question whether Buber would recognize himself in Levinas's interpretation. I take up this latter question of a Buberian response to Levinas in the next section, but here I shall concentrate on Levinas's response to Buber as he formulated it between 1946 and 1961, using Derrida's summary as a starting-point.

The basis for Derrida's summary was Levinas's brief remarks on the I–Thou relation which punctuate *Totality and Infinity* (1961) and the even briefer comments to be found in the earlier works *Time and the Other* (1948) and *Existence and Existents* (1947). Derrida observed that Levinas reproached the I–Thou relationship '(1) for being reciprocal and symmetrical, thus committing violence against height, and especially against separateness, and secretiveness; (2) for being formal, capable of "uniting man to things, as much as Man to man"; (3) for preferring preference, the "private relationship", the "clandestine nature" of the couple which is "self-sufficient and forgetful of the universe" '. And by way of explanation, particularly of this last point, Derrida offered this comment: 'For there is also in Levinas's thought, despite his protests against neutrality, a summoning of the third party, the universal witness, the face of the world which keeps us from the "disdainful spiritualism" of the I–Thou' (ED, p. 156,n1; WD,

p. 314,n37). Derrida thereby touched on the place of *le tiers*, the third, in Levinas's discussion of the face to face and the fact that Levinas characterized as 'complacent' and 'a dual egoism' the relationship between lovers which excludes the third party (TeI, pp. 242–4; TI, pp. 265–6). That the third – and thus the whole of humanity – looks at me in the eyes of the Other is what secures in Levinas's thinking the passage from the Other to the Others, the passage from ethics to justice, from inequality in favour of the Other to equality (TeI, p. 188; TI, p. 213). Levinas specified that this original inequality of asymmetry in favour of the Other is not visible to the third (TeI, p. 229; TI, p. 251) as a kind of external observer. And yet it is this notion of *le tiers*, and also that of *la troisième personne*, which contributed to the development in Levinas of a conception of illeity as 'a way of concerning me without entering into conjunction with me; (AEAE, p. 15; OBBE, p. 12), an 'infinity and divine transcendence, other than the alterity of the Other' (APB, p. 132) – God as trace, not just of the other, but of the others (DEHH, p. 202; TO, p. 46). Derrida was well advised not to distinguish too quickly two (or more) concepts of the *third* in an effort to resolve the ambiguity occasioned by this extraordinary collection of themes around this single word, but it is a topic which extends well beyond the present essay and I shall touch on it later only in so far as it concerns the relation between Buber and Levinas.

Already in *Time and the Other*, his first extended discussion of the relation to the Other, Levinas was at pains to distance his account from Buber's. On the very last page Levinas explicitly distinguished his own use of the phrase 'I–Thou' (*moi–toi*) from that of Buber on the grounds that Buber underestimated 'the ineluctable character of isolated subjectivity' (TA, p. 89). Much of what Levinas said to distinguish his account from the philosophies of communion that may be found in Plato or the Heideggerian *Miteinandersein* clearly does not apply to the relation Buber describes in *I and Thou*. Buber's I–Thou relation is not readily characterized as a 'we' established through participation in a third term. But it is the distance which arises precisely in respect of the Other's proximity, the duality within proximity, which served as Levinas's focus and differentiated the relation he sought to describe from that which preoccupied Buber. Buber is already characterized as a thinker of reciprocity, according to the terms of the first of Derrida's three points. Both in *Time and the Other* and in *Existence and Existents* (where Buber is not mentioned by name) Levinas offered as his own example of the relation with the other the case of so-called 'failure of communication' in love where the absence of the other is something positive – the other's presence as other – and not a deficiency (TA, p. 89 and DEE, p. 163; EE, p. 95). Whether the other is stronger or weaker, the other for Levinas is what I am not: 'intersubjective space is initially asymmetrical'. The references to the poor, the widow, the orphan and the stranger which dominate *Totality and Infinity* are already to be found here – alongside references to the enemy and the powerful one (DEE, p. 163; EE, p. 95).

Although Levinas's treatment of Buber in *Totality and Infinity* (1961) is dispersed throughout the book, there is no difficulty in ascertaining the basis for Derrida's summary. Levinas remained convinced that Buber understood the Thou primarily as partner and friend and thus gave primacy to a relationship of reciprocity, in contrast with his own emphasis on the irreversibility of the relation (TeI, p. 40; TI, p. 68). Alongside it stood a second claim that Buber formalized the I–Thou so that it covered not only the relation between human beings, but also man's relation to things. How well these two claims go together – the claim that Buber understood the I–Thou on the model of friendship and yet at the same time presented it as a 'formalism which does not determine any concrete structure' – is an open question. But perhaps the difficulty seems less acute when one observes that Levinas in making this second point was not saying, as he would later, that a formalism cannot account for an ethics.[5] Rather, the point was that Buber was in no position to account for economy, the search for happiness, the representation of things 'except as an aberration, a fall, or a sickness' (TeI, p. 40; TI, pp. 68–9). These, of course, were precisely the topics with which the second section of *Totality and Infinity* was concerned. The question therefore was not whether Buber lacked a concrete model, so much as whether his distinction between the I–Thou and the I–It was a rich enough tool. The point was therefore not unlike Rosenzweig's complaint on reading the galleys of *I and Thou* that Buber had had to press all authentic life, including the 'authentic It', into the I–Thou.[6]

Finally, Levinas charged the 'I–Thou' relation with being self-sufficient and forgetful of the universe. The passage appeared early in the section on 'The Other and the Others' which focused on the third party. Buber was not mentioned by name at this specific point, but the reference seems unmistakable. 'Language as the presence of the face does not invite complicity with the preferred being, the self-sufficient

"I–Thou" forgetful of the universe; in its frankness it refuses the clandestinity of love, where it loses its frankness and meaning and turns into laughter or cooing' (TeI, pp. 187–8; TI, p. 213).

It might seem that the same point had already been made by Levinas earlier in the book in his statement that the Other as interlocutor was properly speaking not a thou (*tu*), but a you (*vous*) who challenges my freedom (TeI, p. 75; TI, p. 101). And yet Levinas's use of the *vous* for the relation with the Other as height did not mean that he thereby reserved the *tu* or even the *je–tu* to refer to Buber. To attribute such a terminological decision to Levinas would give rise to a dilemma. In the passage at issue where the I–Thou was referred to as self-sufficient, it appeared to be identified with the clandestinity of love. And yet Levinas wrote in the section on 'The Phenomenology of Eros' that 'love . . . grasps nothing, issues in no concept, does not *issue*, has neither the subject–object structure nor the me–thou (*moi–toi*) structure' (TeI, p. 238; TI, p. 261). If Levinas meant here by 'me–thou' the I–Thou relation of Buber, then the point would be that love could not be given a place within either of the alternatives which for Buber were exhaustive. And Levinas went on to say that 'Love does not simply lead, by a more detoured or more direct way, toward the Thou. It is bent on another direction than that wherein one encounters the Thou' (TeI, p. 242; TI, p. 264) where the use of the word 'encounters' (*rencontre*) would again seem to suggest that Buber was still meant. But the I–Thou of Buber could not be meant both in the section 'The Other and the Others' and the section on eros. The confusion arises because Levinas's language was not that of an etablished terminology but of a thinking which was undergoing transformation, a problem no doubt enhanced by the fact that the book was written over a period of years. Another example of this ambiguity is given in the very same paragraph in which Levinas referred to the I–Thou as 'self-sufficient'. He also said there that 'The *Thou* is posited in front of a *we*'. In context this 'thou' who 'commands me as a Master' must be identified with what was called earlier in the book the *vous* of height, but it could not also be the Thou of the self-sufficient I–Thou. In sum, it is simply not clear that Levinas did charge Buber's I–Thou relation with being self-sufficient. Even though Levinas wrote that 'the I–Thou in which Buber sees the category of interhuman relationship is the relation not with the interlocutor but with feminine alterity' (TeI, p. 129; TI, p. 155) the charge of self-sufficiency could have been directed against the clandestinity of love and not the I–Thou of Buber. It is significant that in 'The Phenomenology of Eros' Levinas drew a distinction between love and friendship (TeI, p. 244; TI, p. 266), and it is in terms of friendship, not love, that Levinas presents Buber's I–Thou elsewhere.[7]

Levinas's first essay on Buber and Buber's Response

I noted earlier that in 'Violence and Metaphysics' Derrida expressed some doubt as to whether Buber would recognize himself in Levinas's interpretation. He even speculated as to where one might best find in Buber an appropriate response, thereby suggesting, though only in the briefest outline, the possibility that Levinas might have offered a more sympathetic reading of Buber.

Others will determine, perhaps, whether Buber would recognize himself in this interpretation. It can already be noted in passing that Buber seems to have foreseen these reservations. Did he not specify that the I–Thou relationship was neither referential nor exclusive in that it is previous to all empirical and eventual modifications? Founded by the absolute I–thou, which turns us toward God, it opens up, on the contrary, the possibility of every relationship to Others. Understood in its original authenticity, it is neither detour nor diversion. Like many of the contradictions which have been used to embarrass Buber, this one yields, as the *Postscript to I and Thou* tells us, 'to a superior level of judgement' and to 'the paradoxical description of God as the absolute Person'. (ED, p. 156n; WD, p. 134n37)

Derrida continued the quotation from Buber: 'It is as the absolute person that God enters into the direct relationship to us. . . . The man who turns toward him need not turn his back on any other I–Thou relationship: quite legitimately he brings them all to God and allows them to become transfigured "in the face of God" ' (DP, p. 135/ IT, p. 182).[8]

There is some curiosity in finding Derrida, albeit in 1964, apparently according a special privilege to whether an author recognizes himself in an interpretation of his works. Did Levinas recognize himself when he read Derrida's interpretation and would it have posed a problem for Derrida's reading had he not done so? Did not Derrida himself in the same place insist on the difference between Levinas's 'intentions' and his 'philosophical discourse' (ED, p. 224; WD, p. 151)? Leaving that aside, it is in fact possible to give an exact answer to the question of whether Buber could have recognized himself in Levinas's interpretation of him. At the very time that Derrida was speculating on Buber's likely response to Levinas's treatment of him, Buber published two sets of replies to questions posed to him by Levinas. The first arose in connection with a volume devoted to Buber in the series 'The Library of Living Philosophers'. A feature of the series is the reply the articles elicit from the philosopher to whom the volume is dedicated. In his 55-page 'Reply to my critics' Buber made only two brief comments on Levinas's essay 'Martin Buber and the Theory of Knowledge'.[9] And in fact there are some grounds for believing that Levinas was aware of only one of them, the least interesting.[10] Both comments began by noting that Levinas had misunderstood some crucial point (MB, p. 596; S, p. 697, and MB, p. 619; S, p. 723).

The second response appeared in another volume devoted to the idea of questioning famous philosophers, *Philosophical Interrogations.* There Levinas elicited a more extensive and even less welcoming reply, precisely of the kind Derrida had anticipated. Buber even referred Levinas to the Postscript to *I and Thou*, just as Derrida himself had done. One passage in particular is worth quoting at this point to indicate the tone Buber adopted. Questioning Levinas's understanding of the concepts of the 'between' and the 'primal distance' (*Urdistanz*), Buber wrote that 'Since Levinas, in the first place, accepts a signification for the two concepts which they do not have in the context of my thought and, in the second, equates with each of them other concepts belonging to totally different spheres of this thought, he makes a direct answer to his questions impossible for me' (PI, p. 27). Buber adopted the role of teacher, contenting himself with 'making a few clarifying comments on his objections so far as that fundamental misunderstanding allows'. He did not succeed in answering Levinas's objections if that is understood to mean silencing them. They reappeared in later essays. But there was equally no indication that Levinas was unduly disappointed by Buber's replies, as is particularly clear from a memorial article Levinas published on the occasion of Buber's death.[11]

To begin with Levinas's 'Martin Buber and the Theory of Knowledge', we find there that in the final section Levinas poses three 'objections' to Buber. The first focuses on the question of reciprocity, as in Derrida's reconstruction of Levinas's three objections to Buber in *Totality and Infinity*. In his second objection Levinas is concerned with the fact that although Buber is preoccupied with distinguishing the I–Thou relation from the I–It, Buber does not appear to attend to the fact that it is only in consciousness that we come to know the between (*Zwischen*) (NP, p. 48; S, p. 149). And yet would not this be to refer the I–Thou to the I–It? Levinas's third objection addresses not just Buber but 'any epistemology which bases truth on a non-theoretical activity or on existence'. Here the whole tendency of recent philosophy, as Levinas perceived it, was at issue. I shall begin with this third point as it not only serves to explain why the essay takes the course that it does, but at the same time also clarifies the other two objections.

The essay 'Martin Buber and the Theory of Knowledge' was in the first instance an attempt to assimilate Buber's account of the I–Thou relation to what Levinas calls 'contemporary' philosophical thought. Levinas's presentation of Buber in terms of the problem of knowledge (which he construes as the problem of grasping what is independent so that it maintains its otherness) is questionable because it placed Buber from the outset and without reservation within a philosophical context. Nevertheless it gave Levinas the opportunity to raise the question of separation within a historical framework, a question which in *Totality and Infinity* was posed on the basis of direct description. Ancient ontology was, Levinas said following Plato's *Parmenides*, devoted to the question of how a being subject to error could relate itself to the absolute being without impairing its absolute character. This for Levinas provided the classical formulation of the problem of knowledge. 'Modern' (presumably in the sense of Cartesian and post-Cartesian) discussions of the theory of knowledge were marked by the 'separation' of the subject. But 'contemporary' (Husserlian and post-Husserlian) thought, by contrast, is governed by the rejection of the notion of subject on the grounds that it is an abstraction (NP, pp. 29–30; S, pp. 135–6). It is this development, Levinas suggested, which enabled recent thinking to distinguish knowledge of objects from knowledge of Being, albeit at a high price.[12] For by sacrificing the notion of the subject, contemporary philosophy had deprived itself of the notion of separation, which alone, as he attempted to show in *Totality and Infinity*, made possible 'the relation with the detached, absolute exteriority'. 'Separation opens up between terms that are absolute and yet in relation, that absolve themselves from the relation they maintain, that do not abdicate in it in favour of a totality this relation would sketch out' (TeI, p. 195; TI, p. 220). In *Totality and Infinity*, however, Levinas insisted – following Rosenzweig – on the way in which the ontological tradition of Western philosophy has been conceived as a quest for totality. It is clearly not this conception which Levinas had in mind when in 'Martin Buber and the Theory of Knowledge' he referred to philosophy as 'a rupture of our participation in totality' (NP, p. 49; S, p. 149), so that when philosophy denies separation it denies the impulse which in *Totality and Infinity* is called 'metapysical thought'.

The first of Levinas's objections was formulated in terms of the asymmetry of the ethical relation, the difference of level which is always in favour of the Other. For Levinas a reciprocal relation, such as the I–Thou relation is said to be by Buber, cannot account for this difference of level. Here, as elsewhere, Levinas did not deny the presence of ethical themes in Buber but rather asked whether he made explicit the ethical structure which belongs to the relation with the Other (NP, p. 46; S, p. 147).[13] Levinas at this point referred to a sentence early in *I and Thou* where Buber said that 'I become in the Thou; becoming I, I say Thou' (DP, p. 15; IT, p. 62). Levinas's comment was that

if the I becomes an I in saying Thou, as Buber asserts, I hold the place from my correlate and the I–Thou relation resembles all other relations: as if an outside observer was speaking of the I and of the Thou in the third person. The encounter is formal and is reversible so that it is indifferent whether it is read from left to right or right to left. (NP, p. 47; S, p. 147)[14]

The charge of formalism here – and also as it is repeated in *Philosophical Interrogations* (PI, p. 26) and again in an essay of 1968[15] – arose because the asymmetry of the relation had been allowed to disappear with the loss of separation from Buber's account, as indicated by the phrase referred to by Levinas. Buber, however, challenged this interpretation in his 'Replies to my Critics'. He complained that Levinas was wrong to infer from his statement that I owe my place to my partner, when it should rather be said that I owe my place to my relation to my partner in that the Thou also does not exist outside of the relation. He denied that the relation was reversible and explained further, 'My I – by which here the I of the I–Thou relation is to be understood – I owe to saying Thou, not to the person to whom I say Thou' (MB, p. 596; S, p. 697). Buber would appear to have missed Levinas's point, which was concerned with the question of separation or asymmetry. But the aspect of 'saying Thou' would serve Levinas later as a basis for developing the ethical structure of the relation to the

Other left inexplicit by Buber. There is a sense therefore in which the reply offered by Buber which Levinas did not take up would have provided a better basis for dialogue than that which served as the basis for the article 'Dialogue avec Martin Buber'.

Levinas reformulated the point about reciprocity in the exchange published in *Philosophical Interrogations*. Referring again to the phrase 'I become in the Thou', he asked 'whether the concept of Relation is capable of defining this original structure' (PI, p. 23). Here Buber was again assimilated to the movement of recent philosophical thought, specifically Husserl and Heidegger, where the substantiality and indepedent reality of the self is denied. Levinas's first concern was to put in question Buber's use of the word 'relation' to characterize the basic word I–Thou.[16] Levinas conceded that the question arose only because Buber had conceived the I–Thou as 'a relation in which one of the terms remains absolute' (PI, p. 24). Levinas did not want to charge Buber with contradiction: 'the apparent contradiction between the absolute and the relative is overcome in the case of social relations'. Levinas understood the word 'absolute' in the same sense in which he used it in *Totality and Infinity*, where it refers to a relation in which the terms absolve themselves from the relation while remaining absolute within it (TeI, pp. 35–6; TI, p. 64). Had Levinas read Buber's 1957 Postscript to *I and Thou* – or indeed had he been more attentive to the third part of *I and Thou* instead of focusing largely, like most readers, on the first part – he might not have gone on to ask whether Buber had been aware of 'the logical originality of the relation'. Appealing to the notion of an absolute Person, Buber had in the Postscript explicitly embraced the contradictory nature of the relation as arising out of the supra-contradictory nature of God. This contradiction is met by the paradoxical designation of God as the absolute Person, that is one that cannot be relativized (DP, p. 135; IT, p. 181).

Levinas explained that his suspicions were aroused by Buber's commitment to the two theses, first, that the I derives its *ipseity* from its confrontation with the Thou and, secondly, that the relation is reciprocal. According to Levinas, this would mean that the terms would be related as objects each definable in terms of the other and as constituting a totality from which they could not be separated. Levinas knew very well that Buber would deny the appropriateness of the terms 'object' and 'totality', as indeed he did in his reply (PI, p. 27). Levinas wrote, 'If the terms are related in this way, we must infer that it is logically impossible for them not mutually to define one another, because a term which was absolutely *sui generis* would destroy the relation'. He was not thereby subscribing to this logic. He was presenting Buber with the consequence of failing – as he thought – to specify the inappropriateness of the logic of non-contradiction. In his response Buber claimed that, although he did not insist on reciprocity, he regarded asymmetry as only a special case of the I–Thou relation. 'The asymmetry that wishes to limit the relation to the relationship to a higher would make it completely one-sided: love would either be unreciprocated by its nature or each of the two lovers must miss the reality of the other' (PI, p. 28). It is necessary to consider whether Levinas's account does have that implication. Certainly Levinas says that 'I love fully only if the other loves me' (TeI, p. 244; TI, p. 266). But such assurances are to be regarded as no more final than, for example, Buber's comments about ethics. The issue is, of course, further complicated by Buber's choice of example, which, from a Levinasian standpoint could be said to be a confirmation of Buber's preoccupations. Nevertheless, what is most significant in this context is the question of the judgment which would confirm a relation as symmetrical. From where might it be posed? For Levinas, I cannot make the comparison between my relation to the Other and the Other's relation to me without absenting myself from the relation and looking at it from the outside. And yet, what is visible from outside is not a relation with the Other at all, but only a synthesis of terms. Buber is not saying only that there should be some reciprocity. His point is surely directed against the idea of a relation which amounts to two asymmetries which are nowhere equalized, so that I relate to the Other as to a height and the Other relates to me in the same way. To insist on reciprocity in this sense is to insist on what Derrida in 'Violence and Metaphysics' called 'the transcendental symmetry of two empirical asymmetries' (ED, p. 185; WD, p. 126). Again, if this meant, as Derrida seemed to suggest, that I should recognize myself as other for the other, then Derrida was wrong to say there was no trace of this relationship in Levinas (for example, TeI, p. 56; TI, p. 84). But were not Buber's remarks governed by an ideal of fusion, of presence, just as his model of dialogue was that of transparent communication? Such models make no sense for a relation conceived in terms of separation, because they can only be posed from a transcendental perspective for which the relation to Otherness is in principle inaccessible. It should not be forgotten that Buber's insistence on reciprocity in the sense of an equal or absolute presence of the lovers to each other had already led Levinas in *Existence and Existents* to introduce the example of so-called 'failure of communication' in love where, as I noted earlier, the absence of the other is not a negation or a deficiency, but the other's presence as other.

The course of this discussion in *Philosophical Interrogations* clarifies the relation between the first and second objections in 'Martin Buber and the Theory of Knowledge'. This second objection is that it is only in consciousness that we come to know the between. It was repeated in *Philosophical Interrogations* when Levinas asked this question of the meeting between the I and Thou:

> How does this *Zwischen* or betweenness where it takes place, the 'shock' (*Geschehen*) or 'trust' which defines that meeting encroach on the consciousness that is aware of it? How can this unusual relation of the I–Thou be reflected in our conscious awareness when the latter is essentially awareness of an object, without at the same time leading us to suspect that it involves but a moment of consciousness? (PI, p. 25)

The question was again that of whether the I–Thou relation could be thought except by consciousness, which would be to submit it to the very realm from which it was supposed to be removed. That our knowledge of the I–Thou relation cannot be referred to a secondary act of reflection on an experience or to a consciousness is a constant theme of Levinas's essays on Buber. But what underlay it was the view, most clearly stated in 'Martin Buber and the Theory of Knowledge', that Buber's account of the Other fulfilled the ambitions of the theory of knowledge in its ancient classical form. For Buber, only in the I–Thou relation did one succeed in grasping the independent other (NP, p. 34; S, p. 137); only there did one enter into community with the totality of being (NP, p. 35; S, p. 138). But in consequence Buber offered us a mere union rather than a *synousia*, a social communion (PI, p. 26). That is why Levinas could present Buber's rendering of the I–Thou relation as in some sense a fulfilment of philosophical ambitions, while nevertheless showing how it failed to account for philosophy itself in so far as it was a rupture of the individual with the whole (NP, p. 49; S, p. 149).

The Failed Dialogue Made Good

If the 1958 essay showed Levinas engaged in the task of differentiating his standpoint from that of Buber, the 1978 essay 'Martin Buber,

Gabriel Marcel and Philosophy' indicates how Levinas came to believe that the dialogue between thinkers is not to be limited to such an exercise alone. This latter essay returned to many of the conclusions arrived at in 'Martin Buber and the Theory of Knowledge'. So, for example, in both essays Levinas used the notion of intentionality to contrast the basic word 'I–Thou' with the subject–object relation. Nor was there anything new in the insistence in the 1978 essay that both Buber and Marcel resorted to the language of Being or ontological language, in order to support their descriptions. But the decisive question was now that of the possibility or impossibility of thinking outside or beyond being (BP, p. 508; BMP, p. 318), the very question which had governed Derrida's reading of Levinas in 'Violence and Metaphysics'.

Another important difference between the two essays was that the question of God, which had been virtually ignored in 'Martin Buber and the Theory of Knowledge', now came to play an important role in Levinas's interpretation of Buber. This was not only in conformity with Buber's own insistence in his 1957 Postscript to *I and Thou* that his essential concern in that book had been 'the close association of the relation to God with the relation to one's fellow-men' (DP, p. 122; IT, p. 171). The year 1978, the same one as Levinas's essay, though no doubt too late for him to make use of it, saw the first publication of the text of Buber's 1922 lecures *Religion als Gegenwart* which served as a draft of *I and Thou*.[17] In these lectures Buber began with the theme of the eternal Thou. Had he persisted with this order, the temptation to offer the kind of anthropological interpretation of *I and Thou* which has tended to dominate the secondary literature would have been diminished. But Levinas's interest in the issue of how the relation to God as the invisible and non-given takes place in the relation to the other human being as thou (BP, pp. 493–4; BMP, p. 306) is to be understood less with reference to a change of direction in Buber scholarship than to the fact that this issue had become more prominent in Levinas's own thinking, albeit in a way which led him to think of God as He, in explicit contrast to the Thou of Buber and Marcel (DEHH, p. 202; TO, p. 46).[18] Furthermore, the question of how an alliance might be possible between the singularity of the I and the absolute Thou, a question similar to that which dominated Levinas's contribution to the volume *Philosophical Interrogations*, was now dismissed with the remark that Buber had already transcended the perspective from which the question was posed when he took the relation as his starting-point: 'In the beginning is the relation.' And Levinas here acknowledged the importance of language in Buber. 'Dialogue functions not as a *synthesis* of the relation, but as its very unfolding (*déploiement*)' (BP, p. 496; BMP, p. 309). But it was not only that Levinas came finally to a recognition of the importance of the eternal Thou and of dialogue in Buber. On the question of the formalism of the I–Thou relation, which had previously been such a stumbling block, Levinas repeated that it was indeed in some sense formal, but conceded that in Buber it had at the same time an ethical concreteness (BP, p. 506; BMP, p. 317). The response of dialogue already exhibits the responsibility of 'the one for the other'. Similarly, when Levinas raised once again the question of the reciprocity of the I and the Thou, on this occasion he immediately acknowledged Buber's notion of the between, the *Zwischen* (BP, p. 494; BMP, p. 307). The implication was that the question of the equality of the related terms would no longer arise once attention was paid to the *relation*. So Levinas quoted approvingly Marcel's comment on Buber that 'the encounter does not take place in each of the participants, or in a neutral unity encompassing them, but *between* them in the most exact sense, in a dimension accessible to them alone' (MB, p. 37; S, p. 42). Later in the essay he would acknowledge specifically that, by virtue of the relation to the eternal Thou, elevation could be found in the midst of reciprocity (BP, p. 506; BMP, p. 316), thereby laying to rest the crucial question of asymmetry. And finally, when he repeated the observation that Buber and Marcel both questioned the primacy of the objectifying act, on this occasion it was no longer to place them among the philosophers of existence. The philosophy of existence retained the priority of truth, whereas these 'philosophers of coexistence' maintained a sociality which was 'irreducible to knowledge and to truth' (BP, p. 495; BMP, p. 307). There is no doubting that this is a very different assessment from that given in 'Martin Buber and the Theory of Knowledge'.

In this way Levinas dismissed in just a few sentences the concerns that had preoccupied him in making the first of his three objections in 'Martin Buber and the Theory of Knowlege'. The 1978 essay was more concerned with Marcel's and Buber's reliance on ontological language, a question which was now taken up in a way more reminiscent of Derrida's discussion of Levinas in 'Violence of Metaphysics' than of anything which had appeared in Levinas's previous essays on Buber. The question was whether, having broken with the ontology of objects and substance, Buber and Marcel did not in their descriptions of the encounter hold fast to Being and presence as ultimate referents. The role of presence in Buber's *I and Thou* is pronounced, not surprisingly when one recalls that *Religion as Presence* was the title of the lecture-series in which Buber first developed his ideas on the subject at length. Notwithstanding this, Levinas judged Buber the more successful in breaking with ontology, not least because Buber – unlike Marcel – was clear that sociality could not be reduced to an *experience* of sociality.[19]

Levinas at the beginning of the essay contrasted Buber's rendering of the dialogical 'relation' with that of Marcel, almost as if he was dealing with two readings of the same text. In spite of 'the remarkable community' of their fundamental ideas, Marcel's discussion differentiated itself from Buber's because they came from very different intellectual traditions, even different religions (BP, pp. 492–3; BMP, pp. 305–6). On these same grounds Levinas would be closer to Buber than he would be to Marcel, and indeed in this essay Marcel seems to serve as something of a foil, as if he was introduced to show the superiority of Buber's formulations. When Marcel asked how it was possible for the I–Thou to transpose itself into the realm of language without degenerating thereby (S, p. 45 and BP, p. 497; BMP, p. 309), when he noted that it was impossible to say of the Thou that it was not a thing without reducing it to the status of a thing (S, p. 44), he believed that he was drawing on Buber's own statement that only silence leaves the Thou free (S, p. 47). 'All response binds the Thou into the It-world' (DP, p. 42; IT, p. 89).[20] Levinas, who had earlier characterized the I–Thou as 'an understanding without words, an expression in secret' (TeI, p. 129; TI, p. 155), was now in no mood to dismiss the role of dialogue. 'Buber eliminates the gnoseological foundation of the encounter. It is a pure dialogue, a pure *alliance* which no common pneumatic *presence* envelops. I am destined for the other not because of our *previous* proximity or our substantial union, but because the Thou is absolutely other' (BP, p. 501; BMP, p. 312). It is striking that Levinas with this answer to Marcel also addressed the second objection that he himself had posed in 'Martin Buber and the Theory of Knowledge' about our consciousness of the relation. And it is even more explicitly answered when Levinas later in the essay asked if the I–Thou relation joined being only in a secondary and not always legitimate act of reflection. 'Does not the ethical relation signify precisely the non-significance of being, even if the theologians, reflecting on it, obstinately persist in rediscovering its meaning in the trace of sociality and interpreting sociality as an experience' (BP, pp. 507–8; BMP, p. 318)? At this point it seems that Marcel has been introduced less as a foil for Buber than in order to help Levinas reverse his earlier assessment of *I and Thou*.

Having examined the question of the language of the I–Thou in the context of Marcel's assumption about a more fundamental and silent form of the relation, Levinas then reconsidered the question independently of this assumption. As Levinas posed it, it is the question of whether the immediacy of the I–Thou relation is respected by language as a system of words, language as *said*. The 'said' (*le dit*) is to be understood here in distinction from the 'saying' (*le dire*), although strictly speaking it is not a 'distinction', as the saying and the said are non-synchronizable. The *said* is a language which 'speaks about something and expresses the relation of the speaker to the object of which he speaks, saying what is the case with it' (BP, p. 504; BMP, p. 315). *Saying* says something, says the said, but at the same time says *Thou*. Not that the actual word *Thou* need be said. The *Thou* 'is the said of saying as saying' (BP, p. 505; BMP, p. 315). Thus in the I–Thou, language is not the element of degeneration – or perhaps one should say *not that only*. It is also the element of transcendence (BP, p. 504; BMP, p. 315) and 'thou-saying' (*dire toi*) is directed to the invisible, the unknowable, the unthematizable of which one can say nothing (BP, p. 505; BMP, p. 316). Marcel found all language permeated by the 'I–It'. For Levinas, language is not absorbed irretrievably in the 'I–It', but nor can a language of 'thou-saying' be separated from it to subsist on its own.

Although Buber in his account of the I–Thou relation remained for the most part bound to ontological language (BP, p. 504; BMP, pp. 314–15), Levinas 'awoke' in Buber's *said* a *saying* which was absorbed in it, a speaking beyond the language of Being (cf. AEAE, p. 55; OBBE, p. 43). It was a question, in the time-honoured phrase, not of understanding Buber better than he understood himself, but of rejoining him and recognizing him as the pioneer (BP, p. 505; BMP, p. 316). And this meant to acknowledge Buber as an ethical thinker. 'Surely the immediacy of the I–Thou of which Buber speaks, is not to be found in the negativity of a thought cut off from all recourse to the conceptual systems of the world and of history? Surely it is to be found in the very urgency of my responsibility which precedes all knowing?' (BP, p. 505; BMP, p. 316). Levinas's reading of Buber situated itself – and he used Derrida's word – on the *margin* of Buber's text (BP, p. 505). But it did not stay there very long. Contrary to Levinas's previous reading, 'the whole of Buber's work' was to be regarded as 'a renewal of ethics' (BP, p. 506; BMP, p. 317).

Levinas also returned to the third of the objections raised in his paper 'Martin Buber and the Theory of Knowledge', the question of Buber's relation to the vocation of philosophy. This was now explained, more clearly than had originally been the case, to mean the ability to say 'I', as the call to live in a manner other than that of simple submission to the decisions and commands of society, culture, politics and religion (BP, p. 502; BMP, p. 313). The question was whether the dialogical philosophy of Buber could respond to the traditional vocation for philosophy while at the same time contesting the traditional pre-eminence of ontology, whether the capacity to say 'I' could be secured without basing it on the freedom of a consciousness equal to being (BP, p. 504; BMP, pp. 314–15). Once again Levinas, now equipped with an ethical reading of Buber, was able to fend off a question which seemed so pressing when he was without such an interpretation. I am I not on the basis of my freedom, but as if I had been elected or chosen (BP, p. 507; BMP, p. 317). *I* cannot divest myself of my ethical responsibility.

Levinas closed the essay by returning to the question of the impossibility of thinking outside or beyond being. One could put the question in this way: When Buber says 'all actual life is encounter' (DP, p. 15; IT, p. 62) or when Levinas himself has recourse to the word 'dis-inter-estedness' (*dés-inter-essement*) in an attempt to say 'the uprootedness outside of being' (BP, p. 508; BMP, p. 318) is not the reference to being found to be ineliminable? Levinas answered the question with another question, the counter-question of whether the philosophy of dialogue does not show 'that it is impossible to encapsulate the encounter with the Other in a theory, as if that encounter was an experience whose meaning reflexion would succeed in recovering' (BP, p. 510; BMP, p. 320). The philosophy of dialogue has brought into focus the ambiguity and enigmatic character of that thinking for which the world and the other man, knowledge and sociality, being and God are bound together, as in Husserl, according to the very structure of the experience of consciousness. With Husserl as his example, Levinas focused on the totalizing tendency of solitary, monadological thinking. For Husserl, the urgent needs of the Other, my neighbour who awaits me when I close my book, put down my pen and leave my study, mark a return to the *Lebenswelt* and so a renewal of the thread which binds me to life. But in terms of the transcendental phenomenology which Husserl founded, the call of the neighbour merely represents an interruption. Were we pure intellects like the angels, we would be able to work solidly day and night without distraction.

In order to challenge that attitude, Levinas ended his essay with a story from the Talmud. According to this story, when the divine Torah was about to be given to humanity the angels protested against it being allowed to leave heaven. So an attempt was made to appease the angels. They were reminded that, as they had not been born, they would not die. And because they did not work, eat, have possessions, nor sell them, the Torah did not apply to them. Levinas asks whether the angels were flattered by this answer. Or did they, on the contrary, discover their inferiority to human beings? Humans alone are capable of giving and of being-one-for-the-other. They alone take part in the 'divine comedy' above and beyond the understanding of being to which the pure spirits were dedicated (BP, p. 511; BMP, p. 320). In telling this story and in responding to Husserl in the way outlined above, Levinas did not intend an ethical attack on the philosopher's life-style, although the ethical connotations of the discussion were not inappropriate. In the context of the essay, Levinas should rather be understood as drawing attention to the character of the saying of transcendence as it takes place within the history of ontology. Thinking has come to be construed as the reduction to solitary consciousness or else as the rediscovery of Being, in Heidegger's sense. Failure to conform to this model is conventionally assessed to be the consequence of a certain lack of resolution, an unwillingness to follow thought through to its final conclusions. If thinking fails to reabsorb the Other in the course of thought's return to itself, then this is regarded as a deficiency, the result of blind passion or the consequence of distraction – 'fallenness' in Heidegger's terminology. The significance of the philosophy of dialogue, according to Levinas, is that it challenges this model. The question of whether the angels recognized the superiority of human beings points to the question of whether philosophy can recognize in the human face 'a reasonable significance which Reason does not know' (BP, p. 511; BMP, p. 320). The philosophy of dialogue runs counter to the standard models of thinking and allows us to acknowledge the saying of transcendence as an interruption of ontology.

Reformulations

'Martin Buber, Gabriel Marcel and Philosophy' could be read as a recantation of the essay 'Martin Buber and the Theory of Knowledge', in which case Levinas would be engaged in dialogue with himself as much as with Buber. But I shall try to show in this section how other contemporary essays by Levinas on Buber rule out such an interpretation of the relation between the two essays. Levinas did not withdraw the earlier objections, although in some cases they were reformulated.

The essay 'Martin Buber, Gabriel Marcel and Philosophy' was followed soon after by 'Dialogue', which was written as a contribution to a German encyclopedia of Christianity.[21] The characterization of Buber to be found there emphasized many of the same points: the multiplicity of consciousnesses was not to be regarded as the result of a fall or ontological catastrophe which befell the One any more than sociality was to be considered as compensation for a lost unity (DVI, p. 219); the originality of the I–Thou is understood to be irreducible to experience or knowledge; the eternal Thou is the Thou *par excellence*, invisible, non-objectifiable and non-thematizable (DVI, pp. 220–1); language is the very event of transcendence (DVI, p. 223); the relation where the I encounters the Thou is the place and original occasion of the advent of ethics (DVI, p. 225).

Where the essay 'Dialogue' marks a development over its predecessors is in its application of the notion of an 'absolute distance' to the philosophy of dialogue. It is a term which Levinas had already introduced in *Totality and Infinity* (for example, TeI, p. 116; TI, p. 143) and it served there to describe the separation between the same and the other. Levinas introduced it in 'Dialogue' to acknowledge that Buber had indeed recognized the role of separation. The I and the Thou are said there to be 'separated absolutely by the inexpressible secret of their intimacy' and dialogue transcends this distance without suppressing it (DVI, p. 221). 'Relation' now has a *double meaning* in Levinas's reading of Buber as both 'absolute distance' and 'immediacy' (DVI, p. 228).

It has to be said that, of the two notions, 'immediacy' is the more prominent in Buber's own texts (for instance, DP, p. 15; IT, p. 62). Indeed, when Levinas asked Buber some years earlier in *Philosophical Interrogations* if the reciprocity of the I–Thou relation did not compromise 'the absolute distance of the Thou or Other' (PI, p. 26), Buber, as I documented earlier, complained that Levinas had misunderstood him. Buber had understood Levinas to be equating his two concepts of the 'between' and 'primal distance' and so referred Levinas back to his essay 'Urdistanz und Beziehung'. It seems that he understood Levinas's *la distance absolue* as an attempt to translate into French his own notion of *Urdistanz*. Not that there was anything in Levinas's contribution to *Philosophical Interrogations* to justify that interpretation, although it is just possible that it might have been suggested by the essay 'Martin Buber and the Theory of Knowledge' where Levinas did refer to the essay 'Urdistanz und Beziehung' when construing Buberian man as 'the possibility of both distance and relation' (NP, pp. 37–8; S, p. 140). But Buber's comment should not simply be dismissed as a failure on his part to recognize that Levinas was introducing a concept of his own and not simply translating him into French. Buber specified Levinas's error as a misapplication of the concept of *Urdistanz* to the sphere of the I–Thou relation. The concept of *Urdistanz* is rather an anthropological presupposition for the origination of the duality of the 'primary words', of which the I–Thou is one (PI, p. 27). Even if Buber misidentified Levinas's 'absolute distance' with his own 'primal distance', he was surely correct to recognize a tendency on the part of Levinas – as indeed of many commentators –to confuse the anthropological presuppositions of the I–Thou with the I–Thou itself. This is most clearly apparent in respect of the interpretation of the phrase 'In the beginning is the relation'. But the difficulty is not confined to Buber's interpreters. It reflects an essential ambiguity which permeates Buber's own texts whenever the question of the relative priority and independence of the I–Thou is raised.

In 'Dialogue' Levinas situated this absolute distance less in the failure of one person to know another – a failure of the synthesis which would bring about a coincidence or identity – than in the surplus of the relation. Such a surplus would be exhibited, for example, in a gratuitous gift (DVI, p. 224). Further, Levinas found such a surplus in Buber's notion of grace (DVI, p. 224, and BP, p. 505; BMP, p. 316). So when Buber said that 'The Thou encounters me by grace – it cannot be found by seeking' (DP, p. 15; IT, p. 62) or 'Grace concerns us in so far as we proceed toward it and await its presence; it is not our object' (DP, p. 77; IT, p. 124), he acknowledged the Otherness of the Other and the sense in which the relation is one in which I not only address the Other by saying Thou, but also find myself addressed in a manner which is beyond my control.

Levinas's application of the notion of 'absolute distance' in his reading of Buber made good the lack of an account of separation which in 1958 lay behind many of Levinas's reservations. But had Levinas accomplished this only by a false ecumenism in which the differences were simply concealed and the significant details of their thinking overlooked? At the end of the essay Levinas repeated his charge of reciprocity. Buber sometimes described the I–Thou relation as a harmonious co-presence whereby the relation was in this extreme formalization emptied of its heteronomy (DVI, pp. 229–30). Levinas thereby upset any presumption that he might himself have come to establish a harmonious co-presence with Buber.

This is even more clearly the case in 'A propos de Buber; quelques notes', which was published in 1982. Levinas began this essay by praising Buber for having recognized the ethical relation with the other and having broken thereby with the philosophy of totality. 'It is an order fully cognisant of the ethical relation, a relation with an inassimilable alterity and thus, in the proper sense, in-com-prehensible – foreign to knowledge and to possession – of the Other' (APB, p. 128). As always when Levinas is most positive in his assessment of Buber, language is at the forefront of his interpretation of the encounter. 'The saying which says *Thou*, be it only implicitly' does so in a manner completely different from that of a thought proceeding dialogically from itself or projecting itself towards an object which it gives itself (APB, p. 127). But Levinas in the remainder of the essay presented a series of notes which returned to the task of clarifying the difference between his own perspective and that of Buber. So, for example, Levinas observed that although he himself regarded justice as derivative, Buber began with the I–Thou which, as reciprocal, was a relation of justice (APB, p. 131). So once again the reciprocity, reversibility and equality of the I–Thou 'interpellation' served as a point of contrast with Levinas's own emphasis on the original ethical inequality of a responsibility in which the first person appears not in the nominative but in the accusative (APB, pp. 129–30). But this raises the question of the extent to which Buber could indeed be said to have recognized the ethical relation and have separated himself from the philosophical tradition.

And yet Levinas seemed less concerned with the possibility that he was giving an apparently contradictory assessment of Buber than with taking the opportunity to rehearse his 'objections' or 'questions'. Did not Buber fail to problematize my identity and unicity, drawing these concepts, not from the correlation of a dialogue where the self is concrete, but according to an 'individuation' which is implicitly substantialist (APB, pp. 130–1)? Did not Buber's own thinking fail to break with the intentionality of consciousness and remain rather in the element of consciousness (APB, pp. 131–2)? Was not the very 'for-the-Other' of sociality only concrete in a giving of *things*, without which responsibility for the Other would be an ethereal sociality appropriate only to angels? Did not Buber's language, for all its novelty, fail to break with the priority of ontology (APB, p. 133)? These questions were the same as those which had inspired his initial response to Buber. And unlike 'Martin Buber, Gabriel Marcel and Philosophy' or 'Dialogue', this essay did not show Levinas to be concerned to discover such hidden resources as could be uncovered in Buber's text. So, on this occasion, when Levinas juxtaposed his own conception of *illeity* with Buber's notion of God as the eternal Thou, he seemed more concerned to explain how illeity referred to a divine transcendence which nevertheless returns me to the service of my neighbour, than to see how the eternal Thou functions in Buber's text (APB, p. 132).[22]

Re-reading Buber

When it is said that the question of *separation* and *orientation* (in the sense of asymmetry) governed the dialogue between Buber and Levinas, this should not simply be understood in terms of the way in which Levinas assessed Buber on the extent to which he recognized this twin aspect of the relation to the Other. At that level, the thematic level, the tension in Levinas's account of Buber remains unaddressed. It remains fundamentally unclear why Levinas was so apparently inconsistent in his assessment, sometimes affirming and sometimes denying that Buber recognized the ethical relation of transcendence, but never affirming or denying unambiguously. In particular, it fails to pose the question of the *necessity* whereby Levinas seemed somehow obliged in 'Martin Buber, Gabriel Marcel and Philosophy' to *unsay* the objections of the essay 'Martin Buber and the Theory of Knowledge' only to reformulate them later.

Only when it is acknowledged that Levinas came to practise *separation* and *orientation* or *asymmetry* in his reading of Buber is that necessity addressed. In other words, Levinas's relation to Buber took the form of an ethical relation where, on the basis of that separation from Buber which Levinas established in his early discussions, he subsequently came to exercise an orientation in favour of Buber. Which is not to say that that orientation did not in fact predate the objections. The asymmetry in favour of Buber is not a question of Levinas presenting the formula that he 'does not have the ridiculous pretension of "correcting" Buber' (TeI, pp. 40–1; TI, p. 69). Rather it is much more a matter of awakening the 'saying' of Buber from his said. One could pose the question whether this is not merely to exchange one way of failing to communicate for another. Is not this appeal to a 'saying' just a further way of refusing to listen to what is said, much as when one poses objections against a text from a totally different standpoint or when one assimilates a text to one's own standpoint? The answer is that it will probably always seem so from the neutral standpoint of the observer. This is not to dismiss that standpoint in so far as it represents the demand to do *justice* to the text at issue, but – as in Levinas – justice must ultimately be subordinated to ethics as the awakening of saying.

To do justice to both Buber and Levinas it would be necessary, following this reading of Levinas on Buber, to re-read Buber himself, not so much to confirm or deny the correctness of Levinas's reading which would be to pose the question at a level of simplicity that remains divorced from the 'dialogue between thinkers'. It is more a question of seeing if Buber now reads any differently. In 'A propos de Buber' Levinas invited his reader to return to Buber in this way. He said of the questions and objections that he had raised, 'It is perhaps not impossible to find a response to them – or even to find in the ideas which determine them a place – in Buber's texts' (APB, p. 129). I shall on this occasion forego accepting this invitation exactly as Levinas conceived it, and content myself instead with an examination of Theunissen's discussion of Buber in his book *The Other*. This does not mean that Theunissen is now to serve as a substitute for Buber. My initial justification for turning to Theunissen in this context is that he offered a more detailed reading of Buber than Levinas, while at the same time acknowledging an agreement with 'the general tendency' of Levinas's interpretation as presented in the essay 'Martin Buber and the Theory of Knowledge'.[23] Although Theunissen ultimately took his reading of Buber in a very different direction from that proposed by Levinas, a number of interesting questions are raised by his account which – particularly in their early development – rejoin themes I have already introduced.

Theunissen explicitly followed Levinas in characterizing Buber's work as an 'ontology of the between' (NP, p. 36; S, p. 139), and he took as his starting-point Levinas's account of the I–Thou as the condition for the I–It. But when he came to focus on the question of how the I–Thou relation can be thought as a 'genuine original unity' (DP, p. 22; IT, p. 70), he discovered some of the difficulties which attend this interpretation. Theunissen found that Buber maintained the standpoint of the I in the very displacement of egology, one might almost say *despite himself*. 'The I – despite all Buber's assurances to the contrary – assumes precedence over the Thou' (A, p. 281; O, p. 294). Theunissen based this claim on the observation that Buber, 'regardless of his intention to overcome the supremacy of the I', remained 'true to that inner perspective prescribed by the "mineness" of the I' (A, p. 267; O, p. 279). He had in mind, for example, those formulations of Buber which attempted to explicate the becoming of the I. The problem was that although both the I and the Other are said to originate in the encounter, it remained the case that our access to the encounter is on the part of my I (A, p. 272; O, p. 285) or at least must be expressed as such. Theunissen found Buber's formulations 'intrinsically ambiguous' (A, p. 273; O, p. 286), and attempted a resolution by suggesting that such sentences as 'man becomes an I through the Thou' (DP, p. 32; IT, p. 80) and 'I become through the Thou; becoming I, I say Thou' (DP, p. 15; IT, p. 62) are to be understood in terms of what he calls 'reciprocal constitution'. This guarded against according priority to the Thou, as if the Thou in some way was the origin of the I. But it still left a question about the meaning of the *necessity* whereby, as Theunissen correctly observed, 'in "my" talk about it' reciprocal constitution appeared 'in the shortened perspective of a precedence of the Thou over the I' (A, p. 275; O, p. 287). Theunissen referred it to the methodological orientation toward mineness which leaves me 'only in a position to speak about it from my side and not from the other'. This methodological precedence of the I gave rise to an ontological precedence of the Thou. But Theunissen treated them as if they somehow cancelled each other out. 'The precedence of the Thou over the I . . . is still only the clothing in which the precedence of the between over the I and the Thou manifests itself to me, the one who is met in the meeting.' And yet how was the precedence of the between to be established except by a kind of 'transcendental symmetry' which according to Levinas would inevitably be blind to the ethical orientation of the relation?[24]

In other words, the symmetry was imposed to correct the orientation in favour of the Other. But even so, this only postponed the 'trace of the Other' which re-emerged later in the form of the relation between, on the one hand, 'the precedence of "being spoken to" over "speaking to" ' as it arises in concrete experience and, on the other, the act of 'speaking to' which secures the precedence of the I and which dominates the conceptual unfolding of the relation (A, p. 324; O, p. 339). Buber tended to focus one-sidedly on the 'thou-saying' where 'the initiative goes out from me' (A, p. 286; O, p. 299), even to the point of constituting the I (S, p. 697). But there was also a place in his thinking for the way, for example, in which we are addressed by the eternal Thou (DP, p. 10; IT, p. 57). The notion of grace to which Levinas drew attention in the essay 'Dialogue' was concerned with the way the Other comes to me without my assistance. Hence its role as a 'surplus', as Levinas put it. Not simply because, as Buber wrote, 'What we have to deal with, what we have to be concerned about, is not the other, but our side' (DP, p. 77; IT, p. 124). But also because grace is a 'surplus' over Buber's tendency to dwell on the I saying Thou and which can in no respect be equalized with it in order to establish the between of relation. Even though he was not prepared to abide by the consequences, Theunissen expressed the difficulty well: 'speaking to never flows into being spoken to' (A, p. 324; O, p. 339). Levinas could perhaps be understood to have already pointed in the direction of this difficulty when in his first objection to Buber in 'Martin Buber and the Theory of Knowledge' he wrote, 'If the I becomes an I in saying Thou, I hold the place from my correlate and the I–Thou relation resembles all other relations: as if an outside observer was speaking of the I and of the Thou in the third person' (NP, p. 47; S, p. 147).

Throughout his reading of Buber, Levinas was clear that Buber's fundamental notion was that of the *between* and that his fundamental thesis was that 'In the beginning is the relation'. It was this which kept the I–Thou from being conceived as an alliance (BP, p. 496; BMP, p. 308) and secured the primacy of the relation over the relata. Levinas also understood this insistence on the originality of the relation as an indication that the I–Thou relation was conceived as the condition for the I–It.[25] So, for example, Levinas quoted the fourth paragraph of *I and Thou* where Buber used the classic formula for the explication of Husserlian intentionality: 'I perceive something. I feel something. I imagine something. I want something. I sense something. I think something. . . . All this and its like is the basis of the realm of the It.' Levinas then commented, 'Thus in the measure that the I–Thou relation is distinguished from the I–It relation, the former designates what is not intentional but what for Buber is rather the condition of all intentional relations' (NP, p. 34; S, p. 137). The same interpretation was repeated in other essays so that in 'A propos de Buber', for example, he wrote that 'The basic word I–Thou is in the final analysis the condition of the openness of all language, even of that which announces the relation of pure knowledge expressed by the basic word I–It' (APB, p. 127).

However, in the essay 'Dialogue' Levinas addressed this interpretation rather differently. He took it up in the form of the objection that Buber's descriptions of the dialogue proceed negatively in relation to intentionality and the transcendental structures of consciousness so putting in question their 'philosophical autonomy' (DVI, p. 288). The objection had been presented by Theunissen, who characterized Buber's work as 'a purely negative ontology' on the grounds that the 'sphere of the between' is presented only in abstraction from the 'sphere of subjectivity'. Because Buber pursued 'his quest for a positive categorial elucidation of the I–Thou relationship in a piecemeal fashion', he was unable to think of the I–It and the I–Thou relationships except in a similar manner – that is to say, 'after a model whose ontological basis can only be sustained by the I–It and not only by the I–Thou relationship' (A, pp. 276–77; O, p. 290). In presenting this objection Levinas almost certainly had Theunissen in mind, for the phrases he used echoed those to be found in *The Other*. But it is also worth noting that Derrida in 'Violence and Metaphysics' had brought a similar objection against Levinas (ED, p. 167; WD, p. 113). Whether directed against Buber or Levinas himself, the point is that a thought which proceeds only negatively is without such philosophical autonomy as both Levinas and the so-called 'new thought' of dialogical thinking claimed for themselves. It was in this context that Levinas introduced the idea of the double meaning of relation as both the immediacy of the I–Thou across language and as absolute distance. Furthermore, it is in the concealed – and sometimes unacknowledged – ethical dimension of dialogue that the break with the transcendental model of consciousness is to be found. 'Does it not harbour an ethical dimension where the rupture of dialogue with the transcendental models of consciousness appears most radically' (DVI, p. 228)?

It is not that Levinas replaced the objection that Buber speaks of the I–Thou relation from the outside with an acknowledgment of the ethical affirmation made by Buber. It is not a question of whether Buber's is an ethical discourse or an ontological discourse, but of whether Buber's text *harbours (recéler)* such a dimension. Levinas is not working with a pair of alternatives in opposition to each other, as Buber is when it is always a case of *either* I–Thou *or* I–It – if it is not undifferentiated as in the beginning.[26] The saying and the said are such that each accompanies, supports and yet subverts the other. It is this which enabled Levinas to say that Buber's account was both ontological and yet not ontological, but ethical. The parallel with 'double reading' as Derrida presents it is clear. Levinas acknowledged what draws Buber's text back into the ontological tradition, and yet at the same time he marked what indicates – to recall the phrases of Derrida's essay 'The Ends of Man' – a change of terrain made in a discontinuous and irruptive fashion. But the terms the *saying* and the *said* are not merely ways of designating the two limbs of a double reading. Levinas in reading Buber is in the first instance concerned (this is particularly clear in his contribution to *Philosophical Interrogations*) with recalling certain necessities which govern thinking, his own thinking as much as that of Buber. But he also encountered Buber in an ethical relation. His readings of Buber exhibited the asymmetry and separation of such a relation.

But if there is any sense in which I have succeeded in showing that, how could I have done so? Is not this essay a series of observations from the outside which as such must be blind to the absolute distance so that it disappears into a synthesis of agreement or opposition? And if saying is the openness of a transcendence which can never be reduced to a said and never made a content, how could it be repeated? Could there ever be a saying of saying?[27] I have tried to resolve these dilemmas in what is perhaps the only way open to me: through the intricate complexity of the *said*. It is when there is a break in the dialogue or when Levinas is forced into the apparent contradiction of a yes-and-no saying that a trace of the saying is perhaps to be found in the said, just as the descriptions in *Totality and Infinity* serve to discover a trace of the infinite in the finite. These characteristics of Levinas's dialogue with Buber are not grounds for dismissing it as unclear, confused or inconsistent, but rather evidence that the encounter was genuine. Levinas can be understood as having offered an exemplary reading, one which, instead of seeking to attain self-definition by means of contrast and criticism, sought to reach out to the other without thought of return. And if Buber and Levinas in their communications with each other fell prey to misunderstandings, we should not be disappointed that they did not exhibit some ideal form of unity achieved through philosophical discourse. For our model of dialogue should also recognize the alterity of the other which shows itself in 'the restlesssness of the same disturbed by the other' (AEAE, p. 32; OBBE, p. 25) and in the failure to communicate.

Abbreviations

A   M. Theunissen, *Der Andere*, Berlin, Walter de Gruyter, 1977.

BMM M. Buber, *Between Man and Man*, translated by R. Gregor Smith, London, Fontana, 1968.

DL   M. Buber, *Dialogisches Leben*, Zurich, Gregor Müller, 1947.

DP   M. Buber, *Das dialogische Prinzip*, Heidelberg, Lambert Schneider, 1984.

ED   J. Derrida, *L'Écriture et la différence*, Paris, Seuil, 1967.

IT   M. Buber, *I and Thou*, translated by W. Kaufmann, Edinburgh, T. & T. Clark, 1970.

MB   P. A. Schilpp and M. S. Friedman (eds), *Martin Buber. Philosophen des 20. Jarhunderts*, Stuttgart, Kohlhammer, 1963.

O   M. Theunissen, *The Other*, translated by C. Macann, Cambridge, Mass., MIT Press, 1984.

PI   Sydney and Beatrice Rome (eds), *Philosophical Interrogations*, New York, Harper & Row, 1964.

S   P. A. Schilpp and M. Friedman (eds), *The Philosophy of Martin Buber*, La Salle, Ill., Open Court, 1964.

W   Martin Buber, *Werke, Erster Band. Schriften zur Philosophie*, München, Kösel and Heidelbeg, Lambert Schneider, 1962.

WD   J. Derrida, *Writing and Difference*, translated by Alan Bass, London, Routledge & Kegan Paul, 1978.

Notes

1 M. Heidegger, 'Brief über den Humanismus', in *Wegmarken*, Frankfurt, Klostermann, 1967, p. 167; 'Letter on Humanism', translated by F. A. Capuzzi and J. Glenn Gray in *Basic Writings*, D. F. Krell (ed.), New York, Harper & Row, 1977, p. 216.

2 The fullest study of Levinas's relation to Buber is 'Buber und Levinas. Philosophische Besinnung auf einen Gegensatz' by S. Strasser. It appeared alongside Levinas's BP in the same issue of *Revue Internationale de Philosophie*, vol. 32, no. 126, 1978, pp. 512–25, and so was unable to take account of it. Strikingly, Levinas in APB refers the reader to 'Martin Buber and the Theory of Knowledge' in NP and to 'the fine study' by Strasser, but not to BP itself (APB, p. 133). Philip N. Lawton's 'Levinas's Reading of Buber', *Philosophy Today*, vol. 20, Spring 1976, pp. 77–83, is hampered by the fact that he was apparently unaware of 'Martin Buber and the Theory of Knowlege' and the discussion in PI which were the major sources then available. His account of Levinas closely follows Derrida's footnote on Buber in 'Violence and Metaphysics' which I discuss in the third section of this study. Most of the interest in Andrew Tallon's 'Intentionality, Intersubjectivity, and the Between: Buber and Levinas on Affectivity and the Dialogical Principle', *Thought*, vol. 53, No. 210, 1978, pp. 292–309, resides in the fact that he makes no reference to any of Levinas's discussions of Buber – not even those in TI – and so exhibits in absolute purity the proximity (Tallon calls it 'complimentarity', p. 309) of Buber and Levinas as it appears to the external observer, independent of the observations of the participants themselves.

3 M. Heidegger, *Unterwegs zur Sprache*, Pfullingen, Neske, 1959, p. 188; *On the Way to Language*, translated by P. D. Hertz, New York, Harper & Row, 1971, p. 83.

4 In most cases I follow Kaufmann's translation with minor revisions, but I have not kept with his decision to translate *Du* as 'you'. While granting that this translation has clear advantages for the reading of Buber, the contrast with Levinas makes it essential to maintain the difference between the second person singular and the second person plural, and so I have returned to the 'Thou' which is still more familiar to readers of Buber.

5 See note 15.

6 Levinas would not have known this letter of Rosenzweig, which was not published until 1973. Six years later the letter was republished in a critical edition, F. Rosenzweig, *Der Mensch und sein Werk. Gesammelte Schriften. Briefe und Tagebücher*, The Hague, Martinus Nijhoff, 1979, pp. 824–7, and made the subject of an essay by Bernhard Casper, 'Franz Rosenzweigs Kritik an Bubers "Ich und Du" ', *Philosophisches Jahrbuch*, vol. 86, 1979; 225–38. Levinas praised Casper's article and discussed the letter briefly in 'Façon de Parler' in DVI, pp. 268n–269. For an English translation of the letter, see Rivka Horwitz, *Buber's Way to "I and Thou"*, Heidelberg, Lambert Schneider, 1978, pp. 253–6. See also M. Friedman, 'Martin Buber and Franz Rosenzweig: the Road to I and Thou', *Philosophy Today*, 1981, pp. 210–20.

7 It is significant in this regard that in 'Martin Buber and the Theory of Knowledge' Levinas suggested that spiritual friendship was the apogee of the I–Thou relation for Buber (NP, p. 47; S, p. 148), and referred to the latter's essay 'Education', where, as the third of three forms of the dialogi-

cal relation, Buber wrote of friendship 'based on a concrete and mutual experience of inclusion' (DL, p. 285; W, p. 806; BMM, p. 128). Buber in reply wrote that he regarded this relationship as winning its true greatness 'precisely there where two men without a strong spiritual ground in common even of very different kinds of spirit, yes of opposite directions, still stand over against each other so that each of the two knows and means, recognizes and acknowledges, accepts and confirms the other, even in the severest conflict, as this particular person. In the common situation, even in the common situation of fighting with each other, he holds present to himself the experience-side of the other, his living through this situation. This is no friendship, this is only the comradeship of the human creature, a comradeship that has reached fulfilment. No 'ether', as Levinas thinks, but the hard human earth, the common in the uncommon' (MB, pp. 619–20; S, p. 725). Presumably the comradeship of philosophical debate is included.

8 Buber's Postscript, dated October 1957, first appeared in the special edition of *Ich und Du* prepared in connection with Buber's eightieth birthday on 8 February 1958. Levinas, who wrote 'Martin Buber and the Theory of Knowledge' in the same year, cites there the collection of Buber's writings called *Dialogisches Leben*, which was compiled in 1947.

9 Written in 1958, it was published in German in 1963 (MB, pp. 119–34), in English in 1967 (S, pp. 133–50), but the French original first appeared in 1976 (NP, pp. 29–50). However sympathetic one might be to translators of Levinas, it has to be said that neither of these translations does justice to the original. In their defence it could be said that the translators, working without a knowledge of *Totality and Infinity* where the importance of many of the concepts Levinas uses in the essay are established, were not well placed to know what needed to be preserved and what could be sacrificed in the process of translation. Of course, it would be possible to argue in the same way that in so far as Buber failed to recognize what lay behind Levinas's 'objections' this too was a consequence of his not being aware of the way Levinas developed the notions of asymmetry and separation in *Totality and Infinity*. But even though Buber's comments would no doubt have been different had he had the opportunity to study the thinking from which Levinas's objections arose, we should beware of assuming that it would have brought the thinkers into closer proximity or – and it is not the same thing – would have improved the possibility of dialogue between them. Failure of communicaiton is an essential character of the dialogue between thinkers – as well as lovers – although Buber might well have been among those who would not have understood such an observation.

10 The evidence that half of Buber's reply never reached its destination may be found in the fact that Levinas referred to only one of the two comments – both in a letter he wrote to Buber at the time and in comments that he attached to the letter on the occasion of its publication 13 years later in 1976 (NP, pp. 51 and 53). See also note 14 below.

11 'Dialogue avec Martin Buber', *Les Nouveaux Cahiers*, vol. 1, No. 3, 1965, pp. 1–3; reprinted with the omission of the first two paragraphs in NP, pp. 51–5. The article consisted of an introduction, a further short paragraph introducing a brief extract from his essay 'Martin Buber and the Theory of Knowledge' in which he opposed the notion of solicitude to Buber's model of spiritual friendship (NP, pp. 47–8; S, p. 148), and Buber's reply – an extract from his 'Reply to my Critics' also quoted in note 7 above – which began, 'Levinas errs in a strange way when he supposes that I see in the *amitié toute spirituelle* the peak of the I–Thou relation' (S, p. 723). Alongside these documents Levinas published a respectful letter he had written to Buber in 1963 trying again to explain to Buber his differences together with Buber's reply, a letter which seems to have been addressed to all the contributors to the 'Library of Living Philosophers' volume. This letter contained some Heideggerian reflections on the relation between 'thinking' and 'thanking' and a postscript acknowledging receipt of Levinas's letter. In a short introduction Levinas noted with an exclamation mark the irony in the fact that the 'Library of Living Philosophers' volume on Buber was to appear after his death. But there was no hint of irony or mockery in the way Levinas put together these documents under the title 'Dialogue avec Martin Buber'. One is reminded of Levinas's own words in *Totality and Infinity*: "The claim to know and to reach the other is realized in the relationship with the Other that is cast in the relation of language, where the essential is the interpellation, the vocative. The other is maintained as confirmed in his heterogeneity as soon as one calls upon him, be it only to say to him that one cannot speak to him.' (TeI, p. 41; TI, p. 69). Levinas's only complaint was that following 'la Discourtesie par excellence' – Buber's death – 'the interruption of the dialogue but lately begun was clothed with a profound silence' (NP, p. 51). Again, Levinas does not seem to have regarded failure of communication simply as a deficiency.

12 Levinas here rejoins a theme of his thinking which was already pronounced in *De l'existence à l'existant* in 1947 – the tendency of modern philosophy 'to sacrifice for the sake of the spirituality of the subject its very subjectivity, that is its substantiality' (DEE, p. 168; EE, p. 97).

13 See also the essay 'Transcendance et Hauteur', *Bulletin de la Société française de Philosophie*, vol. 54, 1962, p. 99: 'Our effort does not consist so much in bringing out the originality of the I–Thou relation as in showing the ethical structures of this relation.'

14 The only indication that Levinas was aware of Buber's reply to this specific passage (see also note 10 above) is to be found in the fact that there is nothing in the French text corresponding to the English phrase 'as Buber asserts' (or the German *wie es Buber will*). Did Levinas, when publishing the French original in 1976, drop the phrase in deference to Buber's denial? A rough examination of the English and German translations does not appear to show that Levinas revised the text before publishing the French version, but the translations are so free that it is not always easy to be sure.

15 'La pensée de Martin Buber et le judaïsme contemporain', *Martin Buber, l'homme et le philosophe*, Bruxelles, Editions de l'Institut de Sociologie de l'Université Libre de Bruxelles, 1968, pp. 56–7. Levinas here defends Heidegger, as he had already done in 'Martin Buber and the Theory of Knowledge' (NP, pp. 47–8; S, p. 148), against Buber's charge that *Fürsorge* does not offer access to the Other of itself, but only where that access is already secure (DL, pp. 401–2; W, pp. 367–8; BMM, pp. 296–7 and MB, p. 620; S, p. 723). It is striking to see how quickly Levinas, who wastes no opportunity of his own to attack Heidegger, nevertheless rushes to his defence when he is attacked by someone else or from another perspective.

16 In questioning Buber's use of the word 'relation', Levinas found himself on common ground with Rosenzweig, who had already put the point to Buber when reading *I and Thou* prior to its publication. See R. Horwitz, *Buber's Way to 'I and Thou'*, p. 256. Marcel in his contribution to the volume of the Library of Living Philosophers dedicated to Buber made a similar observation (S, p. 44). For Buber's own defence of his use of the word, see MB, p. 603; S, p. 705.

17 The lectures are published in R. Horwitz, *Buber's Way to 'I and Thou'*, pp. 41–152.

18 See B. Casper, 'Illéité', *Philosophisches Jahrbuch*, vol. 91, 1984, pp. 273–88.

19 Levinas's sensitivity to the ontological character of experience (in so far as it is inscribed with the value of presence) seems to be a consequence of Derrida's remarks in 'Violence and Metaphysics'. For example, 'Has not the concept of experience always been determined by the metaphysics of experience?' (ED, p. 225; WD, p. 152). Before that Levinas himself used the word, albeit with a recognition of certain difficulties. For example, he wrote in the Preface to *Totality and Infinity*, 'The relation with infinity cannot be stated in terms of experience, for infinity overflows the thought that thinks it. . . . But if experience precisely means a relation with the absolutely other, that is, with what overflows thought, the relation with infinity accomplishes experience in the fullest sense of the word' (TeI, p. xiii; TI, p. 25).

20 Buber in his 'Reply to my Critics' dismissed the conclusions Marcel drew from this section of *I and Thou* (MB, p. 604; S, pp. 705–6), but he did not take the opportunity to address the question of how this section should be understood. It is not simply another statement of the 'progressive increase of the It-world', which I discussed briefly in the second section, above, because it joins that theme with the question of the status of dialogue in Buber. This silence of the 'unformed (*ungeformten*), undifferentiated pre-linguistic word' (DP, p. 42; IT, p. 89) – which comes second to the longing for relation – would appear to be the same as the 'wordless anticipation (*Vorgestalt*) of saying Thou' (DP, p. 31; IT, p. 78). But this would serve to show the fragility not just of the I–Thou itself, but also of Buber's distinctions. *Either* the silent anticipation of the I–Thou *or* the response which already subverts the I–Thou. It was this that Buber was denying when he

dismissed Marcel's discussion, but such statements of intent are no final court of appeal.

21 The essay first appeared as 'Le Dialogue. Conscience de soi et proximité du prochain' in *Archivio di filosofia*, vol. 48, 1980, pp. 345–57. The following year it was published in German as 'Dialog' in *Christlicher Glaube in moderner Gesellschaft*, Freiburg, Herder, 1981, pp. 61–85. The French version was republished in DVI. Levinas does not attempt in this essay to divorce himself from so-called 'dialogical thinking' and this raises the question of its relation to his subordination of dialogue to the 'responsibility of being-in-question' elsewhere. When Levinas in AEAE posited the latter as 'prior to dialogue, to the exchange of questions and answers', dialogue was conceived as 'the thematization of the said' (AEAE, p. 142; OBBE, p. 111). In other words, Levinas in this place upheld the priority of saying over the said, just as in 'Dialogue' it is the *saying* of dialogue which is the original mode of transcendence (DVI, p. 225). See also E. Levinas, 'Le mot je, le mot tu, le mot Dieu', *Le Monde*, 19–20 mars 1978, p. 2. However, note Levinas's rather different comment earlier in AEAE. There he contrasted, on the one hand, 'the presence of interlocutors to one another in a dialogue in which they are at peace and in agreement with one another' with, on the other hand, subjectivity as 'the restlessness of the same disturbed by the other' (AEAE, p. 32; OBBE, p. 25). The first phrase describes the conception of 'dialogue' which emerges from the 'philosophy of dialogue'. Levinas's relation to Buber, however, is more readily assimilated to the second of these descriptions.

22 So, for example, instead of voicing his suspicions concerning the appropriateness of situating the divine person in the Thou of dialogue (APB, p. 132 and DEHH, p. 202; TO, p. 46), he might have observed that in so far as all Thou-saying addresses the eternal Thou ('in every Thou we address the eternal Thou', DP, p. 10; IT, p. 57), the relation is asymmetrical. Perhaps it was the way the single Thou provided a glimpse of the eternal Thou (DP, p. 76; IT, p. 123) which led Levinas in *Philosophical Interrogations* to characterize the original relation in Buber as a relation where one of the terms remains absolute. Levinas's reference on that occasion is insufficiently specific to allow for a clear identification.

23 'I agree with him not in his criticism, to be sure, but in the general tendency of his interpretation of Buber. Even Levinas tries to see Buber in the context of the philosophical endeavours of the twentieth century. However, he brings dialogic back too closely to fundamental ontology and does not distinguish sharply enough between Buber's attempt at an overcoming and Heidegger's attempt at a grounding of intentionality' (A, p. 260n27; O, p. 405n27). And again, 'That the interpretation of the "sphere of subjectivity" with the help of Husserlian terminology is not arbitrary and irrelevant is confirmed by Levinas, who insists that it is "characterized in Buber by the same expressions that Husserl utilizes for the designation of the intentional object" ' (A, p. 260n28; O, p. 405n28).

24 Derrida attempted to impose this 'transcendental symmetry' on Levinas in 'Violence and Metaphysics' (ED, p. 185; WD, p. 126).

25 The language of conditions is one that Levinas himself frequently employed in the course of explicating his own thinking, but there are indications that even in *Totality and Infinity* he was not only aware of its problems – pre-eminently within that context that it is an ontological language – but engaged in an effort to counteract or 'unsay' it by employing it only in ways whereby it destroys itself. I shall attempt to show this in my forthcoming book, *Between Levinas and Derrida*.

26 This relates back to the second of the objections in 'Martin Buber and the Theory of Knowledge' where Levinas noted the way that, according to Buber (DP, p. 37; IT, p. 84), the I–It relation corrodes the I–Thou (NP, p. 48; S, p. 149). It can be seen that the saying and the said address this question by not being introduced as in opposition to each other.

27 This is a question which of course addresses itself not only to my efforts here, but more importantly to Levinas's *account* of the 'distinction', an account which can only present the saying and the said as a distinction. Levinas already addressed the problem of giving such a thematic account in *Totality and Infinity*: 'The very utterence by which I state it and whose claim to truth, postulating a total reflection, refutes the unsurpassable character of the face to face relation, nonetheless confirms it by the very fact of stating this truth – of telling it to the Other' (TeI, p. 196; TI, p. 221). See also AEAE, p. 182; OBBE, p. 143 for Levinas's own discussion of 'saying saying the saying itself' (*Dire disant le dire même*).

Levinas, Derrida and Others vis-à-vis

JOHN LLEWELYN

He is Greek, and he speaks Greek, does he not?

Socrates

Ethical Metaphysics

Heidegger frequently links the notion of the physical to a certain Greek conception of what it means to be. He also links it to the idea of emergence into the open and coming to light (*phōs*). So the study of being, ontology, at the time of *Being and Time*, is a phenomenology, a study of appearing (*phainesthai*) and dis-appearing.

Husserl's phenomenology is no less an ontology, a study of essences, than Heidegger's fundamental ontology is a phenomenology. Both Heidegger and Husserl describe what the Greeks called the physical, in the wide sense that Heidegger finds this word to have had for them. If we understand the word in this wide sense we understand why Levinas says that the main topic of his thinking is metaphysical. It is metaphysical because it is ethical. And it is ethical not because he aims to present a code or a metaphysics of ethics. Kant's groundwork of the metaphysics of ethics suggests an analogy between Kantian respect and Heideggerian letting be. But it is being that is to be let be according to Heidegger, and it is the moral law which is to be respected according to Kant. The other person is to be respected, according to Kant, only because the other person is a rational agent, and he is a rational agent only in so far as he personifies the moral law and is capable of exercising a freedom to refrain from following rules of behaviour that could not be universally followed or willed. By the same standard the agent is entitled and obliged to respect himself. He respects the law which, without of course suspending them, transcends the laws of physical nature. Kant's metaphysics of ethics describes the structure of interpersonality, a structure for which his analogy is that of the lawfulness of nature. It describes the foundation of justice.

The ethical, as Levinas describes it, is 'older than' justice as conceived by Kant. It is a condition which is not a foundation of it; so it is more strictly speaking an un-condition which is pre-original and prior to the *intér-esse-ment* which is no less a feature of Kantian deontological morality than it is of the teleological morality of self-interest and general interest. Both of these models of morality are styles of being and being-with, *Mitsein*, notwithstanding the criteria they provide for distinguishing the immoral from the moral and the inauthentic from the authentic. They are both ontological.

The ethical as Levinas would have us understand it is de-ontological, dis-ontological, *ent-ontologisch*. It is prior to all structures of being-with. It is prior to all structures, whether these be the categories of Greek philosophy, of Kant, of Hegel, of Husserl, or the structures of structuralism and of linguistic or economic exchange – prior to all system, to symmetry, to correlation, to the will, to freedom and to the opposition of activity and passivity. It is the superlation of passivity. Because it is prior to the third person.

Without yet knowing what is prior to the third-personal point of view according to Levinas, it is not difficult to see how he stands *vis-à-vis* certain of the other authors whose work has been influential in recent European thinking. The surrationalistic structures of the natural sciences as conceived by Bachelard are third-personal objectivated systems. The disillusioning techniques prescribed in the critical theory of Habermas call for the same objectivation in the social sciences. This third-personal scientific objectivity is demanded by the theories and methods of interpretation advocated by realist critics of Gadamer like Betti and Hirsch. As for the structuralist theories which Lévi-Strauss and others have developed from the teaching of Saussure, these are predicated on a concept of language as a system of opposed terms regarded in isolation from the particular speech acts performed by users of that system. *Langue*, as described by Saussure and his adaptors, fulfils the description that Levinas gives of a system as a coexistence or agreement of different terms in the unity of a theme (AEAE, p. 210; OBBE, p. 165).

So is Levinas in the lineage of those who deny the primacy of *langue*

137

over *parole*? And is he a champion of diachrony against synchrony? The answer to both of these questions is that he is, but in a way which sets him apart. When Merleau-Ponty and Ricoeur re-emphasize the dependence of instituted language upon *parole* they are stressing the intentionality of creative, sense-giving speech acts. When, following Husserl, Merleau-Ponty underlines the importance of anonymous, centripetal intentionality, he is proposing nothing that transcends the general sphere of significance to which the structuralists apply their theories. He, like them, is talking about the universe of discourse in which one thing stands for another, the system of signifier and signified (AEAE, p. 188; OBBE, p. 148). When the system of one thing with another and one thing standing for another is supplemented by the significative intentionality of a speaker we are still short of the non-intentional, pre-intentional or, as Levinas sometimes calls it, reversed intentional, *significance* which, he says, is presupposed by semantic signification. And the diachrony of the speech act is but a difference in the same time in contrast with the radical diachrony Levinas ascribes to my responsibility for the Other, *Autrui*, to whom I address my words and myself. In the essentialist phenomenology of Husserl utterance and all other signifying gestures are noetic-noematic, an intentional projection of subjectivity towards an accusative. This is because for Husserl

all acts generally – even the acts of feeling and will – are 'objectifying' acts, original factors in the 'constituting' of objects, the necessary sources of different regions of being and of the ontologies that belong therewith.[1]

For Husserl the prototype of even non-theoretical acts is perception and the correlation of subjectivity and objectivity, the co-relation of being-with.

Levinas discerns very much the same sort of auto-affection at work in this prototype as is posited by the Kantians and Neo-Kantians from whom Husserl was hoping to move away. These and Husserl are all inheritors of the Cartesian tradition in which consciousness is egological. Another heir of this tradition is Sartre. Although in his existential phenomenology intentionality is interpreted as the for-itself's refusal of the in-itself with which it is correlated, a kind of 'othering', consciousness remains a free recuperation. Its ideal is that of assumption, consumption, digestion, though, in contrast with the Hegelian phenomenology of the concept, fufilment of the ideal is condemned never to be achieved. In Husserl's essentialist phenomenology the

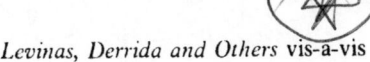

other, although my alter ego and an analogue of myself, resists assimilation because he is only ever appresented; I have no adequate consciousness of his consciousness. Sartre, for different reasons, agrees with this, yet he continues to see the for-itself as consciousness projected towards assimilation.

Somewhat the same assimilative character is ascribed by Gadamer to our efforts to understand each other and the texts and works of art and artifice that others have produced. Understanding is at the same time self-understanding and an interfusion of horizons. It is true that with Sartre cognition is secondary to consciousness and that with Gadamer and Heidegger consciousness is secondary to understanding as a structure of being. However, the Husserlian notion of horizon persists in the accounts that Sartre, Gadamer and Heidegger give of situation or environing world, *Umwelt*. This, Levinas maintains, is incommensurable with the for-the-other which, far from being the mere contingency that is Sartre's being-for-the-other, is an unavoidable and unvoidable human responsibility. Levinas would say that this ethical responsibility is also neglected in the hermeneutic co-responsibility of Gadamer's interpretation of understanding. He does say that it is beyond the reach of the ecstasis of *Verstehen* as this is described in *Being and Time*. It cannot be comprehended by comprehension. Like the infinite of Descartes' third Meditation, it cannot be comprehended. Levinas agrees with readers of the *Meditations* like Martial Gueroult, one of his teachers at Strasbourg, who take as provisional and artificial Descartes' distinction between the consciousness he has of his self and the consciousness he has of his finitude. 'My nature is not only to be a thinking being, thinking itself as thought, but a being thinking itself as finite and consequently thinking the infinite.'[2] The thought of the infinite is implicit in and logically prior to the thought of myself, to the *cogito*.

In thinking the infinite – the self at once *thinks more than it can think*. The infinite does not enter into the *idea* of the infinite; it is not grasped; this idea is not a concept. The infinite is the radically, absolutely other. (DEHH, p. 172)

Whereas Descartes employs causal and ontological arguments to demonstrate that there is a God, the descriptions Levinas gives purport not to be ontological. They take as their cue the axiological function that Descartes attributes to the idea of God's perfection, although, as Gueroult observes, Descartes does not make as clear as

Malebranche does the distinction between judgments of truth or reality and judgments of value or perfection.[3] What Levinas refers to as the most high (*altus*) is the radically other (*alter*). The Other, *Autrui*, is not simply an alter ego, an appresented analogue of myself. He and I are not equals, citizens in an intelligible kingdom of ends. We are not relatives. We are not different as chalk and cheese. There is between us, in the Hegelian phrase which Levinas adapts, an absolute difference. The Other is he to whom and in virtue of whom I am subject, with a subjectivity that is heteronomy, not autonomy, and hetero-affection, not auto-affection. The Other is not the object of my concern and solicitude. Beyond what Heidegger means by *Sorge* and *Fürsorge* is my being con-cerned, *con-cerné*, obsessed by the Other. He is not the accusative of my theoretical, practical or affective intentionality or ecstasis. He is the topic of my regard (*il me regarde*) only because I am the accusative of his look (*il me regarde*) (AEAE, p. 147; OBBE, p. 116). The subject is an accusative, *me*, which is not a declension from a nominative, but an accusative absolute like the pronoun *se* for which, Levinas says, Latin grammars acknowledge no nominative (AEAE, p. 143; OBBE, p. 112). This latter accusative is not a case of the I which accuses itself. The accusative in question is beholden to the Other, but not for any services rendered. He is sub-poenaed by the Other, pursued and persecuted, but not on account of any crime or original sin (AEAE, p. 156; OBBE, p. 121). The persecuted is himself responsible for the persecution to which he is subjected, but his responsibility is beyond free will; and the accusation is not one which he can answer or to which he can respond with an apology, for 'Persecution is the precise moment in which the subject is reached or touched without the mediation of the logos'.[4] It is beyond the spoken word, and beyond or before Christian and Hegelian mediation.

The accused self is categorized beyond free will and beyond the opposition of freedom and non-freedom, where by freedom is understood freedom to choose and initiate. Original ontological freedom, according to Sartre, although prior to deliberation and will, is none the less an unreflective choice. It is also ontological because it is the choice of a way to be. Levinasian ethical responsibility is pre-original and beyond ontology. Sartrian fundamental choice founds the agent's situation. It is a descendant of Fichtean self-positing. Levinasian responsiblity is non-foundational and an-archic. It deposes, ex-poses and de-situates the self. This does not mean, however,

— a choice of a way to be !

that the self is alienated, 'Because the Other in the Same is my substitution for the other through the *responsibility* for which I am summoned as the one who is *irreplaceable*' (AEAE, p. 146; OBBE, p. 114). This substitution is not a derivative of the intersubstitutability of *das Man*.

Through substitution for others, the oneself escapes relations. At the limit of passivity, the oneself escapes passivity or the inevitable limitation that the terms within relation undergo. In the incomparable relationship of responsibility, the other no longer limits the same, it is supported by what it limits. Here the overdetermination of the ontological categories is visible, which transforms them into ethical terms. In the most passive passivity, the self liberates itself ethically from every other and from itself. Its responsibility for the other, the proximity of the neighbour, does not signify a submission to the non-ego; it means an openness in which being's essence is surpassed in inspiration. It is an openness of which respiration is a modality or a foretaste, or, more exactly, of which it retains the aftertaste. Outside of any mysticism, in this respiration, the possibility of every sacrifice for the other, activity and passivity coincide. (AEAE, p.146; OBBE, p. 115)

Since what Levinas here calls 'the most passive passivity' and elsewhere 'the passivity of passivity' is said to be a passivity that coincides with activity, it might be expected that he would refer to this also as a most active activity or the activity of activity. That he never does this marks off the superlative emphatic passivity he does refer to not only from Cartesian freedom, the Kantian rational will and Sartrean originative choice; it mar... it off too from any respect and *Seinlassen* such as would lend itself to articulation in the middle voice. Levinas's beyond of passivity and activity is beyond being, whether being be expressed by a noun, a verb or by a verbal noun; in so far as it can be expressed by a word, it is more correct to call it a passivity than an activity. It follows that this passivity must not be construed as the taking on of suffering, suffering to suffer either a useful passion or a *passion inutile*. It is a passivity that is presupposed by any such assumption or undertaking: assumed by assumption. Contract, engagement and commitment, whether entered into altruistically or from egoistic motives, are still at the level of egoity, and egoity has absolute passivity as its un-condition. Entering into a commitment is subscribing to a project, not something to which the accused is subjected.

For Sartre even the adversity of that which limits my freedom is a function of my freedom,[5] as for Fichte is the resistance, *Anstoss*, of the

not-I. He devotes several paragraphs of *Being and Nothingness* to describing the paradoxes of passivity.[6] These paradoxes arise, he says, from the supposition that passivity is a mode of being-in-itself, whereas both passivity and activity presuppose human beings and the instruments they use: 'man is active and the means which he employs are called passive'. So activity and passivity presuppose being-for-itself, hence non-being. The self-consistency of being-in-itself is beyond both the active and the passive. The absolute passivity of which Levinas writes is indeed sub-jectivity, but subjectivity of the for-others, not of the for-itself. Absolute passivity is also beyond being and nothingness. Levinas agrees with Hegel that meontology is the mirror image of ontology. They occupy the same logical space, the space of the Same. So too does the neutral third value between being and nothingness for which Levinas employs the expression *il y a*, the there is. In *De l'existence à l'existant* this expression carries some of the force carried by the notions of facticity and thrownness in *Being and Nothingness* and *Being and Time*. But this sheer anonymous fact of one's existence is prior to the notion of world or situation. And prior to both the *il y a* and worldhood, availing an exit from them and an exile, is the absolute passivity of passivity.[7]

Facial Expression

The absoluteness of my passivity answers the infinitude of the absolutely other. It fills the place that Descartes gives to the infinitude of the freedom of my will which for him is 'that above all in respect of which I bear the image and likeness of God'. For Levinas and Descartes infinitude is the positive notion in terms of which the notion of man's finitude is understood. Instead of this positive notion of infinity Kant substitutes a regulative idea required to give sense to man's search for more but ever limited knowledge. This notion of infinity is an ideal 'ought'. Heidegger applauds what Kant has to say about human finitude, though where Kant interprets this as man's limitedness by the given, Heidegger interprets it as man's being toward death. Hegel opposes a good infinite to the interminable bad infinite of the Kantian 'ought'. To the finitude of man's being toward his term he opposes the negation of this finitude, the infinity of the end of history. Against this, Levinas says:

We recognize in the finitude to which the Hegelian infinite is opposed, and which it encompasses, the finitude of man before the elements, the finitude of man invaded by the *there is*, at each instant traversed by faceless gods against whom labour is pursued in order to realize the security in which the 'other' of the elements would be revealed as the same. (TeI, p. 171; TI, p. 197)

That is to say, Hegel's good infinite is an infinite of goods. It is an economic infinity of need and the war of each in competition with all where my freedom is limited but also consummated by that of the other. Levinas argues that room must be found also for an infinite of goodness, a peaceful infinite of desire which, instead of limiting and enhancing my freedom, extends my responsibility and exalts it the more I respond to the other's call: 'the absolutely Other does not limit the freedom of the Same. In calling it to responsibility it renews and justifies it.' This renewal, *instauration*, is inspiration, the Levinasian hetero-affective counterpart to the Husserlian auto-affectively intentional animation of the body of the corporeal signifier. Husserl's egological sense-giving *Beseeling* is what Levinas doubtless has in view when he introduces his notion of heteronomous 'psychism'. In Levinas's account of Husserl's semiology signs express meaning only within a horizon against which they are presented much after the manner of objects in a visual field. He gives a similar account of the ready to hand which is accorded priority over the present at hand in Heidegger's analysis of the everyday world as well as in the semiology of *Being and Time*. For Heidegger and Husserl, 'To comprehend the particular being is to grasp it out of an illuminated site it does not fill' (TeI, p. 164; TI, p. 190). For them there is no aspect of a being which is transcendentally foreign to being and comprehension, even if it may be temporarily hidden.

For Levinas the face of the other is beyond being and comprehension. Beyond Husserlian expressive meaning and presupposed by it is the expression of the other's face. This expression is not the expression that is seen. It is heard expression that is the discourse of the Saying (*Dire*) that is presupposed by the Said (*Dit*). The face is not the countenance. It cannot be contained. Like the infinitude of Descartes' God, it cannot be comprehended. Unlike the Look of Sartre's being-for-the-other, the other's face is not a threat to my freedom before which I shrivel. It increases my responsibility and is welcomed.

Under the eye of another, I remain an unattackable subject in respect. It is the obsession by the other, my neighbour, accusing me of a fault which I have not committed freely, that reduces the ego to a self on the hither side of my identity, prior to all self-consciousness, and denudes me absolutely. To revert to oneself is not to establish oneself at home, even if stripped of all one's acquisitions. It is to be like a stranger, hunted down even in one's home, contrasted in one's identity. . . . It is always to empty oneself anew of oneself, and to absolve oneself, like in a haemophiliac's haemorrhage. (AEAE, p. 117; OBBE, p. 92)

The internal haemorrhage in my universe which on Sartre's analysis results from my being seen by the other is the foundation of my unreflective consciousness of myself.[8] The haemorrhage to which Levinas refers is not in the zone of self-consciousness, *Selbstbewusst-sein*, or in any other region of consciousness, unconsciousness or being, *Sein*. It is an emptying out of my consciousness, a *kenosis* commanded by the ethical word of the other which inflicts a wound that never heals (TeI, p. 171; TI, p. 197; AEAE, p. 162; OBBE, p. 126).

The first traumatic word which is the pre-original expression of the face is 'thou shalt commit no murder'.

The epiphany of the face is ethical. The struggle this face can threaten *pre-supposes* the transcendence of expression. The face threatens the eventuality of a struggle, but this threat does not exhaust the epiphany of infinity, does not formulate its first word. War presupposes peace, the antecedent and non-allergic presence of the Other; it does not represent the first event of the encounter. (TeI, pp. 173–4; TI, p. 199)

By war Levinas means a resistance and counter-resistance of energies, an allergy which is an opposition of powers analogous to the reciprocity of forces in the system of Newtonian mechanics. The ethical resistance is 'the resistance of what has no resistance', since it is the weakness of the other which commands me. The other is the poor, the widow and the orphan mentioned in the Book of Job. Paradoxically, it is the vulnerability of the other, the nakedness of the face, which wounds me. The ethical 'thou shalt not' dominates the economic and political 'I can'. The 'I can' and the philosophies of 'I can' are no less egocentric than the philosophies of 'I think', notwithstanding that the ego is correlated with an other. Although Levinas recognizes that in his later writings Husserl explores the limits of the correlation of subject and object, he insists that Husserl never relinquishes the idea that the ego – which Levinas equates with the same – always has its correlative *cogitatum*; that is to say, although, in the track of Brentano, Husserl holds that all intentionality, even non-theoretical intentionality, is the intending of a noematic Object, this other is assimilated into the same. It is the object of my active or passive concern. But this concern is not ultimate since it presupposes a concern beyond activity and passivity. For Heidegger and for Husserl, on Levinas's reading of them, my ultimate concern is the unconcealing of the truth of being.[9] For Hegel and for Husserl the other is assimilated to the same, to the identity of identity and difference. Hegel, Husserl and Heidegger are all three philosophers of possibilities and powers. They are philosophers whose logics of *Aufhebung*, *Erinnerung* and hermeneutic recycling recollect Plato's recollection but forget the *epkeina tēs ousias* which for Levinas is the singular plural *Autrui* rather than the neutral Good of the *Republic*. They forget that ontology presupposes metaphysics (TeI, p. 18; TI, p. 48).

Paradoxical Proximity

In his essay 'Violence and Metaphysics' Derrida asks whether Levinas forgets the ontological difference. He makes the suggestion that Heidegger's notion of letting be may amount to an acknowledgment of the radical alterity which Levinas assigns to the ethical and metaphysical, and that this acknowledgment is perhaps implicit also in Husserl's conception of phenomenology.

In *Speech and Phenomena* Derrida plots the interplay between two themes of Husserl's phenomenology. On the one hand is the principle of all principles which demands that knowledge of any principle be based on 'a primordial dator act' which is an intuition of essence analogous to perception.[10] This theme would lead us to expect an adequation of the act and its object. It is this theme that Levinas has in mind when he says that the model with which Husserl's phenomenological ontology works is that of satisfaction, hence of need rather than of desire in Levinas's sense.

On the other hand Husserl develops the theme that apodicticity of evidence is possible without its being adequate. Derrida cites Husserl's allusions to the countless profiles of physical objects which are not presented to the person looking at the object but which are appresented with those that are presented. More specifically, there are the retentions and protentions involved in my perception of the object, the immediate echo and pre-echo that perception entails. The consciousness directed to my past and to my future is an analogue, Husserl says, of my consciousness of other selves. Which of these, if either, is prior to the other is a question on which Husserl seems to have had different views at different times. In the *Cartesian Meditations* he takes the view that the consciousness of my past self is presupposed by my consciousness of other selves. He also takes the view there that the latter presupposes consciousness of physical things, in particular the other's body. But he insists that my consciousness of the other is different in principle from my consciousness of physical things in that, whereas I cannot have presentations of all of the profiles of the physical thing (although those that I do have will be presentations of profiles that the other person has or could have) I can have no presentations of his presentations. Is not this, Derrida asks, recognition of the infinite transcendence of the other, recognition of his positive infinitude, as against the negative infinitude of my inability to experience the totality of profiles of the physical thing? And is not this recognition of the infinite transcendence of the other possible only if, like Husserl, we conceive the other on analogy with the ego? If we do not, are we not conceiving the other on analogy with a stone? Does not the radical alterity of the other depend on his being another ego? And does not this otherness depend on his sameness, this dissymmetry on this symmetry? The dependence of his otherness on his being another ego does not make the other's ego a dependency of mine. It does not make him part of my real economy, because Husserl is describing a transcendental, not a real, economy.

Derrida is here saying about Levinas what has to be said about those who hold that Husserl embraces metaphysical idealism and those who say that he embraces metaphysical realism. What he calls transcendental phenomenological idealism is neutral in the debate between these alternatives. The transcendental phenomenological reduction aims to suspend matters of empirical and metaphysical factuality. That is why it would be naïve to equate Husserl's appeal to analogical appresentation with the argument from analogy to the existence of other minds. This would be a naïvety comparable with that of supposing that there could be in phenomenology an ontological or causal proof of the existence of God. This would be the naïvety of the natural attitude in favour of the world and its Creator which the successful reduction suspends.

Of course, Levinas is no more intent than Husserl on producing ratiocinative proofs of the existence of other minds or of God. We have seen however that this talk about others is at the same time talk about God. It draws less on Descartes' fifth Meditation than on the third, but it abstracts from the causal terminology of the latter and from the theologicality of both. It abstracts from causality because a cause and an effect are terms within a system. Their causal relation is their way of being together. But the proximity of the face to face is a 'relation' of speaking (*langage*). This is why it can be neither theological nor analogical, hence not a topic of a theology of *analogia entis* or a *theologia negativa*. It is not logical. It is paralogical and paradoxical. That is to say, this strange speech act is beyond the possibility Husserl ascribes to all theoretical and non-theoretical acts of being made the topic of doxic positing.[11] It cannot be named or nominalized. It cannot be said. It would seem then that it cannot be the topic of a phenomenology of the Husserlian kind, despite the indebtedness Levinas acknowledges to Husserl. This is the source of one of the difficulties Derrida warns us we shall find facing Levinas, difficulties of which Levinas himself warns us, for example in his title *Difficult Freedom*.[12]

What sort of discourse can this be which is somehow beyond the scope of logic, exterior to what Derrida calls the logical and phenomenological *clôture*? How can there be any saying where what is said is not said within the framework of a language as systematic as that of cause and effect? And would not the description of the structure of that language be a science or a *logos* of the appearing of meaning: a semiology, to employ Saussure's word, a phenomenology, to employ Husserl's? Although part of the subject matter of phenomenology is the essence of facthood or facticity, empirical and any other factuality is excluded by reduction. Yet Levinas, Derrida suggests, seems to want to combine phenomenology with empiricism. A comparison with Descartes is again relevant. The idea of infinity for Descartes is not adventitious. It is not based on a sensible impression. Nor is it something I make; it is not a fiction, not inventitious. It is innate. But the innateness Descartes attributes to this idea goes along with a sort of adventitiousness in that it comes to me from my Maker – and in so far as Descartes and Malebranche allow that the idea is made by Him, it is to that degree also a fiction. Levinas's account of my idea of the other draws upon Descartes's account of his idea of the infinite. Hence it is not surprising that on Levinas' account the idea of the other is also a hybrid, an unstable amalgam of the phenomenological and the empirical. It is somewhat as though Aristotle, having told us that there is no science of the singular, nevertheless proceeded to present one. Somewhat as though only, because according to Levinas, 'the neighbour concerns me with his exclusive singularity without appearing, not even as a *tode ti*. His extreme singularity is precisely his assignation: he assigns me before I designate him as *tode ti* ' (AEAE, p. 109; OBBE, p. 86). Levinas himself often says that by the standards of formal logic the instability and difficulty of his account would amount to contradiction.

As when 'the Lord spake unto Moses face to face' (Exod. 33: 11), and as when the Lord called Samuel and the latter replied, 'Speak, Master, for thy servant heareth', so does the Other command *me*, and I am ethically and religiously bound to answer, 'Here am I', 'Lo, here am I', '*me voici*', '*hineni*' (Exod. 3: 4, 1 Sam. 3: 4, 6, 8; cf. Gen. 22: 1, 7, 11). I am beholden. I am the One, as Levinas puts it, using the language of the first hypothesis of the *Parmenides*. I am (On) It, as children say when playing hide-and-seek. I am uniquely responsible (AEAE, pp. 124, 126; OBBE, pp. 159, 161). Levinas thinks that this empirical – or, as he would prefer to say, ethical – lopsidedness is in conflict with the symmetry Husserl ascribes to the relationship of the ego and the alter ego in the *Cartesian Meditations*. We have seen that Derrida questions whether there is a conflict here. Is not the so-called empirical dys-symmetry possible only because of the transcendental symmetry? Levinas seems to forget that the ego described in the *Cartesian Meditations* is the transcendental ego, the ego in general. But *qua* philosopher Levinas wants to say something about the essence of the face to face. Perhaps there is little that can be said about this, and what one succeeds in saying appears to leave out what is important. What is important in the discourse of the face to face either does not enter or slips through the net of the said, the *dit*. What is important is the *Dire*, the infinite calling which is never said. Whatever is said about it calls to be unsaid or, better, dis-said, *dédit*. What is significant in the discourse of the face to face is not what is semantically signified. It is not the meaning or the referent of a sign. Nor is it a sign. It is not and never was present and cannot be represented. To call it a trace is to give it not a name but a pro-name.

Maybe a trace of this pronominal trace can be picked up in the signature, and in the call sign a signaller transmits before his message begins. The call sign and the prefatory 'I say' which beckons the person with whom one wants to speak are no more part of the message than is the autograph with which the author signs himself off. Even so, call signs and signatures can be faked, and no single one of them is indubitably authentic. The same applies to them as applies to any pronoun.

The absolutely other [*Autre*] is the Other [*Autrui*]. He and I do not form a number. The collectivity in which I say 'you' or 'we' is not a plural of the 'I'. I, you – these are not individuals of a common concept. . . . Alterity is possible only starting from *me*. (TeI, pp. 9–10; TI, pp. 39–40. Cf. AEAE, p. 202; OBBE, p. 159)

That the most idiosyncratic of token reflexives is essentially imitable is something that has been maintained by philosophers as different as Hegel and Russell. 'I' and 'this' and 'you' and 'that', though they are not common names, are universal in their use. This is what Derrida demonstrates in his meditation on the various moments in *Otherwise than Being or Beyond Essence* when Levinas refers to what he is doing in that book 'at this very moment'.[13]

The Back of Beyond

In his very philosophizing about what is beyond being the author is responding to an ethical call in the face to face with his reader. His reader is therefore, ethically speaking, at that moment his *magister*, his teacher and master. One reader, Derrida, comments on the difficulty of philosophizing about what is otherwise than being and beyond essence. Levinas himself comments on this difficulty. Is it a difficulty that amounts to paradox or incoherence? There is nothing paradoxical or incoherent in the idea of philosophical discourse about, say, incoherence or the illogical. The metalanguage may be perfectly coherent and logical. However, Levinas's predicament is different. His philosophical discourse purports to be about all discourse. So there is a self-referentiality that Levinas compares with that of the arguments for scepticism regarding reason which depend on that very reason regarding which it is sceptical. Levinas's predicament is comparable too with Heidegger's embarrassment at having to assert propositions in order to distinguish the assertoric propounding of thoughts from monstrative saying. Heidegger needs to make this distinction in order to bring into the open the difference between the beingness of beings and the truth of being, in order, that is, to reveal that traditional metaphysics conceals the ontological difference. He sees that this difference is concealed again by its name and by his stating that his aim is to return metaphysics to fundamental ontology. Levinas states that his aim is to return so-called fundamental ontology to ethical metaphysics. It is to penetrate beyond the *logos*, beyond the propositional comprehension of metaphysical ontology, beyond the hermeneutic understanding of Heidegger's fundamental ontology, beyond maieutics, and beyond the coherent discourse of reason to the emphatic rationality of the teaching that makes possible the rationality of the said (Tel, p. 178; TI, p. 203). None the less, in seeking to achieve this aim

one must refer – I am convinced – to the medium of all comprehension and of all understanding in which all truth is reflected – precisely to Greek civilization, and to what it produced: to the logos, to the coherent discourse of reason.... One could not possibly ... arrest philosophical discourse without philosophizing.[14]

Levinas's discourse illustrates this. Whereas Heidegger, without denying that being is always being of a being, believes that there is need to remind ourselves of the priority of being, Levinas aims to show 'The philosophical priority of the existent (*étant*) over being' (Tel, p. 22; TI, p. 51). That surely means that Levinas's discourse is ontic, discourse about beings. It has at least that in common with traditional metaphysical discourse on the being of beings and, despite their declared intentions, with the essentialist ontology of Husserl and the existentialist ontology of Sartre.

However, Levinas's metaphysics is ethical. The ethical would be a mode or region of the ontic as Heidegger uses this term, other modes being the psychological, the biological and so on. But the ethical in Levinas's sense is not even remotely comparable with any natural or human science. And it is 'more original' than fundamental ontology. Yet because the ethical 'dimension' in which man ceases to be the measure of all things is a dimension of a being, albeit a dimension in which that being transcends himself, one cannot help thinking of this as an ontological mode, as, in a phrase to which Levinas often has recourse, a way (*manière*) of being, a *Seinsweise*, to use Heidegger's word. Hence, notwithstanding Levinas's declared intention to convince his reader that 'to exist has meaning in another dimension than that of the perduration of the totality; it can go beyond being' (Tel, p. 278; TI, p. 301), his rhetoric employs statements like 'Being is exteriority' (TeI, p. 266; TI, p. 290). That is, not only does Levinas, as Derrida observes, appear to confirm Heidegger's assertion that one tends to forget the ontological difference, it appears to confirm Heidegger's assertion that language is the house of being. Levinas does not wait for Derrida to tell him that the discourse of the face to face is inscribed within what they both call, following Bataille, the 'general economy' of being.

Of the many other examples of statements one could cite that, like 'Being is exteriority', show that Levinas assumes a fore-understanding of being, here is but one:

A relation whose terms do not form a totality can hence be produced within the general economy of being only as proceeding from the I to the other, as a *face to face*, as delineating a distance in depth – that of conversation (*discours*), of goodness, of Desire – irreducible to the distance the synthetic activity of the understanding establishes between the diverse terms, other with respect to one another, that lend themselves to its synoptic operation. (TeI, p. 9; TI, p. 39)[15]

This is not a Levinasian version of what among English-speaking philosophers is known as the question whether 'ought' can be derived from 'is'. It is a denial that the *being* of alterity can be comprehended. So it is a further contribution toward the destruction of the epistemological and perceptual tradition of metaphysics to which those Greek-speaking philosophers, Parmenides, Plato, Aristotle, Descartes, Kant, Hegel and Husserl, all belong, according to Martin Heidegger. What the philosopher Emmanuel Levinas says seems unable to make the step beyond being and beyond Heidegger announced in the title of the book *Otherwise than Being or Beyond Essence* and previously in a title of a section near the end of *Totality and Infinity*. If the words just cited from the first section of *Totality and Infinity* can be taken at their face value, how can these titles be taken at theirs? If Levinas, as his essay 'Is Ontology Fundamental?' makes clear, is unhappy with the ontology of *Being and Time*, how can this enable him to get outside the thinking of being to which Heidegger himself moved when he became dissatisfied with his earlier programme and put more stress on the thinking of *Ab-grund* and anarchy? True, Levinas stresses a different, ethical, kind of anarchy. But how does this anarchy escape being an anarchy in being rather than exterior to it, *epekeina tēs ousias*, or how does this exteriority escape being an exteriority interior to being? Levinas's response to these questions lies in his statement that the relation of the face to face is not only dreamed of by philosophers because, forgetful of Being, they have cut off 'objective thought' from its deep roots. This relation is accomplished in the welcome of the Other, where, absolutely present, in his face, the Other – without any metaphor – faces me. (DEHH, p. 186)

This response leads Derrida to ask whether it is not the indulgence of the 'etymological empiricism' that he calls, with studied irony, the hidden root of all empiricism (ED, p. 204; WD, p. 139). Exteriority, space, respiration, inspiration: these are all well-worn metaphors for being. Levinas uses them as metaphors for alterity. He uses them also, we have seen, as metaphors for and of being. And they are ontic metaphors which are liable to prevent philosophers remembering the ontological difference, including, Derrida suspects, the philosopher who would have us remember the naked face of the Other.

If to understand Being is to be able to let be (that is, to respect Being in essence and existence, and to be responsible for one's respect), then the understanding of Being always concerns alterity, and par excellence the alterity of the Other in all its originality: one can have to let be only that which one is not. (ED, p. 207; WD, p. 141)

Levinas would reply that respect for radical alterity is accorded only when it is acknowledged that I am ethically responsible to the Other. But could it not be said that this acknowledgment is implicit in Heidegger's inclusion of conscience in his table of existentials? Implicit, because although the voice of conscience in *Being and Time* is the call to responsibility for being, that responsibility is nothing outside the responsibility for existents. Indeed, Derrida remarks, it is precisely because being is nothing outside the existent that being cannot be articulated in language without the resource of ontic metaphor (ED, p. 203; WD, p. 138).

What do we find when we turn from the remarks Derrida makes about Levinas in 'Violence and Metaphysics' to the remarks Levinas makes about Derrida in 'Tout autrement'? There Levinas writes:

What stays constructed after de-construction is surely the severe architecture of the discourse which deconstructs and which employs in predicative propositions the present tense of the verb 'to be'. Discourse in the course of which, at the very moment when it is shaking the foundations of truth, in face of the evidence of a lived present which appears to offer a last refuge to presence, Derrida still has the strength to say 'Is that certain?', as if anything could be certain at that moment, and as if certainty and uncertainty should still matter.

Levinas, Derrida and Others vis-à-vis

It would be tempting to appeal to this use of logocentric language against that very language as an objection to the resulting de-construction. An approach often made in the refutation of scepticism which, nevertheless, having been knocked down and trampled underfoot, gets up again to become once more the legitimate child of philosophy. An approach which perhaps Derrida himself has not always disdained to follow in his polemics.

But in following this approach there is a risk of failing to recognize the signification effected by the very inconsistency of this procedure; of failing to recognize the incompressible non-simultaneity of the Said and the Saying, the dislocation of their correlation: a minimal dislocation, but wide enough for the words of the sceptic to pass through without being strangled by the contradiction between what is signified by what is *said* in them and what is signified by the very fact of uttering something *said*. As if the two significations lacked the simultaneity needed for contradiction to be able to break the knot in which they are tied. As if the correlation of the *Saying* and the *Said* were a dia-chrony of what cannot be united; as if the situation of the *Saying* were already a 'memory of retention' for the *Said*, but without the *lapsed* moments of Saying allowing themselves to be retrieved in this memory.[16]

Otherwise said: Derrida has a keen ear for the diachrony of the said. He locates that diachrony in the dead time of writing with which the living present of the spoken word is engraved. But beyond this diachrony and/or supplementary to it is a radical diachrony that Derrida runs the risk of failing to recognize: a diachrony that is due to the paradoxical tie between the said and the fact of someone's saying something. The paradoxicality is the recalcitrance of the uttering to formulation as a proposition that is said. It is because the saying and the said are in this way 'refractory to the category' that it and the said are *inassemblable*; they are so incomparable that they resist every attempt to bring them together. They resist *Ereignis*. They resist even the limit case of togetherness of logical contradiction. Statements that contradict each other logically are *mutually* contradictory. They are contradictory only because they are posited together in the same time. The contradiction can sometimes be resolved by asserting them at different times. But the saying and the said are neither at the same time nor at different times. They are *in* different times. So the saying cannot be retrieved in the said. And this says something about beyondness and the retrieval of hermeneutic circularity.

The hermeneutic circle is, we are told, the ontological condition of understanding. More precisely, it is the priority of the existential over the apophantic, the recalcitrance of the existential to the category. Assuming that saying is existential and the said categorial, Heidegger,

153

Gadamer and Levinas will be in agreement that the categorial cannot retrieve the existential without a residual existential trace, and they will be in agreement with Merleau-Ponty's judgment that the lesson that the reduction teaches us is the impossibility of a complete reduction. But the Heideggerian existentials are ontological conditions of understanding, whereas saying, Levinas wants to say, is somehow beyond ontology and beyond understanding. Further, the Heideggerian existentials are constitutive of temporality, and although this is not to be confused with the time of the categorized objects and states of affairs about which we assert propositions, the latter is in the former, which is somehow prior. Admittedly, there remains the difficulty of giving an account of this inclusive priority, the difficulty with which Heidegger is occupied in his extrapolation of Kant's doctrine of schematism. This difficulty has not been resolved. It is not resolved by Heidegger, nor has it been resolved in the deconstruction of Heidegger's doctrines undertaken by Derrida and Levinas. Indicative of this difficulty is Levinas's need to have it both ways: to affirm the radical alterity of the time of the other's saying while granting that irretrievable moments of saying are none the less, as it were, immemorial memories retained in the same memory with the said. Metaphorically speaking, so to speak.

The difficulty is the difficulty with metaphor. If, as Derrida says, all metaphors are ontic, they will present a difficulty for anyone, like Heidegger, trying to get beyond ontic metaphysics to fundamental ontology, and for anyone, like Levinas, trying to get beyond ontology to ethical metaphysics. 'The extraordinary word *beyond*' transmits an ontic metaphor (AEAE, p. 16; OBBE, p. 19). No wonder Levinas rings the changes on *au-delà*, 'on the thither side', and *en-deça*, 'on the hither side'. Totality *is* Infinity if we erase this verb 'to be' or raise it, not by *Aufhebung*, but by *emphasis*. When Derrida and Levinas have begun deconstructing the ontic metaphors of priority and transgression we can expect to have difficulty deciding what or who is prior to what or whom. The apparently secure notion of logical priority will begin to quake, and we may consequently fail to find our feet with Levinas when he says, 'The neighbour concerns me outside every *a priori* – but perhaps *prior to every a priori*' (AEAE, p. 109 n20; OBBE, p. 192 n20). When faced with the question whether ontology is beyond metaphysics or metaphysics is beyond being, we may be at a loss for words.[17]

Abbreviations

ED   J. Derrida, *L'Écriture et la différence*, Paris, Seuil, 1967.
WD   J. Derrida, *Writing and Difference*, translated by Alan Bass, London, Routledge & Kegan Paul, 1978.

Notes

1 Edmund Husserl, *Ideen zu einer reinen Phänomenologie und phänomenologischen Philosophie*, I, *Husserliana* 3, edited by Walter Biemel, The Hague, Martinus Nijhoff, 1950; *Ideas*, translated by W. R. Boyce Gibson, London, George Allen and Unwin, 1931, section 117.
2 Martial Gueroult, *Descartes selon l'ordre des raisons*, Paris, Aubier, 1953, I, p. 229.
3 Gueroult, *Descartes*, p. 224.
4 The translation erroneously has 'with'.
5 Jean-Paul Sartre, *L'Être et le néant*, Paris, Gallimard, 1943, pp. 125–6, 135–6; *Being and Nothingness*, translated by Hazel Barnes, London, Methuen, 1969, pp. 83, 92.
6 Ibid., pp. 24f, 31–2; pp. xxxivf, xl–xli.
7 DEE, p. 26; EE, p. 21. See also EI, pp. 45f.
8 Sartre, *L'Être*, pp. 315–8; *Being*, pp. 257–60.
9 DVI, p. 239.
10 Husserl, *Ideas*, section 24. Jacques Derrida, *La Voix et le phénomène*, Paris, Presses Universitaires de France, 1967; *Speech and Phenomena*, translated by David B. Allison, Evanston, Ill., Northwestern University Press, 1973.
11 Husserl, *Ideas*, section 117.
12 Emmanuel Levinas, *Difficile liberté: essais sur le Judaïsme*, Paris, Albin Michel, 1976 (third, corrected, edition).
13 Jacques Derrida, 'En ce moment même dans cet ouvrage me voici', in *Textes pour Emmanuel Levinas*, edited by François Laruelle, Paris, Jean-Michel Place, 1980.
14 Levinas, *Difficile liberté*, pp. 77, 230. Cited at ED, p. 226; WD, p. 152.
15 Other examples are cited at ED, p. 208; WD, p. 141.
16 Emmanuel Levinas, 'Tout autrement', in NP, pp. 85–6, and *L'Arc: Jacques Derrida*, 54, 1973, p. 35.
17 This chapter is a modified version of ch. 10 of John Llewelyn, *Beyond Metaphysics? The Hermeneutic Circle in Contemporary Continental Philosophy*, New Jersey, Humanities Press; London, Macmillan, 1985, and has been adapted for republication with the kind permission of Humanities Press.

· *10* ·

Useless Suffering

EMMANUEL LEVINAS

translated by Richard Cohen

Phenomenology

Suffering is surely a *given* in consciousness, a certain 'psychological content', like the lived experience of colour, of sound, of contact, or like any sensation. But in this 'content' itself, it is in-spite-of-consciousness, unassumable. It is unassumable and 'unassumability'. 'Unassumability' does not result from the excessive intensity of a sensation, from some sort of quantitative 'too much', surpassing the measure of our sensibility and our means of grasping and holding. It results from an excess, a 'too much' which is inscribed in a sensorial content, penetrating as suffering the dimensions of meaning which seem to be opened and grafted on to it. For the Kantian 'I think' – which is capable of reuniting and embracing the most heterogeneous and disparate givens into order and meaning under its *a priori* forms – it is as if suffering were not only a *given* refractory to synthesis, but the *way* in which the refusal opposed to the assembling of givens into a meaningful whole is opposed to it: suffering is at once what disturbs order and this disturbance itself. It is not only the consciousness of rejection or a symptom of rejection, but this rejection itself: a backwards consciousness, 'operating' not as 'grasp' but as revulsion. It is a modality, or the categorial ambiguity of quality and modality. Taken as an 'experienced' content, the denial and refusal of meaning which is imposed as a sensible quality is the *way* in which the unbearable is precisely not borne by consciousness, the way this not-being-borne is, paradoxically, itself a sensation or a given. This is a quasi-contradictory structure, but a contradiction which is not formal like that of the dialectical tension between the affirmative and the negative which arises for the intellect; it is a contradiction by way of sensation: the plaintiveness of pain, hurt [*mal*].[1]

Suffering, in its hurt and its in-spite-of-consciousness, is passivity. Here, 'taking cognizance' is no longer, properly speaking, a taking; it is no longer *the performance of an act of consciousness*, but, in its adversity, a submission; and even a submission to the submitting, since the 'content' of which the aching consciousness is conscious is precisely this very adversity of suffering, its hurt. But, here again, this *passivity* – in the sense of a modality – signifies as a *quiddity*, and perhaps as the place where passivity signifies originally, independent of its conceptual opposition to activity. The latter is an abstraction made from its psycho-physical and psycho-physiological conditions; in its pure phenomenology, the passivity of suffering is in no way the reverse side of activity, as an effect would still be correlative to its cause, or as a sensorial receptivity would be correlative to the 'Obstance' of the object which affects and impresses it. The passivity of suffering is more profoundly passive than the receptivity of our senses, which is already the activity of welcome, and straight away becomes perception. In suffering sensibility is a vulnerability, more passive than receptivity; it is an ordeal more passive than experience. It is precisely an evil. It is not, to tell the truth, through passivity that evil is described, but through evil that suffering is understood. Suffering is a pure undergoing. It is not a matter of a passivity which would degrade man by striking a blow against his freedom. Pain would limit such freedom to the point of compromising self-consciousness, permitting man the identity of a thing only in the passivity of the submission. The evil which rends the humanity of the suffering person, overwhelms his humanity otherwise than non-freedom overwhelms it: violently and cruelly, more irremissibly than the negation which dominates or paralyzes the act in non-freedom. What counts in the non-freedom or the undergoing of suffering is the concreteness of the *not* looming as a hurt more negative than any apophantic *not*. This negativity of evil is, probably, the source or kernel of all apophantic negation. The *not* of evil is negative right up to non-sense. All evil refers to suffering. It is the *impasse* of life and being, their absurdity, where pain does not come, somehow innocently, 'to colour' consciousness with affectivity. The evil of pain, the harm itself, is the explosion and most profound articulation of absurdity.

Thus the least one can say about suffering is that in its own phenomenality, intrinsically, it is useless, 'for nothing'. Doubtlessly this basic sense-lessness that the analysis seems to suggest is confirmed by empirical situations of pain, where pain somehow remains undiluted and isolates itself in consciousness, or absorbs the rest of consciousness. It would suffice, for example, to extract from the medical journals certain cases of persistent or obstinate pain, the neuralgias and the intolerable lumbagos resulting from lesions of the peripheral nerves, and the tortures which are experienced by certain patients stricken with malignant tumours.[2] Pain can become the central phenomenon of the diseased state. These are the 'pain-illnesses' where the integration of other psychological states does not bring any relief but where, on the contrary, anxiety and distress add to the cruelty of the hurt. But one can go further – and doubtless thus arrive at the essential facts of pure pain – by evoking the 'pain-illnesses' of beings who are psychically deprived, backward, handicapped, in their relational life and in their relationships to the Other, relationships where suffering, without losing anything of its savage malignancy, no longer covers up the totality of the mental and comes across novel lights within new horizons. These horizons none the less remain closed to the mentally deficient, except that in their 'pure pain' they are projected into them to expose them *to me*, raising the fundamental ethical problem which pain poses 'for nothing': the inevitable and preemptory ethical problem of the medication which is my duty. Is not the evil of suffering – extreme passivity, impotence, abandonment and solitude – also the unassumable and thus the possibility of a half opening, and, more precisely, the possibility that wherever a moan, a cry, a groan or a sigh happen there is the original call for aid, for curative help, for help from the other[3] ego whose alterity, whose exteriority promises salvation? It is the original opening toward what is helpful, where the primordial, irreducible, and ethical, anthropological category of the medical comes to impose itself – across a demand for analgesia, more pressing, more urgent in the groan than a demand for consolation or a postponement of death. For pure suffering, which is intrinsically meaningless and condemned to itself without exit, a beyond takes shape in the inter-human.[4] It is starting from such situations – we say in passing – that medicine as technique, and consequently the general technology it presupposes, the technology so easily exposed to the attacks of 'right-thinking' rigour, does not merely originate in the so-called 'will to power'. This bad will is perhaps only the price which must sometimes be paid by the elevated thought of a civilization called to nourish persons and to lighten their sufferings. This elevated thought is the honour of a still uncertain and blinking modernity coming at the end of a century of nameless sufferings, but in which the suffering of suffering, the suffering for the useless suffering of the other person, the just suffering in me for the unjustifiable suffering of the Other, opens upon suffering the ethical perspective of the inter-human. In this perspective a radical difference develops between *suffering in the Other*, which for *me* is unpardonable and solicits me and calls me, and suffering *in me*,[5] my own adventure of suffering, whose constitutional or congenital uselessness can take on a meaning, the only meaning to which suffering is susceptible, in becoming a suffering for the suffering – be it inexorable – of someone else. It is this attention to the Other which, across the cruelties of our century – despite these cruelties, because of these cruelties – can be affirmed as the very bond of human subjectivity, even to the point of being raised to a supreme ethical principle – the only one which it is not possible to contest – a principle which can go so far as to command the hopes and practical discipline of vast human groups. This attention and this action are so imperiously and directly incumbent on people – on their selves – that it makes waiting for the saving actions of an all-powerful God impossible without degradation. To be sure, consciousness of this inescapable obligation makes the idea of God more difficult, but it also makes it spiritually closer than confidence in any kind of theodicy.

Theodicy

In the ambiguity of suffering which the above phenomenological essay brings out, its modality also shows the content or sensation that consciousness 'supports'. This adversity-to-all-harmony, as quiddity, enters into conjunction with other 'contents' which it disturbs, to be sure, but where it is given reasons or produces a reason. Already within an isolated consciousness, the pain of suffering can take on the meaning of a pain which merits and hopes for reward, and so lose, it seems, in diverse ways, its modality of uselessness. Is it not meaningful as a means with an end in view, when it tallies with the effort which leads to a work or in the fatigue which results from it? One can discover in it a biological finality: the role of an alarm signal manifesting itself for the preservation of life against the cunning dangers which menace life in illness. 'He that increaseth knowledge increaseth sorrow', says Ecclesiastes (1:18), where suffering appears at the very least as the price of reason and of spiritual refinement. It would also temper the individual's character. It would be necessary to the teleology of community life, where social unrest awakens a useful attention to the health of the collective body. The social utility of suffering is necessary to the pedagogic function of Power in education, discipline and repression. Is not fear of punishment the beginning of wisdom? Is it not believed that sufferings, submitted to as sanctions, regenerate the enemies of society and man? This political teleology is founded, to be sure, on the value of existence, on the perseverance of society and the individual in being, on their successful health as the supreme and ultimate end.

But the unpleasant and gratuitous non-sense of pain already pierces beneath the reasonable forms which the social 'uses' of suffering assume. These, in any case, do not make the torture which strikes the psychically handicapped and isolates them in their pain any less scandalous. But behind the rational administration of pain in sanctions distributed by human courts, immediately dressing up dubious appearances of repression, the arbitrary and strange failure of justice amidst wars, crimes and the oppression of the weak by the strong, rejoins, in a sort of fatality, the useless sufferings which spring from natural plagues as if effects of an ontological perversion. Beyond the fundamental malignity of suffering itself, revealed in its phenomenology, does not human experience in history attest to a malice and a bad will?

Western humanity has none the less sought for the meaning of this scandal by invoking the proper sense of a metaphysical order, an ethics, which is invisible in the immediate lessons of moral consciousness. This is a kingdom of transcendent ends, willed by a benevolent wisdom, by the absolute goodness of a God who is in some way defined by this super-natural goodness; or a widespread, invisible goodness in Nature and History, where it would command the paths which are, to be sure, painful, but which lead to the Good. Pain is henceforth meaningful, subordinated in one way or another to the metaphysical finality envisaged by faith or by a belief in progress. These beliefs are presupposed by theodicy! Such is the grand idea necessary to the inner peace of souls in our distressed world. It is called upon to make sufferings here below comprehensible. These will make sense by reference to an original fault or to the congenital finitude of human being. The evil which fills the earth would be explained in a 'plan of the whole'; it would be called upon to atone for a sin, or it would announce, to the ontologically limited consciousness, compensation or recompense at the end of time. These supra-sensible perspectives are invoked in order to envisage in a suffering which is essentially gratuitous and absurd, and apparently arbitrary, a signification and an order.

Certainly one may ask if theodicy, in the broad and narrow senses of the term, effectively succeeds in making God innocent, or in saving morality in the name of faith, or in making suffering – and this is the true intention of the thought which has recourse to theodicy – bearable. By under-estimating its temptation one could, in any case, misunderstand the profundity of the empire which theodicy exerts over humankind, and the *epoch-making* character – or the *historical* character, as one says today – of its entry into thought. It has been, at least up to the trials of the twentieth century, a component of the self-consciousness of European humanity. It persisted in watered-down form at the core of atheist progressivism, which was confident, none the less, in the efficacy of the Good which is immanent to being, called to visible triumph by the simple play of the natural and historical laws of injustice, war, misery and illness. As providential, Nature and History furnished the eighteenth and nineteenth centuries with the norms of moral consciousness. They are associated with many essentials of the deism of the age of Enlightenment. But theodicy – ignoring the name that Leibniz gave to it in 1710 – is as old as a certain reading of the Bible. It dominated the consciousness of the believer who explained his misfortunes by reference to the Sin, or at least by reference to his sins. In addition to the Christians' well-established reference to Original Sin, this theodicy is in a certain sense implicit in the Old Testament, where the drama of the Diaspora reflects the sins of Israel. The wicked conduct of ancestors, still non-expiated by the sufferings of exile, would explain to the exiles themselves the duration and the harshness of this exile.

The End of Theodicy

Perhaps the most revolutionary fact of our twentieth-century consciousness – but it is also an event in Sacred History – is that of the destruction of all balance between the explicit and implicit theodicy of Western thought and the forms which suffering and its evil take in the very unfolding of this century. This is the century that in thirty years has known two world wars, the totalitarianisms of right and left, Hitlerism and Stalinism, Hiroshima, the Gulag, and the genocides of Auschwitz and Cambodia. This is the century which is drawing to a close in the haunting memory of the return of everything signified by these barbaric names: suffering and evil are deliberately imposed, yet no reason sets limits to the exasperation of a reason become political and detached from all ethics.

Among these events the Holocaust of the Jewish people under the reign of Hitler seems to us the paradigm of gratuitous human suffering, where evil appears in its diabolical horror. This is perhaps not a subjective feeling. The disproportion between suffering and every theodicy was shown at Auschwitz with a glaring, obvious clarity. Its possibility puts into question the multi-millenial traditional faith. Did not the word of Nietzsche on the death of God take on, in the extermination camps, the signification of a quasi-empirical fact? Is it necessary to be surprised, then, that this drama of Sacred History has had among its principal actors a people which, since forever, has been associated with this history, whose collective soul and destiny would be wrongly understood as limited to any sort of nationalism, and whose *gesture*, in certain circumstances, still belongs to Revelation – be it as apocalypse – which 'provokes thought' from philosophers or which impedes them from thinking?[6]

Here I wish to evoke the analysis which the Canadian Jew, the philosopher Emil Fackenheim, of Toronto, has made of this catastrophe of the human and the divine, in his work, and notably in his book *God's Presence in History*:

The Nazi Genocide of the Jewish people has no precedent within Jewish history. Nor . . . will one find a precedent outside Jewish history. . . . Even actual cases of genocide, however, still differ from the Nazi holocaust in at least two respects. Whole peoples have been killed for 'rational' (however horrifying) ends such as power, territory, wealth. . . . The Nazi murder . . . was annihilation for the sake of annihilation, murder for the sake of murder, evil for the sake of evil. Still more incontestably unique than the crime itself is the situation of the victims. The Albigensians died for their faith, believing unto death that God needs martyrs. Negro Christians have been murdered for their race, able to find comfort in a faith not at issue. The more than one million Jewish children murdered in the Nazi holocaust died neither because of their faith, nor despite their faith, nor for reasons unrelated to the Jewish faith [but] because of the Jewish faith of their great-grandparents [who brought] up Jewish children.[7]

The inhabitants of the Eastern European Jewish communities constituted the majority of the six million tortured and massacred; they represented the human beings least corrupted by the ambiguities of our world, and the million infants killed had the innocence of infants. Theirs is the death of martyrs, a death given in the torturers' unceasing destruction of the dignity which belongs to martyrs. The final act of this destruction is accomplished today in the posthumous denial of the very fact of martyrdom by the would-be 'revisers of history'. This would be pain in its undiluted malignity, suffering for nothing. It renders impossible and odious every proposal and every thought which would explain it by the sins of those who have suffered or are dead. But does not this end of theodicy, which obtrudes itself in the face of this century's inordinate distress, at the same time in a more general way reveal the unjustifiable character of suffering in the other person, the scandal which would occur by my justifying my neighbour's suffering? So that the very phenomenon of suffering in its uselessness is, in principle the pain of the Other. For an ethical sensibility – confirming itself, in the inhumanity of our time, against this inhumanity – the justification of the neighbour's pain is certainly the source of all immorality. Accusing oneself in suffering is undoubtedly the very turning back of the ego to itself. It is perhaps thus; and the for-the-other – the most upright relation to the Other – is the most profound adventure of subjectivity, its ultimate intimacy. But this intimacy can only be discreet. It could not be given as an example, or be narrated as an edifying discourse. It could not be made a predication without being perverted.

The philosophical problem, then, which is posed by the useless pain which appears in its fundamental malignancy across the events of the twentieth century, concerns the meaning that religiosity and the human morality of goodness can still retain after the end of theodicy. According to the philosopher we have just quoted, Auschwitz would paradoxically entail a revelation of the very God who nevertheless was silent at Auschwitz: a commandment of faithfulness. To renounce after Auschwitz this God absent from Auschwitz – no longer to assure the continuation of Israel – would amount to finishing the criminal enterprise of National-Socialism, which aimed at the annihilation of Israel and the forgetting of the ethical message of the Bible, which Judaism bears, and whose multi-millennial history is concretely prolonged by Israel's existence as a people. For if God was absent in the extermination camps, the devil was very obviously present in them.

From whence, for Emil Fackenheim comes the obligation for Jews to live and to remain Jews, in order not to be made accomplices of a diabolical project. The Jew, after Auschwitz, is pledged to his faithfulness to Judaism and to the material and even political conditions of its existence.

This final reflection of the Toronto philosopher, formulated in terms which render it relative to the destiny of the Jewish people, can be given a universal signification. From Sarajevo to Cambodia humanity has witnessed a host of cruelties in the course of a century when Europe, in its 'human sciences', seemed to reach the end of its subject, the humanity which, during all these horrors, breathed – already or still – the fumes of the crematory ovens of the 'final solution' where theodicy abruptly appeared impossible. Is humanity, in its indifference, going to abandon the world to useless suffering, leaving it to the political fatality – or the drifting – of the blind forces which inflict misfortune on the weak and conquered, and which spare the conquerors, whom the wicked must join? Or, incapable of adhering to an order – or to a disorder – which it continues to think diabolic, must not humanity now, in a faith more difficult than ever, in a faith without theodicy, continue Sacred History; a history which now demands even more of the resources of the *self* in each one, and appeals to its suffering inspired by the suffering of the other person, to its compassion which is a non-useless suffering (or love), which is no longer suffering 'for nothing', and which straightaway has a meaning? At the end of the twentieth century and after the useless and unjustifiable pain which is exposed and displayed therein without any shadow of a consoling theodicy, are we not all pledged – like the Jewish people to their faithfulness – to the second term of this alternative?[8] This is a new modality in the faith of today, and also in our moral certainties, a modality quite essential to the modernity which is dawning.

The Inter-human Order

To envisage suffering, as I have just attempted to do, in the inter-human perspective – that is, as meaningful in me, useless in the Other – does not consist in adopting a relative point of view on it, but in restoring it to the dimensions of meaning outside of which the immanent and savage concreteness of evil in a consciousness is but an abstraction. To think suffering in an inter-human perspective does not amount to seeing it in the coexistence of a multiplicity of consciousnesses, or in a social determinism, accompanied by the simple knowledge that people in society can have of their neighbourliness or of their common destiny. The inter-human perspective can subsist, but can also be lost, in the political order of the City where the Law establishes mutual obligations between citizens. Properly speaking, the inter-human lies in a non-indifference of one to another, in a responsibility of one for another. The inter-human is prior to the reciprocity of this responsibility, which inscribes itself in impersonal laws, and becomes superimposed on the pure altruism of this responsibility inscribed in the ethical position of the self as self. It is prior to every contact which would signify precisely the moment of reciprocity where it can, to be sure, continue, but where it can also attenuate or extinguish altruism and disinterestedness. The order of politics – post-ethical or pre-ethical – which inaugurates the 'social contract' is neither the sufficient condition nor the necessary outcome of ethics. In its ethical position, the self is distinct from the citizen born of the City, and from the individual who precedes all order in his natural egoism, from whom political philosophy, since Hobbes, tries to derive – or succeeds in deriving – the social or political order of the City.

The inter-human lies also in the recourse that people have to one another for help, before the marvellous alterity of the Other has been banalized or dimmed in a simple exchange of courtesies which become established as an 'inter-personal commerce' of customs. We have spoken of this in the first paragraph of this study. These are expressions of a properly ethical meaning, distinct from those which the *self* and *other* acquire in what one calls the state of Nature or civil society. It is in the inter-human perspective of *my* responsibility for the other person, without concern for reciprocity, in my call to help him gratuitously, in the asymmetry of the relation of *one* to the *other*, that we have tried to analyze the phenomenon of useless suffering.

'La Souffrance inutile' first appeared in *Giornale di Metafisica* 4 (1982), 13–26, and was reprinted in *Les Cahiers de la Nuit Surveillé, Numéro 3; Emmanuel Levinas,* edited by Jacques Rolland, Paris, Editions Verdief, pp. 329–38. It is translated here with the permission of the author.

Notes

1 The French term '*mal*' means both 'hurt' and 'evil', and both words have been used to translate it.

2 See the article by Dr Escoffier-Lambiotte in *Le Monde*, 4 April 1981, entitled 'Le premier centre français de traitement de la douleur a été inauguré à l'hôpital Cochin' ['The First French Center for the Treatment of Pain has been Opened at the Cochin Hospital'].

3 With regard to this point we refer to Philippe Nemo's fine book, *Job et l'excess du Mal* [*Job and the Excess of Evil*] (Paris, Grasset, 1977): the very resistance of suffering to synthesis and order is interpreted as the rupture of pure immanence where, essentially, the psychism is enclosed, and as the event of transcendence, and even as an interpellation of God. Cf., also, our analysis of this book, 'Transcendance et mal' ['Transcendence and Evil'], reprinted in *De Dieu qui vient à l'idée*, Paris, J. Vrin, 1982, pp. 189–207.

4 There is a talmudic dialogue or apologue (tractate Berakhot of the *Babylonian Talmud*, 5b) which reflects the conception of the radical hurt of suffering, its intrinsic and uncompensated despair, its confinement and its recourse to the other person, to medication *exterior* to the immanent structure of hurt.

Rav Hiya bar Abba falls ill and Rav Yohanan comes to visit him. He asks him: 'Are your sufferings fitted to you?' 'Neither them nor the compensations they promise.' 'Give me your hand', the visitor of the ill man then says. And the visitor lifts the ill man from his couch. But then Rav Yohanan himself falls ill and is visited by Rav Hanina. Same question: 'Are your sufferings fitted to you?' Same response: 'Neither them nor the compensations they promise.' 'Give me your hand', says Rav Hanina, and he lifts Rav Yohanan from his couch. Question: Could not Rav Yohanan lift himself by himself? Answer: The prisoner could not break free from his confinement by himself.

5 This suffering *in me* would be so radically mine that it could not become subject to a predication. It is as suffering *in me* and not as suffering in general, that *welcome* suffering, attested in the spiritual tradition of humanity, can signify a true idea: the expiatory suffering of the just suffering for others, the suffering that illuminates, the suffering that is sought after by Dostoevsky's characters. I think also of the Jewish religious tradition which is familiar to me, of the 'I am love-sick' of the *Song of Songs*, of the suffering about which certain talmudic texts speak and which they name 'Yessourine shel Ahava', sufferings through love, which is joined to the theme of expiation for others. This suffering is often described at the limit of 'its usefulness'. Cf. note 3, where, in the test of the just, suffering is also what 'does not fit me' – 'Neither it, nor the "recompense" attached to it'.

6 Maurice Blanchot, who is known for his lucid and critical attention to literature and events, notes somewhere: 'How philosophize, how write in the memory of Auschwitz, of those who have said to us sometimes in notes buried near the crematories: "Know what has happened", "do not forget", and, at the same time, "You will never know"?' I think that all the dead of the Gulag and all the other places of torture in our political century are present when one speaks of Auschwitz. [Blanchot's words appear in his article 'Our Clandestine Companion', translated by David Allison, in *Face to Face with Levinas*, edited by Richard Cohen, Albany, State University of New York Press, 1986, p. 50: translator's addition.]

7 Emil Fackenheim, *God's Presence in History: Jewish Affirmations and Philosophical Reflections after Auschwitz*, New York, New York University Press, 1970, pp. 69–70. This work has been translated into French by M. Delmotte and B. Dupuy (Lagrasse, Veridier, 1980.): translator's note.

8 We said above that theodicy in the broad sense of the term is justified by a certain reading of the Bible. It is evident that another reading of it is possible, and that in a certain sense nothing of the spiritual experience of human history is foreign to the Scriptures. We are thinking here in particular of the book of Job which attests at once to Job's faithfulness to God (2:10) and to ethics (27:5 and 6), despite his sufferings without reason, and his opposition to the theodicy of his friends. He refuses theodicy right to the end and, in the last chapters of the text (42:7), is preferred to those who, hurrying to the safety of Heaven, would make God innocent before the suffering of the just. It is a little like the reading Kant makes of this book in his quite extraordinary short treatise of 1791, *Uber das Misslingen aller philosophischen Versuche in der Theodicee* ['On the Failure of all the Philosophical Attempts at a Theodicy'], where he demonstrates the theoretical weakness of the arguments in favour of theodicy. Here is the conclusion of his way of interpreting what 'this ancient book expresses allegorically': 'In this state of mind Job has proven that he did not found his morality on faith, but his faith on morality; in which case faith, however weak it may be, is nonetheless one of a pure and authentic kind, a kind which does not found a religion of solicited favours, but a well conducted life ('*welche eine Religion nicht der Gunstbewerbung, sondern des guten Lebenswandels grundet*').

· 11 ·

The Paradox of Morality: an Interview with Emmanuel Levinas

TAMRA WRIGHT, PETER HUGHES, ALISON AINLEY

translated by Andrew Benjamin and Tamra Wright

The interview which follows took place at Levinas's home in the summer of 1986, when Alison Ainley, Peter Hughes and Tamra Wright, graduate students at the University of Warwick, went to Paris to discuss with Levinas several questions which had arisen at weekly seminars on *Totality and Infinity* during the course of the preceding academic year. The questions were sent to Levinas before the interview, with the result that his responses frequently refer to more than one question at a time.

Is the face a simple or a complex phenomenon? Would it be correct to define it as that aspect of a human being which escapes all efforts at comprehension and totalization, or are there other characteristics of this phenomenon which must be included in any definition or description of the face?
The face is a fundamental event. Among the many modes of approach and diverse ways of relating to being, the action of the face is special and, for this reason it is very difficult to give it an exact phenomenological description. The phenomenology of the face is very often negative.

What seems essential to me is, for example, the manner in which Heidegger understood the *zeug* – that which comes to hand, the instrument, the thing. He understood it as irreducible proto-type. The face is similar in that it is not at all a representation, it is not a given of knowledge, nor is it a thing which comes to hand. It is an irreducible means of access, and it is in ethical terms that it can be spoken of. I have said that in my analysis of the face it is a demand; a demand, not a question. The face is a hand in search of recompense, an open hand. That is, it needs something. It is going to ask you for something. I don't know whether one can say that it is complex or simple. It is, in any case, a new way of speaking of the face.

When I said that the face is authority, that there is authority in the face, this may undoubtedly seem contradictory: it is a request and it is an authority. You have a question later on in which you ask me how it could be that if there is a commandment in the face, one can do the opposite of what the face demands. The face is not a force. It is an authority. Authority is often without force. Your question seems to be based on the idea that God commands and demands. He is extremely powerful. If you try not doing what he tells you, he will punish you. That is a very recent notion. On the contary, the first form, the unforgettable form, in my opinion, is that, in the last analysis, he can not do anything at all. He is not a force but an authority.

But is there something distinctive about the human face which, for example, sets it apart from that of an animal?
One cannot entirely refuse the face of an animal. It is via the face that one understands, for example, a dog. Yet the priority here is not found in the animal, but in the human face. We understand the animal, the face of an animal, in accordance with *Dasein*. The phenomenon of the face is not in its purest form in the dog. In the dog, in the animal, there are other phenomena. For example, the force of nature is pure vitality. It is more this which characterizes the dog. But it also has a face. There are these two strange things in the face: its extreme frailty – the fact of being without means, and, on the other hand, there is authority. It is as if God spoke through the face.

Is it necessary to have the potential for language in order to be a 'face' in the ethical sense?
I think that the beginning of language is in the face. In a certain way, in its silence, it calls you. Your reaction to the face is a response. Not just a response, but a responsibility. These two words [*réponse, responsabilité*] are closely related. Language does not begin with the signs that

one gives, with words. Language is above all the fact of being addressed ... which means the saying much more than the said.

In the word 'comprehension' we understand the fact of taking [*prendre*] and of comprehending [*comprendre*], that is, the fact of englobing, of appropriating. There are these elements in all knowledge [*savoir*], all familiarity [*connaissance*], all comprehension; there is always the fact of making something one's own. But there is something which remains outside, and that is alterity. Alterity is not at all the fact that there is a difference, that facing me there is someone who has a different nose than mine, different colour eyes, another character. It is not difference, but alterity. It is alterity, the unencompassable, the transcendent. It is the beginning of transcendence. You are not transcendent by virtue of a certain different trait.

In totalization there is certainly the fact of inclusion, of adding up. Men can be synthesized. Men can easily be treated as objects. We speak to the other who is not encompassed, who, on the contrary, is the one who offers his face to you.

The analysis can go further. I'm not saying that it is completed. The idea that is very important to me is frailty, the idea of being in a certain sense much less than a thing. One can kill, annihilate. It is easier to annihilate than to possess the other.

For me, these two starting points are essential: the idea of extreme frailty, of demand, that the other is poor. It is worse than weakness, the superlative of weakness. He is so weak that he demands. This, of course, is the beginning of the analysis, because the way in which we behave concretely is different. It is more complex. In particular because, what seems to me very important, is that there are not only two of us in the world. But I think that everything begins as if we were only two. It is important to recognize that the idea of justice always supposes that there is a third. But, initially, in principle, I am concerned about justice because the other has a face.

What is the role of the phenomenological method in relation to the conception of the face that is presented in Totality and Infinity? *Does phenomenology lead us, by means of a detailed construction of the diverse aspects of the phenomenon, to a new understanding of the face? Or is the phenomenology of the face only a systematic description of what is always revealed when we encounter the other?*

Totality and Infinity was my first book. I find it very difficult to tell you, in a few words, in what way it is different from what I've said

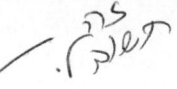

afterwards. There is the ontological terminology: I spoke of being. I have since tried to get away from that language. When I speak of being in *Totality and Infinity*, what remains valuable is that, above all, it indicates that the analyses should not be taken as psychological. What is described in these human states is not simply empirical, but it is an essential structure. And in the word 'essential' there is the word '*esse*', being. It is as if it were an ontological structure.

In *Totality and Infinity* I used the word 'justice' for ethics, for the relationship between two people. I spoke of 'justice', although now 'justice' is for me something which is a calculation, which is knowledge, and which supposes politics; it is inseparable from the political. It is something which I distinguish from ethics, which is primary. However, in *Totality and Infinity*, the word 'ethical' and the word 'just' are the same word, the same question, the same language. When I use the word 'justice' there it is not in the technical sense as something opposed to or distinct from the moral.

The face is fundamental. It does not have any systematic character. It is a notion through which man comes to me via a human act different from knowing.

Do you think that there is room for an enlarged phenomenology of the face? Are there interesting characteristics of this phenomenon that you have not deal with in Totality and Infinity?

I am not at all sure that the face is a phenomenon. A phenomenon is what appears. Appearance is not the mode of being of the face. The face is, from the start, the demand of which I was just speaking. It is the frailty of the one who needs you, who is counting on you. This is where the idea of dissymmetry – which is very important to me – comes from. It is not at all a question of a subject faced with an object. It is, on the contrary, that I am strong and you are weak. I am your servant and you are the master. Consequently, I am not frightened by the idea that the one with power is always the master; no, it is not in that sense that I use these terms.

According to your analysis, the commandment 'Thou shalt not kill' is revealed by the human face; but is the commandment not also expressed in the face of an animal? Can an animal be considered as the other that must be welcomed? Or is it necessary to possess the possibility of speech to be a 'face' in the ethical sense?

I cannot say at what moment you have the right to be called 'face'. The

human face is completely different and only afterwards do we discover the face of an animal. I don't know if a snake has a face. I can't answer that question. A more specific analysis is needed.

But there is something in our attraction to an animal. . . . In the dog, what we like is perhaps his child-like character. As if he were strong, cheerful, powerful, full of life. On the other hand, there is also, even with regards to an animal, a pity. A dog is like a wolf that doesn't bite. There is the trace of the wolf in the dog. In any case, there is here the possibility of a specific phenomenological analysis. . . . Children are often loved for their animality. The child is not suspicious of anything. He jumps, he walks, he runs, he bites. It's delightful.

If animals do not have faces in an ethical sense, do we have obligations towards them? And if so, where do they come from?
It is clear that, without considering animals as human beings, the ethical extends to all living beings. We do not want to make an animal suffer needlessly and so on. But the prototype of this is human ethics. Vegetarianism, for example, arises from the transference to animals of the idea of suffering. The animal suffers. It is because we, as human, know what suffering is that we can have this obligation.

The widespread thesis that the ethical is biological amounts to saying that, ultimately, the human is only the last stage of the evolution of the animal. I would say, on the contrary, that in relation to the animal, the human is a new phenomenon. And that leads me to your question. You ask at what moment one becomes a face. I do not know at what moment the human appears, but what I want to emphasize is that the human breaks with pure being, which is always a persistence in being. This is my principal thesis. A being is something that is attached to being, to its own being. That is Darwin's idea. The being of animals is a struggle for life. A struggle for life without ethics. It is a question of might.  Heidegger says at the beginning of *Being and Time* that *Dasein* is a being who in his being is concerned for this being itself. That's Darwin's idea: the living being struggles for life. The aim of being is being itself. However, with the appearance of the human – and this is my entire philosophy – there is something more important than my life, and that is the life of the other. That is unreasonable. Man is an unreasonable animal. Most of the time my life is dearer to me, most of the time one looks after oneself. But we cannot not admire saintliness. Not the sacred, but saintliness: that is, the person who in his being is more attached to the being of the other than to his own. I believe that it is in saintliness that the human begins; not in the accomplishment of saintliness, but in the value. It is the first value, an undeniable value. Even when someone says something bad about saintliness, it is in the name of saintliness that he says it.

Does your conception of the face have roots in Jewish theology?
Not so much in Judaism as in the Bible. The Bible has diverse levels. There is a level on which the importance of the other is taught as being, ultimately, favourable to me as well. That is, you are told that you will be rewarded for ethical actions. There is that in the Bible as well. But there is also the idea of saintliness in the Bible. Not only in Christianity. In the Old Testament there is the sixth commandment, 'Thou shalt not kill'. This does not mean simply that you are not to go around firing a gun all the time. It refers, rather, to the fact that, in the course of your life, in different ways, you kill someone. For example, when we sit down at the table in the morning and drink coffee, we kill an Ethiopian who doesn't have any coffee. It is in this sense that the commandment must be understood. There is also the phrase 'Thou shalt love thy neighbour'. It is expressed in several ways. There is also 'Thou shalt love the stranger'.

But, more specifically, does the image of the face have Judaic or Biblical roots?
No. The word *'panim'*, which means 'face' in Hebrew, is not a philosophical term in the Bible. I would say that the conception of the face is a certain way of expressing philosophically what I mean when I speak of the *conatus essendi*, the effort to exist which is the ontological principle. . . . I didn't find this in a Biblical verse. But, in my opinion, that is the spirit of the Bible, with all its concern for weakness, all the obligation towards the weak. But I didn't find that in a verse. You see, my terminology does not come from the Bible. Otherwise it would be the Bible to the very end.

Although there is a very clear distinction between your philosophical texts and your writings on religion, your philosophy seems to express the Jewish values which you affirm in your essays on Judaism. Do you think that familiarity with the Jewish tradition would help a reader to understand Totality and Infinity?
There is a very radical distinction between them; they are not even published by the same publishers. In the philosophical texts, the Bibli-

cal verse never serves as a proof, but as an illustration. On the other hand, there are the texts which I call confessional. The non-philosophical texts are exegeses. But there is certainly a relationship between them.

It is sometimes suggested that your philosophy is difficult for non-Jews to understand because it is more 'Judaic' than 'Greek' in orientation.
I think that Europe is the Bible and Greece. This is not colonialism – the rest can be translated. Nevertheless, the first intelligibility, the first meaning of all speech is the face. You could not speak without a face. One speaks to someone. That is even a first truth. And to speak to someone is not simply to speak in front of the plastic form that the other is. And in this sense I do not at all think that there is any negation of Greece in insisting on the priority of the face. The interlocutor is first of all in this ethical posture by which my lips open for speech, or by which I am addressed. I am called upon to respond. I think that the first language is the response. But, with the appearance of the third – the third must also have a face. If the third is also a face, one must know whom to speak to first. Who is the first face? And, in this sense, I am led to compare the faces, to compare the two people. Which is a terrible task. It is entirely different from speaking to the face. To compare them is to place them in the same genre.

The other is unique, unique to such an extent that in speaking of the responsibility for the unique, responsibility in relation to the unique, I use the word 'love'. That which I call responsibility is a love, because love is the only attitude where there is encounter with the unique. What is a loved one? He is unique in the world. In *Totality and Infinity* I do not often use the word 'love' because by love is often understood what Pascal called love with concupiscence.

Now, when there are two unique beings, the genre reappears. From this moment on, I think of the other in the genre. I am Greek, it is Greek thought. The thought of comparison, of judgment, the attributes of the subject, in short, the entire terminology of Greek logic and Greek politics appear. Consequently, it is not true that my thought isn't Greek. On the contrary, everything that I say about justice comes from Greek thought, and Greek politics as well. But, what I say, quite simply, is that it is, ultimately, based on the relationship to the other, on the ethics without which I would not have sought justice. Justice is the way in which I respond to the face that I am not alone in the world with the other.

If everything terminates in justice, why tell this long story about the face, which is the opposite of justice? The first reason is that it is ethics which is the foundation of justice. Because justice is not the last word; within justice, we seek a better justice. That is the liberal state. The second reason is that there is a violence in justice. When the verdict of justice is pronounced, there remains for the unique I that I am the possibility of finding something more to soften the verdict. There is a place for charity after justice. The truly democratic state finds that it is never democratic enough. It always wants to improve its institutions. The third reason is that there is a moment when I, the unique I, along with other unique I's, can find something else which improves universality itself. I think for example, that the abolition of the death penalty certainly results from that.

There is no necessity for expressing these ideas in Biblical terms; and *Totality and Infinity* can therefore be read without any familiarity with either Judaism or the Bible.

If we understand your text correctly, the relationship to the other is fundamentally and originally an ethical relation. The face of the other always presents itself as a commandment, as the prohibition of murder. The face commands that one welcome it. Now, if the commandment is absolute, how can people act unethically? Does a violent action indicate that the person has not recognized the commandment? Or is it possible to recognize an absolute commandment as such and to disobey it in spite of this recognition?

Certainly. That is the distinction I made at the beginning between authority and force. In the *conatus essendi*, which is the effort to exist, existence is the supreme law. However, with the appearance of the face on the inter-personal level, the commandment 'Thou shalt not kill' emerges as a limitation of the *conatus essendi*. It is not a rational limit. Consequently, interpreting it necessitates thinking it in moral terms, in ethical terms. It must be thought of outside the idea of force. It is in the human being that a rupture is produced with being's own law, with the law of being. The law of evil is the law of being. Evil is, in this sense, very powerful. Consequently, it is the unique force. Authority is a paradox. Both authority and morality are paradoxes.

If there is an explicitly Jewish moment in my thought, it is the reference to Auschwitz, where God let the Nazis do what they wanted. Consequently, what remains? Either this means that there is no reason for morality and hence it can be concluded that everyone should act like the Nazis, or the moral law maintains its authority. Here is freedom; this choice is the moment of freedom.

It still cannot be concluded that after Auschwitz there is no longer a moral law, as if the moral or ethical law were impossible, without promise. Before the twentieth century, all religion begins with the promise. It begins with the 'Happy End'. It is the promise of heaven. Well then, doesn't a phenomenon like Auschwitz invite you, on the contrary, to think the moral law independently of the Happy End? That is the question. I would even ask whether we are not faced with an order that one cannot preach. Does one have the right to preach to the other a piety without reward? That is what I ask myself. It is easier to tell myself to believe without promise than it is to ask it of the other. That is the idea of asymmetry. I can demand of myself that which I cannot demand of the other.

The essential problem is: can we speak of an absolute commandment after Auschwitz? Can we speak of morality after the failure of morality?

If it is the case that the person who acts unethically has not recognized the commandment which comes from the face, how is this lack of recognition to be explained?

The truly difficult thing to understand is that one can hear and understand [*entendre*] this commandment. Being persisting in being, that is nature. And that there can be a rupture with nature, yes; but one must not attribute to it the same force as nature has. There is a moment where the idea of freedom prevails – it is a moment of generosity. Here there is a moment where someone plays without winning. That is Charity. For me, this is very important. Something that one does gratuitously, that is grace. Grace begins there. It is gratuitous, a gratuitous act. You are reasoning as if the act were not gratuitous. The idea of the face is the idea of gratuitous love, the commandment of a gratuitous act. Commanding love. Commanding love signifies recognizing the value of love in itself.

The face does not give itself to be seen. It is not a vision. The face is not that which is seen. I began today by saying that the face is not an object of knowledge [*une connaissance*]. There is no evidence with regards to the face; there is, rather, an order, in the sense that the face is a commanded value. Consequently, you could call it generosity, in other terms, it is the moment of faith. Faith is not a question of the existence or non-existence of God. It is believing that love without

reward is valuable. It is often said 'God is love'. God is the commandment of love. 'God is love' means that He loves you. But this implies
that the primary thing is your own salvation. In my opinion, God is a
commandment to love. God is the one who says that one must
love the other.

But, to return to your question, it is not difficult to recognize the
face. There is the commandment, the form in which its excellence
appears. It is a commanded excellence because it is not an excellence
given simply, in an intuition. It is the being that we are, being itself,
which prevents us from recognizing our ethical duties.

*How can one learn to recognize and welcome the face of the other? We
share your view that the Jewish religion, for example, can teach this to
its adherents. But what about atheists? How can they learn to welcome
the face?*
I do not preach for the Jewish religion. I always speak of the Bible, not
the Jewish religion. The Bible, including the Old Testament, is for me
a human fact, of the human order, and entirely universal. What I have
said about ethics, about the universality of the commandment in the
face, of the commandment which is valid even if it doesn't bring salvation, even if there is no reward, is valid independently of any
religion.

*How would you respond to the suggestion that your ethics is too ideal-
istic, because it does not offer any practical advice for solving political
problems? Would you say that the importance of ethics is that it provides
ideals towards which we may work, and which allow us to evaluate the
morality of our society?*
That is the great separation that there is between the way the world
functions concretely and the ideal of saintliness of which I am speaking. And I maintain that this ideal of saintliness is presupposed in all
our value judgments. There is no politics for accomplishing the moral,
but there are certainly some politics which are further from it or closer
to it. For example, I've mentioned Stalinism to you. I've told you that
justice is always a justice which desires a better justice. This is the way
that I will characterize the liberal state. The liberal state is a state
which holds justice as the absolutely desirable end and hence as a perfection. Concretely, the liberal state has always admitted – alongside
the written law – human rights as a parallel institution. It continues to
preach that within its justice there are always improvements to be

made in human rights. Human rights are the reminder that there is no justice yet. And, consequently, I believe that it is absolutely obvious that the liberal state is more moral than the fascist state, and closer to the morally ideal state.

There is a utopian moment in what I say; it is the recognition of something which cannot be realized but which, ultimately, guides all moral action. This utopianism does not prohibit you from condemning certain factual states, nor from recognizing the relative progress that can be made. Utopianism is not a condemnation of everything else. There is no moral life without utopianism – utopianism in this exact sense that saintliness is goodness.

Do you think that the 'deconstruction' of Greek metaphysics will enable philosophers to reflect better on the ethical dimension of human existence?

I believe that Greek philosophy cannot be eliminated. Even in order to criticize the ultimate character of Greek philosophy, one needs Greek philosophy. That is not at all a contradiction. The Greeks have taught us how to speak. Not to speak, not the saying [*le dire*] but to rediscover ourselves in the said. Greek philosophy is a special language which can say everything to everyone because it never presupposes anything in particular. Greek philosophy is the way that people speak in the modern university the world over. That is speaking Greek. They all speak Greek, even if they don't know the difference between alpha and beta. It is a certain way of presenting things. It is a way of using a language which everyone can enter. The second quality of this language is that one is not obliged to take the forms of the language for the actual forms of the meaning it represents. In spite of the fact that something has been said in a certain way, the forms of this saying do not leave a trace in what has been shown. And, consequently, one can show what goes beyond the universality of comprehension. It is a form which leaves no trace in the matter it presents. You can unsay what you have said.

What do you think of the Husserlian position on the question of the alterity of the other which is presented by Derrida in his essay 'Violence and Metaphysics'? Derrida seems to think that one can only recognize the face of the other if the other is considered an alter ego, and therefore that the other cannot be absolutely other. According to him, the dis-symmetry of the ethical relation is dependent upon a prior symmetry. He

writes that 'The other is for me an ego of which I know that he relates to me as to an other'. For you, this 'knowledge' would already be violence, would it not?

Derrida has reproached me for my critique of Hegelianism by saying that in order to criticize Hegel, one begins to speak Hegel's language. That is the basis of his critique. To which I respond that for me, on the contrary, the Greek language is a language which does not imprint itself in what it says, and consequently that there is always the possibility of unsaying that to which you were obliged to have recourse in order to show something.

The idea of dissymmetry seems very important to me; it is, perhaps, the most important way of conceiving of the relationship between self and other which does not place them on the same level. You know my quotation from Dostoevsky: 'Everyone is guilty in front of everyone else and me more than all the others.' That is the idea of dissymmetry. The relationship between me and the other is unsurpassable; it is modified by the fact that there is justice and that, with justice, there is a state, and as citizens we are equal. But, in the ethical act, in my relationship to the other, if one forgets that I am guiltier than the others, justice itself will not be able to last. But the idea of dissymmetry is another way of saying that in the perseverance in being we are all equal, but the idea that the death of the other is more important than my own is an affirmation that we are not being looked at from outside, but the essential difference between me and the other remains in my look.

There are two alterities. There is logical alterity; if there is a series, each term is other in relation to the rest. The alterity of which I am speaking is the alterity of the face, which is not a difference, not a series, but strangeness – strangeness which cannot be suppressed, which means that it is my obligation that cannot be effaced.

In the section 'Beyond the Face' of Totality and Infinity *you present fecundity as a means of access to a vista of infinite time. You write that it is biology that makes this opening possible, but that biology does not limit it. Does this mean that the model of potentiality is only found in heterosexual relationships? In other words, is there a type of 'fecundity' that has nothing to do with biology?*

The father–son relationship, for example, should not be thought of only in biological terms. The father–son relationship can exist between beings who, biologically, are not father and son. Paternity and filiality, the feeling that the other is not simply someone I've met, but that he is, in a certain sense, my prolongation, my ego, that his possibilities are mine – the idea of responsibility for the other can go that far.

Levinas: an English Bibliography

compiled by
ROBERT BERNASCONI

The standard bibliography of studies both by and on Levinas is by Roger Burggraeve. He regularly updates his bibliography, the most recent edition of which is *Emmanuel Levinas. Une bibliographie primaire et secondaire (1929–1985)*, Leuven, The Centre for Metaphysics and Philosophy of God, 1986. Inevitably, the present bibliography is greatly indebted to the work of Roger Burggraeve, to whom it is dedicated. Nevertheless all references have been independently verified and a substantial number of additions have been made. I would be pleased to receive corrections and additions to this list.

I Levinas in English Translation

'About Blanchot: an interview', translated by Garth Gillan, *Sub-Stance*, No. 14, 1976, 54–7.

'Bad Conscience and the Inexorable', translated by R. Cohen, in *Face to Face with Levinas*, edited by R. Cohen, Albany, State University of New York Press, 1986, pp. 35–40.

'Balance Sheet', in *American Jewish Year Book 1977* edited by Morris Fine and Milton Himmelfarb, vol. 77, The American Jewish Committee, New York, and The Jewish Publication Society of America, Philadelphia, 1976, pp. 383–4.

'Beyond Intentionality', translated by Kathleen McLaughlin, in *Philosophy in France Today*, edited by A. Montefiore, Cambridge, Cambridge University Press, 1983, pp. 100–15.

Collected Philosophical Papers, translated by A. Lingis, The Hague, Martinus Nijhoff, 1987.

'The Contemporary Criticism of the Idea of Value and the Prospects for Humanism', in *Value and Values in Evolution*, edited by Edward A. Maziarz, New York, Gordon and Breach, 1979, pp. 179–87.

Discovering Existence with Husserl, translated by R. Cohen, Bloomington, Ind., Indiana University Press, 1988.

Ethics and Infinity, Conversations with Philippe Nemo, translated by R. Cohen, Pittsburgh, Pa., Duquesne University Press, 1985.

'Ethics of the Infinite', in *Dialogues with Contemporary Continental Thinkers* by R. Kearney, Manchester, Manchester University Press, 1984, pp. 47–69.

Existence and Existents, translated by A. Lingis, The Hague, Martinus Nijhoff, 1978.

'Franz Rosenzweig', translated by R. Cohen, *Midstream*, vol. 29, No. 9, Nov. 1983, 33–40.

'God and Philosophy', translated by R. Cohen, *Philosophy Today*, vol. 22, 1978, 127–45. (Revised version in *Collected Philosophical Papers*.)

'Ideology and Idealism', *Modern Jewish Ethics*, edited by Marvin Fox, Columbus, Ohio, Ohio State University, 1975, pp. 121–38.

'Interrogation of Martin Buber conducted by Maurice S. Friedman', in *Philosophical Interrogations*, edited by Sydney and Beatrice Rome, New York, Harper & Row, 1970, pp. 23–6.

'Intervention by Levinas', *A Short History of Existentialism*, by John Wahl, translated by Forrest Williams and Stanley Maron, New York, Philosophical Library, 1949, pp. 47–53.

'Intuition of Essences', translated by J. Kockelmans, in *Phenomenology: the Philosophy of Edmund Husserl and Its Interpretation*, edited by J. Kockelmans, Garden City, New York, Doubleday Anchor, 1967, pp. 83–105 (A translation of ch. 6 of the book subsequently translated as *The Theory of Intuition in Husserl's Phenomenology*)

'Judaism and the Feminine Element', translated by E. Wyschogrod, *Judaism*, vol. 18, No. 1, 1969, 30–8.

'A Language Familiar to Us', translated by Douglas Collins, *Telos*, No. 44, 1980, 199–201.

'Martin Buber and the Theory of Knowledge', in *The Philosophy of Martin Buber*, edited by Paul Schilpp and Maurice Friedman, La Salle, Ill., Open Court, 1967, pp. 133–50.

'Martin Buber, Gabriel Marcel and Philosophy', translated by Esther Kameron, in *Martin Buber. A Centenary Volume*, edited by Haim Gordon and Jochanan Bloch, New York, Ktav Publishing House for the Faculty of Humanities and Social Sciences Ben Gurion University of the Negev, 1984, pp. 305–21.

'On the Trail of the Other', translated by Daniel J. Hoy *Philosophy Today*, vol. 10, No. 1, 1966, 34–46. (See 'The Trace of the Other' for a new translation.)

Otherwise than Being or Beyond Essence, translated by A. Lingis, The Hague, Martinus Nijhoff, 1981.

'Present Problems of Jewish Education in Western Lands', *Community*, No. 12, Nov. 1960, 1–6.

'Signature', translated by Mary Ellen Petrisko and edited by Adriaan Peperzak, *Research in Phenomenology*, vol. 8, 1978, 175–89. (Replaces 'Signature', translated by William Canavan, *Philosophy Today*, vol. 10, No. 1, 1966, 30–3.)

The Theory of Intuition in Husserl's Phenomenology, translated by André Orianne, Evanston, Ill., Northwestern University Press, 1973.

Time and the Other, translated by Richard Cohen, Pittsburgh, Pa., Duquesne University Press, 1987. (Also includes 'The Old and the New' and 'Diachrony and Representation'.)

'To Love the Torah more than God', translated by Helen A. Stephenson and Richard I. Sugarman, *Judaism*, vol. 28, No. 2, 1979, 216–23.

Totality and Infinity, translated by A. Lingis, Pittsburgh, Pa., Duquesne University Press, 1969.

'The Trace of the Other', translated by A. Lingis, *Deconstruction in Context*, edited by Mark Taylor, Chicago, Ill., University of Chicago Press, 1986, pp. 345–59.

'Transcendence and Evil', translated by A. Lingis, *The Phenomenology of Man and of the Human Condition*, edited by A-T. Tymieniecka, *Analecta Husserliana*, vol. 14, Dordrecht, D. Reidel, 1983, pp. 153–65.

'Transcendence and Height', translated by Tina Chanter, to be included in a volume of essays by Levinas she is co-editing with Adriaan Peperzak.

Annette Aronowicz is preparing a translation of *Quatre Lectures Talmudiques* and *Du Sacré au Saint* to be published by Indiana University Press.

II Selected Secondary Literature in English

Awerkamp, Don, *Emmanuel Levinas: Ethics and Politics*, New York, Revisionist Press, 1977.

Bernasconi, Robert, 'Levinas Face to Face – with Hegel', *Journal of the British Society for Phenomenology*, vol. 13, No. 3, Oct. 1982, 267–76.

— — —, 'Levinas on Time and the Instant', in *Time and Metaphysics*, edited by D. Wood and R. Bernasconi, Coventry, Parousia Press, 1982, pp. 199–217.

— — —, 'The Trace of Levinas in Derrida', in *Derrida and Differance*, edited by D. Wood and R. Bernasconi, Coventry, Parousia Press, 1985, pp. 17–44.

— — —, 'Hegel and Levinas: the Possibility of Reconciliation and Forgiveness', *Archivio di Filosofia*, vol. 54, 1986, 325–46.

— — —, 'Deconstruction and the Possibility of Ethics', in *Deconstruction and Philosophy*, edited by John Sallis, Chicago, Ill., Chicago University Press, 1987, pp. 122–39.

— — —, 'Levinas: Philosophy and Beyond', *Continental Philosophy*, vol. 1, New York, Routledge & Kegan Paul, 1988.

— — —, 'The Silent Anarchic World of the Evil Genius', *The Collegium Phaenomenologicum: the First Ten Years*, edited by G. Moneta, J. Sallis and J. Taminiaux, Dordrecht, Martinus Nijhoff, 1988, forthcoming.

Blum, Roland Paul, 'Emmanuel Levinas' Theory of Commitment', *Philosophy and Phenomenological Research*, vol. 44, No. 2, 1983, 145–68.

— — —, 'Deconstruction and Creation', *Philosophy and Phenomenological Research*, vol. 46, No. 2, 1985, 293–306.

Bouckaert, Luk, 'Ontology and Ethics: Reflections on Levinas' Critique of Heidegger', *International Philosophical Quarterly*, vol. 10, 1970, 402–19.

Burggraeve, Roger, 'The Ethical Basis for a Humane Society according to Emmanuel Levinas', translated by C. Vanhove-Romanik, in *Emmanuel Levinas*, Leuven, The Centre for Metaphysics and Philosophy of God, 1981, pp. 5–57.

— — —, *From Self-Development to Solidarity: an Ethical Reading of Human Desire in its Socio-Political Relevance according to Emmanuel Levinas*, translated by C. Vanhove-Romanik, Leuven, The Centre for Metaphysics and Philosophy of God, 1985.

Burke, John Patrick, 'The Ethical Significance of the Face', *Proceedings of the American Catholic Philosophical Association*, vol. 56, 1982, 194–206.

Casey, E., 'Levinas on Memory and Trace', *The Collegium Phaenomenologicum: the First Ten Years*, edited by G. Moneta, J. Sallis and J. Taminiaux, Dordrecht, Martinus Nijhoff, 1988, forthcoming.

Chanter, Tina, 'The Alterity and Immodesty of Time: Death as Future and Eros as Feminine in Levinas', in *Writing the Future*, edited by Andrew Benjamin and David Wood, London, Warwick Studies in Philosophy and Literature, Routledge, forthcoming.

Cohen, Richard A., 'Review of *Existence and Existents*', *Man and World*, vol. 12, 1979, pp. 521–526.

Cohen, Richard A., 'Emmanuel Levinas: Happiness is a Sensational Time', *Philosophy Today*, vol. 25, No. 3, 1981, 196–203.

———, 'The Privilege of Reason and Play: Derrida and Levinas', *Tijdschrift voor Filosofie*, vol. 45, No. 2, 1983, 242–55.

———, (ed.), *Face to Face with Levinas*, Albany, State University of New York Press, 1986.

De Boer, Th., 'Beyond Being: Ontology and Eschatology in the Philosophy of Emmanuel Levinas', *Philosophia Reformata*, vol. 38, 1973, 17–29.

———, 'Judaism and Hellenism in the Philosophy of Levinas and Heidegger', *Archivio di Filosofia*, vol. 53, 1985, 197–215.

De Greef, Jan, 'The Irreducible Alienation of the Self', *The Self and the Other*, edited by A-T. Tymieniecka, *Analecta Husserliana*, vol. 6, Dordrecht, D. Reidel 1983, 27–30.

Derrida, Jacques, 'Violence and Metaphysics', in *Writing and Difference*, translated by Alan Bass, Chicago, Ill., Chicago University Press, and London, Routledge & Kegan Paul, 1978, 79–153.

Durfee, Harold A., 'Emmanuel Levinas' Philosophy of Language', in *Explanation: New Directions in Philosophy*, The Hague, Martinus Nijhoff, 1973, pp. 89–120.

———, 'War, Politics, and Radical Pluralism', *Philosophy and Phenomenological Research*, 35, 1975, 549–58.

Ehman, Robert R., 'Emmanuel Levinas: the Phenomenon of the Other', *Man and World*, vol. 8, No. 2, 1975, 141–5.

Gans, Steven, 'Ethics or Ontology', *Philosophy Today*, vol. 16, No. 2, 1972, 117–21.

Gerber, Rudolph J., 'Totality and Infinity: Hebraism and Hellenism – the Experiential Ontology of Emmanuel Levinas', *Review of Existential Psychology and Psychiatry*, vol. 7, No. 3, 1967, 177–88.

Gilkey, Langdon, 'Comments on Emmanuel Levinas's *Totalité et infini*', *Algemeen Nederlands Tijdschrift voor Wijsbegeerte*, vol. 64, 1972, 26–38.

Kelbley, Charles A., 'An Introduction to Emmanuel Levinas', *Thought*, vol. 49, No. 192, 1974, 81–6.

Keyes, C. D., 'An Evaluation of Levinas' Critique of Heidegger', *Research in Phenomenology*, vol. 2, 1972, 121–42.

Lawton, Philip, 'Levinas' Notion of the "There Is" ', *Tijdschrift voor Filosofie*, vol. 37, No. 3, 1975, 477–89. (Also published in *Philosophy Today*, vol. 29, No. 1, 1976, 67–76.)

———, 'A Difficult Freedom: Levinas' Judaism', *Tijdschrift voor Filosofie*, vol. 37, No. 4, 1975, 681–91.

———, 'Love and Justice: Levinas' Reading of Buber', *Philosophy Today*, vol. 20, No. 1, 1976, 77–83.

Libertson, J., 'Levinas and Husserl: Sensation and Intentionality', *Tijdschrift voor Filosofie*, vol. 41, No. 3, 1979, 485–502.

———, *Proximity, Levinas, Blanchot, Bataille and Communication*, Phaenomenologica, 87, The Hague, Martinus Nijhoff, 1982.

Lichtigfeld, A., 'On Infinity and Totality in Hegel and Levinas', *South African Journal of Philosophy*, vol. 2, 1983, 31–3.

Lingis, Alphonso, 'Emmanuel Levinas and the Intentional Analysis of the Libido', *Philosophy in Context*, vol. 8, 1978, 60–9.

———, 'Face to Face: a Phenomenological Meditation', *International Philosophical Quarterly*, vol. 19, No. 2, 1979, 151–63.

———, 'Intuition of Freedom, Intuition of Law', *Journal of Philosophy*, vol. 79, No. 10, 1982, 588–96.

———, *Libido: the French Existential Theories*, Bloomington, Ind., Indiana University Press, 1985, pp. 58–73 and 103–20.

Llewelyn, John, 'Levinas, Derrida, and Others vis-à-vis', in *Beyond Metaphysics*, Atlantic Highlands, New Jersey, Humanities Press, 1985, pp. 185–206.

———, 'Jewgreek or Greekjew', *The Collegium Phaenomenologicum: the First Ten Years*, edited by G. Moneta, J. Sallis and J. Taminiaux, Dordrecht, Martinus Nijhoff, 1988, forthcoming.

Lyotard, Jean-François, 'Jewish Oedipus', in *Driftworks*, New York, Semiotext(e), 1984, pp. 35–55.

Masterson, Patrick, 'Ethics and Absolutes in the Philosophy of E. Levinas', *Neue Zeitschrift für Systematische Theologie und Religionsphilosophie*, vol. 25, 1983, 211–23.

McCollester, Charles, 'The Philosophy of Emmanuel Levinas', *Judaism*, vol. 19, 1970, 344–54.

O'Connor, Noreen, 'The Meaning of "Religion" in the Work of Emmanuel Levinas', *Proceedings of the Irish Philosophical Society*, 1977.

———, 'Exile and Enrootedness', *Seminar*, Journal of the Philosophical Seminar, University College, Cork, vol. 2, 1978, 53–7.

———, 'Being and the Good: Heidegger and Levinas', *Philosophical Studies*, The National University of Ireland, vol. 27, 1980, 212–20.

———, 'Intentionality Analysis and the Problem of Self and Other', *Journal of the British Society for Phenomenonology*, vol. 13, No. 2, 1982, 186–92.

Ogletree, Thomas W., 'Hospitality to the Stranger: the Role of the "Other" in Moral Experience', in *Hospitality to the Stranger: Dimensions of Moral Understanding*, Philadelphia, Pa., Fortress Press, 1985, pp. 35–63.

Peperzak, Adriaan, 'Beyond Being', *Research in Phenomenology*, vol. 8, 1978, 239–61.

———, 'Emmanuel Levinas: Jewish Experience and Philosophy', *Philosophy Today*, vol. 27, No. 4, 1983, 297–306.

———, 'Phenomenology – Ontology – Metaphysics: Levinas' Perspective on Husserl and Heidegger', *Man and World*, vol. 16, 1983, 113–27.

Smith, Steven G., 'Reason as One for Another: Moral and Theoretical Argument in the Philosophy of Levinas', *Journal of the British Society for Phenomenology*, vol. 12, No. 3, 1981, 231–44.

———, *The Argument to the Other: Reason Beyond Reason in the Thought of Karl Barth and Emmanuel Levinas*, American Academy of Religion: Academy Studies, No. 42, Chico, Cal., Scholars Press, 1983.

Strasser, Stephan, 'The Unique Individual and his Other', *The Self and the Other*, edited by A-T. Tymieniecka, *Analecta Husserliana*, vol. 6, Dordrecht, D. Reidel 1983, pp. 9–26.

———, 'Emmanuel Levinas (Born 1906); Phenomenological Philosophy', in *The Phenomenological Movement* by Herbert Spiegelberg, 3rd revised and enlarged edition, Phaenomenologica 5/6, The Hague, Martinus Nijhoff, 1982, pp. 612–49.

Tallon, Andrew, 'Intentionality, Intersubjectivity, and the Between:

Buber and Levinas on Affectivity and the Dialogical Principle',
Thought, vol. 53, No. 210, 1978, 292–309.

———, 'Emmanuel Levinas and the Problem of Ethical Metaphysics',
Philosophy Today, vol. 20, No. 1, 53–66.

———, 'Review of *Autrement qu'être ou au-delà de l'essence*', *Man and
World*, vol. 9. 1976, 451–62.

Vasey, Craig R., 'Review of *Existence and Existents*', *Thought*, vol. 44,
1980, 466–73.

———, 'Emmanuel Levinas: From Intentionality to Proximity',
Philosophy Today, vol. 25, No. 3, 1981, 178–95.

Watson, Stephen, 'Reason and the Face of the Other', *Journal of the
American Academy of Religion*, vol. 54, No. 1, 1986, 33–57.

Webb, Mark, 'The Rape of Time', *Southwest Philosophical Studies*
(San Marcos, Texas), vol. 7, 1982, 147–54.

Wolosky, Shira, 'Derrida, Jabès, Levinas: Sign-Theory as Ethical
Discourse', *Prooftexts: Journal of Jewish Literary History*, 1982,
No. 2, pp. 283–302.

Wyschogrod, Edith, 'Review of *Totality and Infinity*,' *Human
Inquiries*, vol. 10, 1971, 185–92.

———, 'Emmanuel Levinas and the Problem of Religious Language',
The Thomist, vol. 26, No. 1, 1972, 1–38.

———, *Emmanuel Levinas: the Problem of Ethical Metaphysics*, The
Hague, Martinus Nijhoff, 1974.

———, 'The Moral Self: Emmanuel Levinas and Hermann Cohen',
Daat: a Journal of Jewish Philosophy, vol. 4, 1980, 35–58.

———, 'Doing Before Hearing: On the Primacy of Touch', in *Textes
pour Emmanuel Levinas*, edited by François Laruelle, Paris, Jean-
Michel Place, 1980, pp. 179–203.

———, 'God and "Being's Move" in the philosophy of Emmanuel
Levinas', *The Journal of Religion*, vol. 62, No. 2, 1982, 145–55.

Index

absence, 3, 7, 22, 41, 45, 51, 85, 94,
    105, 113
absolute distance, 77, 120–1, 127–8;
    see also Urdistanz
absolution/the absolute, 88, 103,
    109, 111, 144
Ainley, A., 3, 4, 70–82, 168–80
alienation, 2, 32, 48, 93–8, 141
alterity, 3, 6, 13, 15, 16, 18, 36, 46,
    53, 63, 68n(22), 77, 103–6, 122,
    129, 145–8, 151–2, 154, 158, 165,
    170, 178–9
Aristotle, 57, 148, 151
asymmetry (dissymmetry), 7, 45,
    62, 104–5, 110, 112, 115, 123–4,
    128, 146, 148, 165, 171, 176,
    178–9

de Beauvoir, S., 3, 35, 45, 52–4;
    The Second Sex, 54
Being, 18–26, 29, 38, 42, 50–1, 58,
    62–4, 77, 85–6, 93, 97, 102, 109,
    113–19, 136, 138–9, 141–4, 149–
    52, 154, 157, 160–1, 168, 171–2,
    175–7, 179
Being-for-Others, 93, 143, 163

Bernasconi, R., 3, 100–35; *Between
    Levinas and Derrida*, 135n(25)
between (the)/zwischen, 88–9, 108–
    9, 113, 115, 121, 125–7
Boothroyd, D., 3, 15–31
Buber, M., 2, 3, 100–35; *I and
    Thou*, 101, 104–5, 107–8, 110–11,
    114–17, 120, 126, 129, 134n(22),
    135n(26); *Between Man and Man*,
    131n(7), 133n(15); *Das dialogische
    Prinzip*, 101–2, 107, 110–11, 114,
    120, 125–6, 129, 133n(20),
    134n(22), 135n(26); *The
    Philosophy of Martin Buber*, 108–
    10, 126–7, 129, 131n(7), 133n(15);
    Philosophical Interrogations, 108,
    110–11, 113–14, 120–1, 128–9;
    'Reply to my critics', 108, 110,
    132n(11), 133n(20); *Dialogisches
    Leben*, 129, 131n(8); *Martin
    Buber, Philosophen Des Jarhun-
    derts*, 108; *Werke, Erster Band.
    Schriften Zur Philosophie*, 129,
    131n(7), 133n(15); *Religion Als
    Gegenwart*, 114–15; 'Urdistanz
    und Bezeihung'*, 121

189

Printed in Great Britain
by Amazon